PRAISE FOR *STRATEGIC REPUATIO*

'Amanda Coleman says that she's "often wrestled with the concept of reputation management". Me too. How can we claim to manage something that's controlled by others rather than by us? How should it be measured? Is reputation the same as trust? And what's the connection between reputation, relationships and issues management in the practice we call public relations? This is a topic ready for review, and Coleman is a wise, informed and sensible guide to this contested terrain. A thoughtful and useful contribution to the literature on this subject.'
Richard Bailey Hon FCIPR, public relations editor and former university lecturer

'You can build a reputation for 20 years and destroy it in 20 seconds. This simple truth, valid for the era of social media, is the thin message that goes slowly through this wonderful book and is a lesson to learn. The book is well structured and the story is told in a business language that all speak these days. Simply – it is a must to be on your desk in the office.'
Maxim Behar, CEO and Chairman of the Board, M3 Communications Group

'Good books on reputation management are rare. This is one of them. Amanda Coleman mixes practical advice, case studies, academic research and decision-making frameworks to help practitioners make the right choices about reputation management. It's great to see a chapter dedicated to ethics and its relationship to managing reputations over the long term.'
Ben Verinder, MD, Chalkstream, and AI and reputation leadership trainer

'A welcome book about the contemporary role of reputation management within organizations and wider society. Amanda Coleman argues that reputation is earned through behaviour and rejects the notion that reputation can be manipulated through media or public relations practice. It is the responsibility of every aspect of an organization, supported by ethical and expert corporate communications or public relations practice, to build trust with stakeholders through relationship management. A practical book that

firmly makes the case that organizations must operate transparently and within cultural and societal norms to build reputation.'
Stephen Waddington, Director, Wadds Inc, and PhD researcher, Leeds Business School

'Amanda Coleman's practical guide to reputation management is characterized by its experience-based approach. It covers important topics such as inclusiveness, cultural intelligence and ethical challenges that are often overlooked in other texts. Essential reading for communications professionals.'
Philippe Borremans, risk, crisis and emergency communication consultant

'Packed full of wisdom and the latest thinking, this book helps communicators bring reputation management into the heart of any business. Amanda Coleman's insightful advice and experience creates a practical guide, which I recommend you keep close.'
Rachel Miller, Founder, All Things IC, and author of *Internal Communication Strategy*

'Bringing your PR team into the decision-making process when a crisis has already emerged is a losing move and often ends up with reputation-washing. This book sets out a much better alternative, providing a framework for how PR professionals can help their clients work constructively on their reputation when there is yet no sign of trouble. Much has changed in the dynamics of how modern reputations are built up and broken down, and Amanda Coleman provides a fresh and experienced view on the approaches that will work in our uncertain times.'
Alastair McCapra, Chief Executive, Chartered Institute of Public Relations

ALSO BY AMANDA COLEMAN

Crisis Communication Strategies: How to prepare in advance, respond effectively and recover in full

Everyday Communication Strategies: Manage common issues to prevent a crisis and protect your brand

Strategic Reputation Management

Identify strengths, manage performance and protect your brand

Amanda Coleman

KoganPage

First published in Great Britain and the United States in 2025 by Kogan Page Limited

2nd Floor, 45 Gee Street
London
EC1V 3RS
United Kingdom
www.koganpage.com

8 W 38th Street, Suite 902
New York, NY 10018
USA

Kogan Page books are printed on paper from sustainable forests.

ISBNs
Hardback   978 1 3986 1731 5
Paperback   978 1 3986 1730 8
Ebook   978 1 3986 1732 2

British Library Cataloguing-in-Publication Data
A CIP record for this book is available from the British Library.

Library of Congress Cataloging-in-Publication Data
Names: Coleman, Amanda, author.
Title: Strategic reputation management : identify strengths, manage
   performance and protect your brand / Amanda Coleman.
Description: London ; New York, NY : Kogan Page, 2025. | Includes
   bibliographical references and index.
Identifiers: LCCN 2024032914 (print) | LCCN 2024032915 (ebook) | ISBN
   9781398617308 (paperback) | ISBN 9781398617315 (hardback) | ISBN
   9781398617322 (ebook)
Subjects: LCSH: Public relations. | Reputation. | Corporate image. | Crisis
   management.
Classification: LCC HD59.2 .C646 2025 (print) | LCC HD59.2 (ebook) | DDC
   659.2–dc23/eng/20240808
LC record available at https://lccn.loc.gov/2024032914
LC ebook record available at

Typeset by Hong Kong FIVE Workshop
Print production managed by Jellyfish
Printed and bound by CPI Group (UK) Ltd, Croydon CR0 4YY

This book is dedicated to all those who have believed in me and kept me focused on my writing. My Dad (Philip) for his constant reminders of the deadlines that were looming, and to those who kept nudging me along particularly Lucy Easthope, Sandra Edwards and my PA Linda O'Neil.

CONTENTS

ABOUT THE AUTHOR

Amanda Coleman is a PR and communication professional with extensive experience of managing communication for organizations under pressure. She is the director of her own crisis communication and issues management consultancy and works internationally with a range of businesses, organizations and brands.

Amanda is a Fellow of both the Chartered Institute of Public Relations and the Public Relations and Communications Association, as well as being a Chartered PR Practitioner. She is the author of two books *Crisis Communication Strategies* and *Everyday Communication Strategies*, both also published by Kogan Page. She writes a newsletter *Under Pressure* (https://underpressure.substack.com/) and a blog under the name Amandacomms's Blog (amandacomms1.wordpress.com).

PREFACE

Throughout my career I have often wrestled with the concept of reputation management. Is it really what good public relations is about or has the world moved on from the 1950s approach to promoting goods and services? And if PR is not about reputation management, what is it? This book is the culmination of many years challenging myself in relation to what I am doing at work and reviewing the existing publications about reputation management. In writing this I want to challenge some of those accepted views that have been with us for many years, and I ask you to consider if in a post-Covid, trust deficit era we need to take a different approach to reputation management.

The time is right for a new and updated definition of reputation and a change to the way reputation management is implemented. It has to be more than effective PR and communication activity. It has to be more than the social media and online views of the business. It has to be more than manipulating people to have a particular view. It has to be more than avoiding problems when they occur. Reputation management is about the whole of the business, brand or organization. It is something everyone needs to be aware of and be working to support. Throughout the book I aim to take a broader look at reputation and how it fits into the working of a business. This starts with what comprises a good reputation and the factors that we should be considering. I have also considered what happens when a business has a bad reputation or becomes a toxic brand. Is there a way back and if so, what does that look like and how should a business move positively forward?

A huge challenge to reputation management is quantifying a reputation and being able to recognize what it is. This requires more than just one measure and is about a range of important factors that need to be identified and considered. The factors will vary from business to business depending on who you are, what you do and how you operate. There should be a suite of indicators that can be identified, monitored and assessed to support the business' understanding of what the reputation is. This also allows it to be tracked over time. Understanding reputation should be part of the business measures alongside profitability, recruitment figures and productivity. It needs to be considered in the same business development conversations and be taken seriously by the C-suite and in the boardroom. Measuring reputation becomes essential for the moments when an issue or problem threatens the business. How can we understand the impact that a situation is having, or has had, if we don't have ways to quantify it? Being able to effectively respond to problems, issues or crises is essential to a business. It supports resilience and can ensure that an effective operational response is recognized. It can mean the difference between a business or brand that survives and one that disappears. In a quarter of a century dealing with crisis situations, I can honestly say that I have never been concerned about reputation in the first moments of a response. What matters at that point is that the business recognizes the problem exists and takes steps to address it. The impact of the incident and the response on reputation comes later. It should not be about trying to cover up or present a false view, but about demonstrating and giving insight into an effective response.

Reputation management does face many ethical dilemmas. They happen on a daily basis and often we deal with them without fully recognizing what we have done. It is important to understand the pitfalls and problems that need to be navigated when providing PR and communication support and advice. It is why I dedicate a full chapter to the issue of ethical challenges. Most PR and communication professionals have been asked to do things that they do not feel are appropriate. There are moments we are uncomfortable, and we need to understand why, and what it means to how we act or advise others. In an increasingly complex and swiftly changing world, societal norms and attitudes need to be considered and a business really needs to understand its customers or service users. There are further challenges ahead with the developments in technology and the expansion of artificial intelligence. This will put further pressure on the ethical approaches to PR and communication that we need to be ready to address.

As with my other books *Crisis Communication Strategies* and *Everyday Communication Strategies* this book is not meant to be an academic study of the issue of reputation management. I hope instead it can be a practical book that gives tips, insights, checklists and a toolkit for how to effectively consider and implement reputation management. There are also a range of case studies to consider how businesses and organizations are affected by issues and incidents and what can be taken from reviewing the situation, the impact and the approach taken to respond. As you read the book, I ask you to take the opportunity of challenging yourself about how you view reputation and what role it plays both in a business and the communication of that business. Are we using the term correctly or is it overused and misunderstood? Reputation remains an important asset for any business or organization if it is managed the right way. The strategic management of reputation helps to build a strong business that performs well, is innovative and forward thinking and can withstand those moments of stress. This is the time for a fresh look at both what we do and how we do it so that we build reputations for now and the future.

ACKNOWLEDGEMENTS

Writing this book has given me the opportunity to speak to a number of leading minds in the world of PR and communication. I am grateful for the support that they have given me and also for the support from the Chartered Institute of Public Relations. I want to thank Professor Anne Gregory, Advita Patel, Sandra Macleod, Andy Green, Marc Whitt, Stephen Waddington and Ben Verinder who have shared their thoughts with me and helped to shape the book.

A special thank you to the Kogan Page team for the help in putting the book together and their continued faith in me to undertake the work. I especially want to thank Jeylan Ramis and Donna Goddard for their support throughout the production of the book.

1

Reputation – what is it and how can it be managed?

Introduction

Being talked about, being written about and being recognized in a crowded marketplace have been seen by many to underpin reputation. But where it comes from, what it is and importantly how it can be managed is more complex. Reputation has also been placed at the centre of many definitions of public relations and remains the driving force behind much of the work that takes place. In a world that is increasingly driven by technological developments and where there is instability and uncertainty, is our understanding of reputation management still appropriate? Is reputation still what we thought it was? Does the definition require changing and updating? In the post-Covid world have views and attitudes moved on and are they leaving the PR and communication profession behind?

Reputation management needs to change and adapt to the developments in society and the world of communication. External factors have created the need to update the approach to reputation management for it to be effective. The challenge is to understand whether the elements that comprise a positive reputation have also changed over the years. If this change has happened, then what elements are involved in creating a positive reputation for any business or organization? How much is it influenced by the experiences that people have and how much is it driven by perceptions? And importantly has this changed in a world where technological advances have given people the ability to share any thoughts, views and opinions instantly?

For those outside the PR and communication profession there is a misunderstanding about what reputation and reputation management is. It is often equated to manipulation and the attempt to present a positive image regardless of whether it matches the reality. This is a position that is often propagated by the mainstream media who depict reputation management and public relations as the art of spin. For some, the word reputation has been dropped to break the connection to this commonly held view of PR. It appears that reputation and reputation management have themselves developed a bad reputation. To understand what it is and how relevant it is to modern day communication, it is important to dissect the constituent parts of reputation. This should be followed by looking at what a positive reputation means and whether there is a need to establish an updated definition of reputation and reputation management.

What is reputation?

It is helpful to start with some definitions of both reputation and reputation management with a consideration of what they mean for the world of public relations and communication. A common definition of reputation is the general opinion or description of a person's character or other qualities and the opinion people usually have, or the perceived admiration or respect for someone or something, determined by past character or behaviour. The elements within these definitions that are important are: opinion and perception, qualities, behaviours and characters. If organizations are going to be able to effectively manage their reputation it is important to understand each of these elements in the context of the business.

Some views of reputation are that it is intangible, based on levels of trust in the organization, or that it is about actions and behaviour. However, there are ways that it can be quantified by taking account of a range of variables some of which may be normative but others that will be defined by the business. This will be explored in future chapters. Noted public relations theorist James E Grunig and academic Chun-ju Flora Hung highlight that reputation, image, brand, perception and impression are often used interchangeably to define reputation.[1] So it is important to consider what is bound up in reputation to make it tangible and quantifiable for organizations and businesses. Grunig and Hung offered an updated definition of reputation in the 2002 paper. In it they said, 'We defined reputation as a distribution of cognitive representations, may or may not include an attitudinal or evaluative component, held by members of a collectivity – such as the general population or a specific public of an organization.'[2]

In Grunig and Hung's definition, reputation can be shaped by both attitudes and facts and is how we internalize the external perception of something or someone. This roots reputation in the cognitive processes of the individual, which is critical to understand when considering how to manage and evaluate it, as well as respond when it is under pressure.

A final definition that needs to be considered comes from John Doorley and Helio Fred Garcia in their book, *Reputation Management*. Doorley had established a process known as 'Comprehensive Reputation Management'[3] which 'defined reputation as the sum of perceptions of the stakeholder groups and was based on the proposition that to manage the parts is to manage the whole'.[4] It included the formula for reputation management, which brought performance, behaviour and communication together, adding a multiplier of the authenticity factor at a later date. This includes a number of the constituent parts that influence or impact on reputation, but it lacks the human interpretation that was postulated by Grunig in his work. The role of people within the definition of reputation and reputation management is a critical element that needs to be reflected in the modern era. It is when views of reputation are shared and made public that they have the most impact. The position goes from influencing one person's decisions and actions to potentially influencing multiple people including family, friends and unknown individuals through social media and other technology. This was highlighted by Diermeier who stated that 'reputations are public by nature'.[5]

The reputation of a business is comprised of both good and bad experiences, of the moments when things work well and when things have gone wrong. This means it can change and develop over time, either with those views becoming more entrenched or changing in light of new experiences, actions or perceptions. Reputation is not a static thing that defines a business or organization continuously in the same way. It is therefore something that is transient and is tied to a point in time, so action can be taken to move it further up or down the scale. It is that action that will be detailed in Chapter 4, which looks at how to rescue a bad reputation.

Multiple reputations

The situation is further complicated with the potential for multiple reputations to be in place depending on who is assessing the situation, and at what point in time it happens. This can also be seen with multinational organizations where reputations may vary due to geographical differences. Actions and behaviour of companies will be perceived differently due to a range of external factors and the community values and norms. For example, the approach to censoring the media that exists in China would not be accepted in other parts of the world. This in turn will influence views and perceptions of the way authorities, organizations and businesses operate.

The definition of what reputation is, will be different from within the company or business and from those outside the business, whether customers or consumers. Internal and external groups will apply different weightings to what is seen as most important to establishing a good reputation and where they place value will be subject to change. Where the business will put a lot of focus on the financial viability, investment and innovation to secure a positive reputation, people will look to the behaviours, attitudes and product or service quality. In Chapter 3 the impact of this difference will be seen when looking at how to measure reputation and quantify any risk or challenge to the reputation of a business. It is also important to identify how reputation may change and develop over time due to external factors. This includes the impact of societal and organizational norms on what is acceptable and what is prioritized.

Personal reputation does have an impact in certain cases on the reputation of the organization or business. In those situations where the founder, CEO or C-suite are very vocal, publicly recognized and connected to the business their actions and behaviour will affect that of the whole organization. Even when the CEO may be low key their behaviour will still have an impact once it is recognized and scrutinized. Corporate reputation, which this book is concerned with, is made up of a number of elements which will be discussed later in this chapter. It is developed from the past, present and future operation and behaviour of the business. It can be affected by myths and legends related to the history of the business. Organizations essentially cannot unilaterally own their reputation as it is owned by those whose views shape it. Online reputation may also be highlighted as a separate element to the business' reputation, but it does not stand alone. Whether online or offline the reputation will be comprised of a number of critical factors.

Lenses to view reputation

Reputation is, as stated earlier, created from both experience and perceptions. The views people have can and do have an effect on how they define a business' reputation. This can also change over time and with developments. The business' reputation is not a one-size-fits-all situation and needs to be categorized by those who are assessing it. Different groups will be looking at it through a variety of lenses. For example, if I am a customer then how a business deals with my purchase, any challenges, complaints and providing updates on future products will be central to how the reputation is perceived.

Corporate reputation can be seen through lenses including the financial reputation, customer reputation, legal reputation, online reputation, political reputation, investor reputation, supplier reputation, community reputation. There may be others such as governance reputation which could involve the views of boards, non-executive directors and trustees. If any of these groups perceive the business' reputation as poor, then it can impact on the views of others and the overall corporate reputation. But the severity of the impact will depend upon how significant that problematic element is seen to be to the operation of the organization. If there is a recently established technology company that has a number of investors, and those investors view the relationship they have in a negative way then the investor reputation will be poor. On a severity assessment it may also have a significant impact on the overall reputation of the business by highlighting challenges with innovation. The details of conducting severity assessments will be covered in Chapter 4.

When attempting to define the business' reputation, first understand which of the factors are critical to it and how it operates. One of the most important factors is the purpose. What is it and do the staff and others understand it? Alongside this are the associated vision and values of the organization. Is the business demonstrating its values in how it operates? For example, if excellent customer service is part of the vision, then the reputation among customers is a critical part of the reputation. Understanding this is also a crucial factor when developing an approach to issues management and crisis communication, as will be explained in Chapter 6.

Identifying the audiences that are most significant to the business is the starting point. The perceptions these priority audiences have will matter the most whether they are consumers, service users or potential employees. Other perceptions cannot be ignored but they will potentially be of less direct significance to the way the business develops. Using stakeholder mapping, audiences can be categorized into those with the most influence and with the most interest. Reputation is comprised of a tapestry of different views from different groups. For example, in December 2023 a doctor's surgery in Doncaster, England texted all patients with a message that they had 'aggressive lung cancer'. It was sent in error and should have been a message wishing people happy holidays.[6] The story very quickly went viral and was published as far afield as Australia, India and the US. The impact to the reputation of the doctor's surgery from the views of those reading it outside the UK would not be as important as the views and perceptions of the patients.

What is reputation management?

Reputation management is the ability to manage the perceptions, views and attitudes that are in place about a business or organization. It is built from experience as well as perception which requires the involvement of the whole business to address. The fact that public relations defines itself as managing reputation can lead to silo working. The PR and communication function can be seen as where reputation is managed. In Chapter 2 the impact of reputation management across businesses will be considered.

Grunig moves the position from talking about reputation management to that of influence. He sees that influence better reflects the approach and activities that will be undertaken, and puts this alongside the importance placed upon building relationships.[7] This definition moves PR from being the delivery mechanism for establishing and maintaining a good reputation to the strategic advisory role to organizations. According to Grunig, PR needs to operate at a strategic level to achieve the required impact on developing and maintaining a positive reputation.

If reputation is defined as comprising both views and facts, then attempting to manage it becomes challenging to achieve. In reality, organizations can manage their approach to reputation, and to responding to issues when they occur rather than reputation itself. Businesses are not able to manage people's views and attitudes. Instead, they are able to influence how those perceptions are developed.

PR is a key element of reputation management and does need to be recognized by senior leaders as having a strategic impact. It requires a structure or framework to be developed that will bring reputation management into the heart of the business and of importance to all. This system will carefully consider the situation, the risks, the areas to develop and the actions that need to be taken. If there is a reputational problem it is not enough to throw

PR and communication activity at it, which will be assessed in Chapter 7. When a threat to the reputation of a business is detected, communication needs to support the strategic response to the situation. The principles of reputation management are that it needs to be planned and integrated in an organization with all employees having a role to play in developing and maintaining a positive reputation.

Reputation management needs to be taking place all day, every day. It is linked to integrity, which will be considered within Chapter 8 looking at the ethical challenges. It is what we should be doing even when no one is looking. It is not a one-off activity linked to a new product, campaign or initiative. The work is continuous using established systems and processes. If there is a change in CEO, or a new product or service developed, the approach to reputation management needs to be adjusted as necessary but still maintained. However, reputation management is different to crisis management but does play a part in how a business attempts to avoid facing a crisis in the first place.

The role of trust in reputation management

Reputation is affected by how much trust people have in organizations and businesses. If the business has a good reputation people are more likely to use the service or purchase the product. Ratings on Trustpilot or Google can influence confidence in the business.

Trust in organizations is a golden thread. It impacts all aspects of the business operation, and affects internal, external and stakeholder relationships. Do employees believe that they will be supported if something goes wrong? Do customers believe they are receiving value for money in purchasing the product? Are stakeholders confident that the business is viable and sustainable for the long-term future? Each of these questions has trust at the heart of it and driving views and perceptions. If employees do not feel they will be supported if a genuine problem emerges then they will potentially attempt to hide situations and cover up problems. Ultimately, this affects the culture of the organization, presents risks and threats to its operation, and the impact on its reputation will follow. If stakeholders do not believe the business is viable, they will seek alternatives to work with. If customers do not believe they are receiving value for money, they will move to competitors.

For public services and any organizations involved in supporting people, this lack of trust can have bigger consequences. If people do not trust what you are saying in response to an emergency, they may fail to take the actions required to save lives and property. For example, reports into the devastating impact of Hurricane Katrina in 2005, highlighted that people either did not receive the warnings or they chose to ignore them.[8] Warnings of impending disasters and the need to leave homes, move away or take other action may be ignored if the organization that is providing them is not trusted. In the world of social media and online sources of news they may look to other more trusted sources of information. As will be detailed later in Chapter 7, this is where fake news, and the rise of self-appointed experts has the potential to do the most damage to the reputation of a business.

Building trust has been seen to be the most important task during a reputational crisis.[9] Daniel Diermeier in his book *Reputation Rules* detailed the Trust Radar that highlighted four key constituent parts of trust – transparency, commitment, expertise and empathy. Each of these needs to be reflected in the response to a reputational crisis. But these elements are also important to the development of trust and ultimately to building a positive reputation before any crisis situation has emerged.

Organizations that can demonstrate the following are moving towards a positive reputation:

- transparent when they can be, recognizing that not everything can be shared for many operational, legal, financial or other reasons

- have a commitment to develop and produce the best and most affordable product, or the most effective service

- are demonstrably experts in the field that they are operating within

- listen and respond to situations with honesty, empathy and as human beings not just as a faceless corporate entity

---

In addition to the points in Diermeier's Trust Radar, the following could be added: authenticity, engagement, reliability, consistency and integrity. All these can be part of how trust is built and how reputations are improved. More details of these strategies and approaches to a reputation in crisis are discussed in Chapter 7.

The history of reputation management

From the very dawn of civilized societies, people will have been viewed and categorized as trustworthy, reliable and someone to do business with or not. This was the start of reputation being recognized as a key factor in society. But it was with the arrival of print media that it became more relevant as mass advertising meant that views could be shared with larger numbers of people. This was recognized with the dawn of the public relations industry in the 1900s. When Edward Bernays published his book *Propaganda* in 1928, he highlighted that public relations was becoming a necessity in modern life.[10] At this point the activities as part of public relations were linked to promotional campaigns focusing on convincing people that they required the products. This developed into the role of reputation management as brands and business grew, and television and radio began to broadcast.

It was the growth of the internet in the 1990s and the subsequent advent of social media in the 2000s onwards that put even more focus on reputation. Perceptions could be shared instantly and were able to be broadcast over a larger area. Social media and the development in smartphone technology brought the ability to broadcast thoughts, feelings, perceptions and concerns in a global way. It is with these developments that the position of reputation management accelerated in importance. However, it has also skewed views of reputation management, which is often seen as how to address online perceptions.

In the post-Covid pandemic era, the situation has developed further with the proliferation of fake news and a trust deficit in 'authorities' that has impacted on how reputation and reputation management is perceived. Rebuilding after the pandemic led to additional challenges financially, globally and politically. This uncertainty and chaos placed further pressure on approaches to reputation management. Developments within artificial intelligence and automated bots are expected to drive reputation management in the future. The challenge of trust and establishing accurate views of reality is becoming more complex as technology blurs many of the boundaries that had previously existed.

Throughout these years the views of what makes a positive reputation have changed and developed. In Bernays' time, approaches that were considered to be acceptable are now considered to be ethically challenging. Through the years, society has developed; acceptable behaviour and the way values are weighted have changed. Inclusive communication is now important for communication but in earlier years this was not a priority. This demonstrates that what is valued and prioritized will change and develop over time. The challenge for the communicator is to keep up to date with these developments so reputation can be managed effectively. For those working in global businesses the need to understand the norms, values and accepted behaviour in different communities is a critical part of how to conduct effective communication and reputation management. Monitoring these developments within societies is essential. Watching how issues develop, crises emerge and how actions and responses are viewed will assist in recognizing at an early stage any changes in how reputation is being viewed and assessed.

Monitoring political developments within a country is an important part of the horizon scanning that will assist in understanding and evaluating reputation. Are there new laws that are in place and have created new regulations to work within? Have politicians made announcements that may impact on what you do? Are political representatives commenting on the sector or industry that you work in? Do those politicians have a recognized standing within society or are they viewed with distrust? It is important to recognize the impact that these situations can have on a business reputation as well as that of a whole sector. When electioneering is taking place, the challenges can become even greater with politicians seeking to either gain from organizations that have a good reputation or to show action on sectors that are viewed as underperforming, particularly when they impact on the lives of the electorate.

A framework for a positive reputation

Establishing a positive reputation requires a framework to be in place across the whole organization and involving all employees. Creating a positive reputation needs to be linked to the organization's values, behaviour and culture. This must be seen as important to the operation of the business and being able to quantify it. Details of how to approach evaluating and quantifying reputation will be set out in Chapter 3. Communication and PR professionals have a key role in ensuring the value of reputation to the operation of the business is recognized.

There are six steps that can be taken to develop this framework: understand the composition of the reputation; define the key principles; outline the organizational framework; create a structure to support reputation management; establish communication within the business; and develop the training and development offer:

1 **Understand the composition of the reputation**

As outlined earlier, the elements that are important within reputation will vary between organizations and businesses. Understanding what matters to the business and therefore the reputation is the starting point of creating the framework to support development of a positive reputation. There will be factors involving people, finance, relationships, products and services, and organizational resilience that will be relevant. Each of these elements will have more or less significance to the business depending on what you do, where you do it and how long you have been doing it for. Define and understand what matters to the reputation for the business. It is important at this stage to be clear about the purpose of the organization and what it is established to do. The values of the business should be central to this stage.

2 **Define the key principles**

Outlining what matters and how it relates to the reputation of the organization will allow the development of the key principles to create a positive reputation. Doorley identified 10 precepts for reputation management which include building a strong culture, understanding people, prioritizing honesty, taking a long-term strategic approach, and being prepared for a crisis.[11] While organizations will have their own key principles related to the activity they undertake and the sector they are working within there are broad principles that apply to every business looking to establish a positive reputation. Some are reflected in what Doorley has outlined and in the post-Covid world with trust being under pressure, others are developed from assessing societal norms.

The eight principles of reputation management are:

– 1. *Nurture trust in the business through what you say and what you do* – trust is a valuable commodity and should be protected wherever possible. What you say should be supported by what you do to avoid accusations of manipulation or attempting to misrepresent the organization. Once trust is damaged or lost it is a long road back to regain it both from the public, staff and others.

– 2. *Establish boundaries within the organization to support the creation of a positive culture* – having a strong framework of governance with clear expectations and accepted behaviours is important. This requires organizations to ensure they are operating within legal and moral boundaries, as well as reinforcing the purpose and values so they are understood by staff. Build a positive culture where people are able to highlight problems and suggest improvements, and where leaders live the values on a daily basis.

- *3. Prioritize having a clear purpose and your organizational values –* these are what define the business and what sets it apart from competitors. There needs to be a clear understanding of what the business has been established to do. In addition, the values need to be threaded throughout everything the organization does and says. It needs to be found in what is monitored and measured, what is rewarded and what is delivered. It is also important to use creativity and storytelling techniques to embed these values within the organization. In addition, the values should not be compromised as it will damage trust, break the boundaries and ultimately damage the culture.

- *4. Be honest and transparent –* these principles are important to all forms of communication and to approaching communication at a time of crisis. The two principles are also key to building trust both within and outside an organization. Any attempts to hide, cover up, dupe or manipulate will be uncovered at some point either by staff such as whistleblowers, or through the actions of those outside the business. Once that happens it will impact on trust and ultimately will damage the reputation of the business. This will be discussed in Chapter 8.

- *5. Be authentic –* this is key in the modern world where being true to your values and what you believe in is highly rewarded. A business that attempts to portray itself in a way that is not genuine will face challenges. Authenticity is essential when managing issues or delivering crisis communication. It is another factor that helps to build trust and confidence as the business' words then match the actions. This is an issue that will be covered in Chapter 8 when ethics are considered.

- *6. Build relationships that are open and involve two-way communication –* leaders in organizations need to be ready to listen to feedback in an open and positive way. Effective leaders will not believe they have all the answers and will put ego aside for the benefit of the business. The culture within the business will be influenced by those at the top and they should aspire to an organization where communication is two-way, and employees feel able to raise concerns and offer improvements. Relationships that are valued and cultivated will support the creation of a positive reputation.

- *7. Establish reputation within strategic and long-term planning* – building a reputation cannot be achieved overnight. It takes time, commitment and planning to create the culture and business operation that will support positive reputation management. The approach to reputation management needs to be strategic for it to be effective and it should not be developed in response to a challenging situation.

- *8. Be risk aware and crisis prepared* – when a problem emerges seek a resolution at an early opportunity. Understand where the biggest risks are that may affect the business and be ready to spot them immediately. Issues management is a way to avoid crises occurring by mitigating problems before they grow and develop. Effective issues management across the organization and strong crisis management procedures are vital to be ready to respond effectively when the reputation is threatened. This will be covered in detail in Chapter 7, looking at strategies to respond to situations that threaten the reputation of the business.

3 Outline the organizational framework
A business needs to have clear and understandable operating procedures. The principles by which it works should be understood by the whole organization and be underpinned by the values and the purpose. This should detail the systems for identifying and managing risks, how the business will innovate and change, the expectations of staff at all levels, and where and how decisions are made. It is also essential to determine the business' legitimacy to operate. In a research paper from the University of Alberta the following definition of organizational legitimacy was provided: 'Organizational legitimacy is the perceived appropriateness of an organization to a social system in terms of rules, values, norms, and definitions.'[12] It requires organizations to understand the framework that they work within, the legislation and regulations as well as the moral and societal expectations on them. This should drive the systems and processes that are in place.

4 Create a structure to support reputation management
As has been stated, reputation management is something that affects and should involve all parts of the business. With that in mind, there needs to be a structure that will support the day-to-day activity and the long-term

strategic overview of reputation management. This will involve the risk management processes, business development and product innovation, employee engagement and reward processes, and communication and marketing. There may be other elements that are required such as investment and investor relations, stakeholder engagement, lobbying and political relationships, and staff training. All these aspects should be connected together with an understanding of how they relate to, and impact on, reputation management.

5 Establish communication within the business

The role of the communication, PR and marketing teams within any business is often seen to be the only area that needs to focus on reputation management. However, they are the team that deal with the public-facing manifestation of reputation and will spot problems on the horizon. The whole business, as stated earlier, needs to be involved in the management of the business' reputation. The communication team must have a strategic position within the business so that they can help develop and drive the framework around reputation management. If they do not have a seat at the top table where they can advise the C-suite, they should ensure there are ways that they can influence the decision-making. At the heart of the communication activity should be the focus on building and maintaining confidence in the business. Communication should work both strategically and tactically, advising about the problems, identifying areas to develop, and considering how to promote the business. Communication needs to see across the whole of the business so they are able to identify areas of concern or problems from within before they develop, and so they can provide external feedback to aid the development of the business.

6 Develop the training and development offer

The final section of the framework that will support the development of a positive reputation is the training and development offer for employees. If those employed by the business do not feel supported and equipped to do their role it can lead to them becoming disconnected and disengaged. Problems from within the workforce are one of the primary areas where reputational risks and issues emerge. Ensuring employees are engaged with the vision and purpose for the business is essential but so is providing them with ongoing training and development so they can achieve their full potential. It is through training that the culture and expectations can be reinforced, and staff can understand the importance of getting things right or highlighting problems at an early stage.

The new definition of reputation

There are many definitions of reputation that have been identified and included earlier in this chapter. But in a world of chaos, crises and where there is a trust deficit in those in authority, should there be a new definition of reputation? From history, Abraham Lincoln is quoted as saying: 'Character is like a tree and reputation like its shadow. The shadow is what we think of it, the tree is the real thing.' While this may have been true in the 1800s the definition feels out of touch with the modern life challenges of social media, developments in technology, and fake news. Views may be given of the tree and what it is, even that it is not a tree, which can impact both on the character of the tree and how its reputation is viewed. The simplicity of Lincoln's position adds little to the complexity of modern life.

Doorley's equation of reputation as the sum of perception, behaviour and communication with a multiplier of authenticity also feels that it is failing to take account of the factors that are relevant in the post-Covid era to reputation and reputation management. It needs to include a recognition of the societal norms and values that are impacting on the way reputation is viewed, as well as the personal position that can change how a business is perceived. It may be too simplistic to try to distil the definition of reputation to an equation. The benefit of defining reputation is that it should be clear how it plays a part in the development or in the case of a poor reputation, the demise of the business. The factors that should be included are the impact of external issues and the development of modern technology, as these have required an expanded and further developed definition of reputation. In addition, the role of people in defining and establishing reputation should be included in any definition. In modern communication, relationships are crucial to defining and improving reputation.

A revised definition of reputation could be that it is the way an organization or business is viewed by individuals and groups. The views are shaped by a variety of factors including experiential data and attitudinal perspectives which may be based in facts or opinions that have been interpreted by the individual or others. Opinions and perceptions may or may not be rooted in facts and verifiable data. Reputation is about what an organization says and does and the congruence and adherence to the outlined vision and purpose as well as societal norms. At its core, reputation will be ultimately defined by those who are viewing the business, whether or not this has been derived through influence, experience or unfounded views.

From understanding the way a reputation can be developed, an organization can then move to identifying the steps to take to build a positive reputation and how to influence the way people perceive the business, which will be covered in Chapter 2.

CASE STUDY
Confederation of British Industry (CBI)

Background

The Confederation of British Industry (CBI) claims on its website that it 'speaks on behalf of 170,000 businesses of all sizes and sectors, across every region and nation of the UK'.[13] It is a member organization that was established in 1965. It was established to share the views of member businesses to the government and has been involved in lobbying. The CBI is also a Royal Charter organization so has oversight from the CBI Council, which is comprised of members of regional and national councils and committees.

Situation

In March 2023, *The Guardian* newspaper ran an article that the CBI's Director-General Tony Danker had 'stepped aside' following them asking questions about a formal complaint that had been made in January of that year about Mr Danker's behaviour, and additional allegations that had been made by other members of staff.[14] The CBI President Brian McBride was reported as saying that the complaint was investigated and determined it did not require escalating into a disciplinary process. However, in response to the fresh allegations an independent investigation was launched by the CBI who brought in an external law firm.

The situation escalated a few weeks later when additional serious allegations emerged which sparked a police investigation by the City of London police. The independent investigation reported findings in late April and made a number of recommendations in relation to governance, structure, policies, management, employee relations and the management or risk. In a summary document the investigation found:

> that it is apparent that staff did not come forward at the time with their concerns; and that there were obstacles to the communication of concerns about employee behaviour from the HR team to the Executive Committee or to the Board level, such that they were not consistently escalated and discussed when they ought to have been.[15]

It led to the CBI suspending membership and policy activity until June 2023 when an Extraordinary General Meeting was held to decide on the future. At the same time, some of the biggest names in business were distancing themselves from the organization.[16] There had been further allegations during April that led to media reports of a 'toxic culture' at the CBI.[17] The allegations reported by *The Guardian* included that of an 'unchecked culture of misogyny'.

The CBI created a plan of reform following the recommendations within the investigation report. It was approved by members at the June Extraordinary General Meeting.[18] In the months that followed, the CBI provided updates on the progress through their website on the page Scorecard for Change[19] and provided some commentary with the publication of the 2022 Annual Report. The President Mr McBride wrote a preface in an annual report that talked of the challenges and how they had informed the organization. It highlighted the programme of change that was underway including to governance, systems and processes.[20] The annual report also referenced the 'material uncertainty' that lay ahead.[21] There remains discussion about whether the CBI can withstand the long-term damage to its reputation that happened in 2023.

Reputation lessons

- The damage began when the complaint was not dealt with through the disciplinary process. It represented a serious risk to the organization and could have been handled more sensitively and with a recognition of steps that may need to be taken. Issues and problems that may damage the reputation of the organization must be recognized at the earliest opportunity so that appropriate action can be taken before the issue becomes public.

- The culture of the CBI was highlighted, and internal systems and processes appear not to have allowed employees to raise concerns in a supportive environment. It is a reminder that the views and experiences of staff need to be heard by management and be considered in decision-making.

- Building a supportive environment where there is trust and staff have confidence in management requires the support of those at the top of the organization. Trust is an important part of reputation management and that is for both employees and the public.

- The CBI found that member businesses distanced themselves from the organization as the crisis escalated. Stakeholder engagement remains an important strategy when managing a potentially damaging situation. Expect those closely aligned to the business at risk to look for reassurance and to publicly protect themselves by building some distance if required as an organization responds to the situation. Rebuilding the stakeholder support takes time and requires significant investment of time and energy to achieve results.

- The President recognized that this was not about rebranding or putting out communication but required the organization to be 'sorted out'.[22] The future of the CBI will be due to the organizational change and framework that is put in place; not changing its name or putting out items of positive news and developments.

- The situation has developed over many months and impacted on the businesses who are, or would be, members of the CBI. In rebuilding the reputation the CBI needs to invest in a whole organization approach for a considerable period of time. It needs to embed reputation management as part of the organization's development moving forward.

CASE STUDY

Policing and law enforcement in the UK and US

Background

A series of challenging situations and criminal cases involving police officers hit the headlines in the UK. The murder of Sarah Everard by a serving police officer sparked protests and concerns about the culture within the Metropolitan Police. It led to an independent report being commissioned assessing the standards of behaviour and internal culture of the Metropolitan Police Service. The review was led by Baroness Casey and reported in March 2023.

In the US there have been similar concerns raised following the murder of George Floyd in 2020. The response to the school shooting in Uvalde in May 2022 was another high-profile incident where the police response was heavily criticized.[23] But many cities and communities were affected by incidents and issues involving local law enforcement officers. For example, in Antioch, a small city outside San Francisco, an investigation into police misconduct found more than 45 officers, half of the city's squad, was implicated in racist behaviour. The investigation concerned text messages between law enforcement officers between 2019 and 2022 that were 'violently racist, misogynistic and anti-gay'. The city council voted to audit the department, which had not conducted internal reviews since 2017.[24]

Situation

The combination of a number of high-profile cases of misconduct, corruption and criminal activity has had an impact on levels of trust and confidence in policing. The Casey report into the Metropolitan Police Service found there were 'systematic and fundamental problems in how the Met is run' and that 'deep-seated cultures' needed to be tackled. It also concluded that 'discrimination is tolerated, not dealt with and has become baked into the system'. In her foreword Baroness Casey said:

> The police want to earn our trust. And we want to trust the police. It is what great police officers deserve. It is what the great city of London deserves. Words alone cannot do that. It is only through actions that the Met can now begin to re-earn that trust. This is the moment for it to do so.[25]

Following the publication of the report the Metropolitan Police Commissioner detailed a programme of change and has regularly reported on its impact.

In December 2023, the IPSOS Veracity Index that assesses levels of trust in different professions found that the 'views of the truthfulness of the police continue to decline'. Between 2019 and 2023 levels of trust in the police had fallen by 20 points to the lowest level in 40 years.[26] At the same time a Gallup survey in the US saw a drop in confidence in local police forces from 73 per cent in 2021 to 69 per cent in 2023. But among Black Americans confidence was considerably lower at 56 per cent. Three-quarters of the Black Americans involved in the survey said they wanted to see major changes in policing.[27] Action was taken in many of the cases with officers being sacked, investigated or police teams disbanded.

Reputation lessons

- Industry-wide concerns have the ability to impact everyone involved in the work. As the case study shows, there was a widespread drop in the confidence levels in law enforcement. All working in the sector needed to take notice, review how they operate and make changes where necessary. This may include revising any communication or public activity that may appear out of step with the stated values.

- As Baroness Casey stated, the response and approach to rebuild reputation was about more than words. The key in rebuilding trust and confidence had to be a visible change in the way police operated, conducted investigations and connected with communities. When reputation is challenged, the actions need to be put in place and this can then be supported by the strategic communication.

- Addressing damage to a business' reputation cannot be achieved by just pushing out good-news stories. It is important to understand what the concerns are linked to, what has happened to cause the damage? How important is the area of concern to the overall reputation of the business? What is the short- and long-term impact of this loss of confidence? This should be used to take a strategic look at the communication activity over time.

- Understanding internal behaviour and the culture of the business is essential to identify issues and make changes, as necessary. In both situations there appears to have been a lack of awareness of the emerging problems. In the Antioch situation the lack of any internal audit, inspection and oversight has allowed the behaviour to continue without challenge for many years. Strong governance and clear expectations and behaviour that staff should adhere to, and that is reinforced, is critical to avoiding reputational crises.

- Even with strong internal systems and processes, problems can still develop if the business does not take account of views and issues raised by diverse communities. The surveys from the US show that the response needs to be focused in different ways for different communities. Understanding the views and perceptions has to be more detailed than just one universal position. Methods to listen to external perceptions are a critical part of the business infrastructure.

- In both the UK and US the work to rebuild trust and confidence cannot be achieved overnight. Figures for the UK show a drop to a 40-year low, and this will not be turned around with just communication activity, or some positive stories being shared. The changes need to be structural and institutional and flow through every area of the organization. It requires sustained behaviour change among officers and staff, and above all this change needs to be visible in the actions and approaches that people experience.

- Law enforcement in the US and the UK also need to have contingency plans and crisis communication plans in place throughout the long road to rebuilding a positive reputation. Any one incident, miscommunication, error or problem could be a setback and further damage the reputation of policing. The structured response that is used for operational emergencies can be used to provide a whole organization response to future challenges linked to perceptions.

Conclusion

Reputation has become misunderstood, and its definition has added to the challenge of what it is and what it means. In the modern world it is important to recognize that reputation management really means reputation influencing, as Grunig highlighted. Businesses need to be clear about their purpose and what it is that they both do and want to be seen to do. This is more than PR and communication and is about the whole business operating effectively, within boundaries and with clear expectations.

Being able to impact on the reputation of the business can only be effective when the groups that matter have been identified. Reputation can then be dissected to a number of constitutional parts of the reputation with those identified communities. How they view the business will not be static as the world and societies are constantly changing. It is a challenge for the business, its reputation management processes and communicators but one that must be managed to be able to develop effective reputation management. Societal changes, external developments and internal operational developments can all impact on the way a business and its reputation are perceived.

Before considering how to improve the reputation of any business there are key factors that need to be in place. The eight principles of reputation management need to be in place and widely understood by those in the business. Without the processes, systems and culture in place to support a positive reputation, the efforts of the business and its communication team can fail to bring the required results. But with a clear focus and drive to improve, live the purpose and values, and be responsive to problems and issues a business can start to look at ways to improve their reputation, which will be covered in Chapter 2.

References

1   James E Grunig and Chun-ju Flora Hung. The Effect of Relationships on Reputation and Reputation on Relationships: A cognitive behavioural study [pre-print], 2022, www.researchgate.net/publication/247855482_The_effect_of_relationships_on_reputation_and_reputation_on_relationships_A_cognitive (archived at https://perma.cc/W78M-UM2V)

2   James E Grunig and Chun-ju Flora Hung. The Effect of Relationships on Reputation and Reputation on Relationships: A cognitive behavioural study [pre-print], 2022, www.researchgate.net/publication/247855482_The_effect_of_relationships_on_reputation_and_reputation_on_relationships_A_cognitive (archived at https://perma.cc/W78M-UM2V)

3   J Doorley and H F Garcia (2021) *Reputation Management: The key to successful public relations and corporate communication*, Routledge, New York

4   J Doorley and H F Garcia (2021) *Reputation Management: The key to successful public relations and corporate communication*, Routledge, New York

5   D Diermeier (2011) *Reputation Rules: Strategies for building your company's most valuable asset*, McGraw-Hill, New York

6   M Drummond. GP surgery accidentally texts patients that they have 'aggressive lung cancer' – instead of Happy Christmas, *Sky News*, 29 December 2022, https://news.sky.com/story/gp-surgery-accidentally-texts-patients-they-have-

aggressive-lung-cancer-instead-of-happy-christmas-12776352 (archived at https://perma.cc/U297-7GUZ)

7 James E Grunig and Chun-ju Flora Hung. The Effect of Relationships on Reputation and Reputation on Relationships: A cognitive behavioural study [pre-print], 2022, www.researchgate.net/publication/247855482_The_effect_ of_relationships_on_reputation_and_reputation_on_relationships_A_cognitive (archived at https://perma.cc/W78M-UM2V)

8 T Cole and K Fellows. Risk Communication Failure: A Case Study of New Orleans and Hurricane Katrina, *Southern Communication Journal*, 2008, 73 (3), www.tandfonline.com/doi/full/10.1080/10417940802219702 (archived at https://perma.cc/4N5Z-BTXC)

9 D Diermeier (2011) *Reputation Rules: Strategies for building your company's most valuable asset*, McGraw-Hill, New York

10 R Gunderman. The manipulation of the American mind: Edward Bernays and the birth of public relations, *The Conversation*, 9 July 2015, https://theconversation.com/the-manipulation-of-the-american-mind-edward-bernays-and-the-birth-of-public-relations-44393 (archived at https://perma.cc/ 5WGH-9ZWS)

11 J Doorley and H F Garcia (2021) *Reputation Management: The key to successful public relations and corporate communication*, Routledge, New York

12 D Deephouse, J Bundy, L Plunkett-Tost and M Suchman. Organizational Legitimacy: Six key questions, SSRN, https://ssrn.com/abstract=2849636 (archived at https://perma.cc/K3LX-JAE3)

13 The CBI 'About Us', www.cbi.org.uk/about-us/ (archived at https://perma.cc/ G8ST-5DEY)

14 A Isaac. CBI boss Tony Danker steps aside amid allegations of misconduct, *The Guardian*, 6 March 2023, www.theguardian.com/business/2023/mar/06/ cbi-boss-tony-danker-steps-aside-amid-allegations-of-misconduct (archived at https://perma.cc/P5LM-3LTM)

15 CBI: Annex: The Fox Williams Report, 2023, www.cbi.org.uk/media/ m0pcest1/annex-to-open-letterapril23.pdf (archived at https://perma.cc/ 6BJE-MMWW)

16 A Isaac, G Wearden and D Hajjaji. CBI to suspend operations until June after exodus of top UK businesses, *The Guardian*, 21 April 2023, www.theguardian. com/business/2023/apr/21/cbi-suspend-operations-top-uk-businesses-john-lewis-natwest (archived at https://perma.cc/MR8D-85QC)

17 A Isaac. Revealed: new claims of sexual misconduct and 'toxic culture' at CBI, *The Guardian*, 3 April 2023, www.theguardian.com/business/2023/apr/ 03/revealed-new-claims-of-sexual-misconduct-and-toxic-culture-at-cbi (archived at https://perma.cc/WV3F-LJRH)

18 K Rawlinson and G Wearden. CBI members back reform package at extraordinary general meeting – as it happened, *The Guardian*, 6 June 2023, www.theguardian.com/business/live/2023/jun/06/cbi-future-crunch-vote-extraordinary-general-meeting-rain-newton-smith-brian-mcbride-today-business-live (archived at https://perma.cc/Z8Y7-MD87)

19 CBI. CBI Scorecard for change, 22 Feb 2024, www.cbi.org.uk/articles/scorecard-for-change/ (archived at https://perma.cc/WA7W-TTFB)

20 CBI. CBI Annual Report and Accounts 2022, 1 December 2023, www.cbi.org.uk/media/udtfnjiz/cbi-annual-report-and-accounts-2022.pdf (archived at https://perma.cc/PAN2-E22J)

21 R Neate. CBI warns of 'material uncertainty' over future after sexual misconduct claims, *The Guardian*, 4 December 2023, www.theguardian.com/business/2023/dec/04/cbi-warns-of-material-uncertainty-over-future-after-sexual-misconduct-claims (archived at https://perma.cc/NHU3-XS8A)

22 A Isaac. CBI president says it failed to 'filter out culturally toxic people' from ranks, *The Guardian*, 24 April 2023, www.theguardian.com/business/2023/apr/24/cbi-president-says-it-failed-to-filter-our-culturally-toxic-people-from-ranks (archived at https://perma.cc/7825-7QZ2)

23 Z Despart. 'Systemic failures' in Uvalde shooting went far beyond local police, Texas House report details, *Texas Tribune*, 17 July 2022, www.texastribune.org/2022/07/17/law-enforcement-failure-uvalde-shooting-investigation/ (archived at https://perma.cc/AT9W-HTFV)

24 R Buller. In racist police text scandal, US town sees echoes of an intolerant past, *The Guardian*, 27 April 2023, www.theguardian.com/us-news/2023/apr/27/antioch-california-police-text-scandal (archived at https://perma.cc/2TTY-G43F)

25 Baroness Casey Review, Final Report: An independent review into the standards of behaviour and internal culture of the Metropolitan Police Service, March 2023, www.met.police.uk/SysSiteAssets/media/downloads/met/about-us/baroness-casey-review/update-march-2023/baroness-casey-review-march-2023a.pdf (archived at https://perma.cc/WQ7L-PU9Q)

26 Ipsos. Trust in politicians reaches its lowest score in 40 years, 14 December 2023, www.ipsos.com/en-uk/ipsos-trust-in-professions-veracity-index-2023 (archived at https://perma.cc/EE64-PA2H)

27 M C Brown and C Lloyd. Black Americans less confident, satisfied with local police, Gallup.com, 18 September 2023, https://news.gallup.com/poll/511064/black-americans-less-confident-satisfied-local-police.aspx (archived at https://perma.cc/U8QJ-3KHB)

2

Building a positive reputation – what does it take?

Introduction

The importance of a positive reputation has been underestimated by many. There is a school of thought that places any publicity, and possibility to increase the recognition of a business, as beneficial. The 'all publicity is good publicity' approach would accept that infamy can be a part of reputation management. Infamy arises when there is a negative reaction when the name of an organization or individual is mentioned.[1]

In a world of influencers that has become more polarized in relation to issues, the position of being infamous may be seen as favourable. Being a controversial celebrity figure may lead to additional bookings and opportunities to add a different perspective to topics under discussion. However, for businesses this is a dangerous position to try to inhabit as will be outlined later.

There are many benefits to establishing a positive reputation for the business or organization. The business that has a positive reputation in relation to how it treats and rewards staff will find it easier to recruit and be able to choose the best people for the positions. This can also include attracting trustees, non-executive directors and board members to fill vacancies. If those employees feel motivated and supported, they are more likely to be invested in the vision of the business. This helps to create a positive culture and ultimately the staff can become advocates to continue to build the positive reputation. Staff who feel engaged with the organization they work for will be more productive and potentially will help to innovate and develop the business.

An organization that has a positive reputation as being financially stable will be able to access investment more easily as it is viewed as sustainable, prudent and well-managed. It will also attract more customers and service users and be able to retain them as they return due to effective customer relations and having a strong productive or service offer. Businesses that have a positive reputation are also able to command higher prices for the product or service, which can be seen as desirable. Organizations that have a positive reputation can also have share prices boosted.

In addition to the financial, customer and staffing benefits, a business with a positive reputation will be able to choose the suppliers and third parties that they want to work with. Other businesses will want to work with them. They may be able to agree favourable deals on the purchase of raw materials as other businesses want to benefit from being associated with them. Organizations that have a good reputation will avoid unwarranted media scrutiny as they face fewer issues, problems and crises. When they do face problems, they will have the required structure and approach that allows them to manage the situation effectively and swiftly. They can dodge being labelled as a problematic or a crisis-hit business within media coverage of any situations that emerge. This means that establishing a positive reputation gives a business a competitive advantage, and this is a valuable and non-transferable asset.

The benefits of a positive reputation are significant enough to assist the business in establishing its legitimacy to operate and building its market position and share. Quantifying the benefit of a positive reputation will be outlined in more detail in Chapter 3. But the benefits identified make building a positive reputation an aspiration for businesses. From the definition of reputation in the previous chapter it is clear; building a positive reputation requires more than just communication, PR and marketing activity.

What creates an effective organization?

Before considering the elements that are required to establish a positive reputation, it is important to be clear what aspects create an effective business or organization. The business has to be able to function effectively for there to be a chance of establishing a positive reputation. There are six qualities that are identified in systems theory as being required. Systems theory considers the development of a unification across all systems within an organization. The six qualities are 'wholeness, hierarchy, self-regulation, openness, adaptability and stability and flexibility'.[2] Seeing the organization and its systems as a whole rather than as individual parts is essential when considering the development of a positive reputation. It avoids the silo approach that may prioritize only certain aspects of the organization. However, the qualities may appear to be values or principles rather than tangible factors of an effective organization.

An effective organization does need to operate in a unified way and this means focusing on eight areas working together. These eight key areas are: product, service, staff, strategy, governance, operation, finances and communication:

1 *Product* – whatever the product or service provided by the business, it needs to be the best it can be and subject to continued development and innovation.

2 *Service* – there needs to be an understanding of the customer requirements and the ability to respond to their needs by offering the best possible service.

3 *Staff* – employees need to be connected to the purpose of the business and help to deliver a quality service and make improvements as necessary.

4 *Strategy* – the business needs to have a clear strategy based in the purpose that it has established. This strategy considers how to weather the potential uncertainties and also to remain ahead of competition by developing the product or service.

5 *Governance* – strong governance is a critical part of a successful organization. It ensures everyone understands their roles and responsibilities and that decision-making is carried out in a timely and effective manner.

6 *Operation* – the day-to-day activities of the business are subject to policies and procedures that ensure smooth working. Any problems are identified and managed quickly, and opportunities to develop and improve are grasped.

7 *Finances* – the business needs to be financially viable, solvent and profitable with money invested in the future operation and development of the business and its products and/or services.

8 *Communication* – communication is a strategic function that can advise on the development and delivery of effective activities both internally and externally.

A strong business is developed from what it does and how it does it. Each of these eight elements are part of the framework that creates a robust business. With these factors in place it can then support the establishment of a positive reputation by putting key pieces of the jigsaw together. Even with a problem in one or two of these areas a business can still develop a positive reputation, but it may be heading for challenging times if those issues are not addressed. For example, a bakery business that has a strong product line, supportive staff and a structure that will support development and future investment but that fails to listen to negative customer feedback will struggle to maintain a positive reputation. People will expose the business to negative online reviews and comments that could damage the reputation. Establishing the eight aspects of the business and ensuring that they are working needs to be the first step to building a positive reputation.

Reputation is more than good PR

Building a positive reputation cannot be achieved by developing PR campaigns, communication and marketing activity alone. As has been outlined, reputation comes from what is done, as well as what is said, by businesses. Approaching the challenge of developing a good reputation by creating campaigns and PR only is fundamentally flawed. In the worst case it will lead to a backlash against the business and potentially damage the reputation as what is being promoted is contrary to people's experiences. In all cases it will get called out by others who recognize that the portrayal of the business is not accurate or appropriate. Remember that reputation is a combination of both direct experiences and indirect views.

PR and campaigns have a part to play in supporting the development of a positive reputation but should not be the first thought for a business that wants to establish itself or to improve its position. Reputation needs to be a golden thread through the organization, how it is established, how it operates and what it does. The way a business conducts itself is critical to that positive reputation. Are decisions made in an appropriate way considering the needs of customers as well as shareholders and the future of the business? Is there a strong governance framework in place that ensures accountability? Are staff treated well and is there a strong offer for those who join as employees? Are products and services developed to be the best they can be, and do they listen to customer feedback? All of these questions outline areas that can make an impact positively or negatively on the reputation of the business. The corporate framework and operation of a business needs to understand the role that reputation plays in ensuring its future.

A positive reputation is not just something that is developed over many years. Being in existence for a number of years does give an opportunity to have established a strong reputation but it does not mean it is a given position. Time served is no guarantee of a positive reputation. In the technology sector, companies can grow quickly and have a strong reputation that develops swiftly; for example, OpenAI and its artificial intelligence products have become leaders in the sector building its reputation. At the same time businesses that have been in existence for many years have disappeared from high streets regardless of their reputation, for example Debenhams and Woolworths in the UK. They may have had a reputation that was neutral or positive but if that did not translate into sales it would never secure their future.

It is important to understand what the business looks like to others when considering reputation management and development. Ensuring there is accurate data and insight into how customers, the public and others view the business is critical to building a positive reputation. If there is no clear understanding of what people think, it will be a huge challenge to take any steps to address inaccuracies or to promote a different perspective. Building a positive reputation has to come from a clear knowledge of what others think or believe when they hear the business' name. And breaking that down into audiences that are segmented. Communicators must avoid considering reputation in a narrow context from their own perspective, as it provides just one view. Different groups will have different views and it is important to understand each of them and which are the most crucial to business development using stakeholder and audience mapping.

Data, brand awareness and other factors need to be measured on an ongoing basis so that the position is understood at any point in time. This is critical when a problem occurs, and a possible issue or crisis emerges. There will be no opportunity to run reputation monitoring data before the impact of the situation affects the reputation. Without data, it is impossible at that point to really understand the full extent of the damage that the situation has done to the reputation of the business.

What is needed for a positive reputation?

The elements that are identified as necessary for a positive reputation can depend on the way that reputation is viewed and defined. Six key aspects for a great reputation are identified in the book *Reputation Management* where Nitin Mantri focuses on 'retaining the customer's trust, consistent innovation, happy employees, an able leadership team, social responsibility and continuous engagement'.[3] These do raise some important elements that are needed within a good reputation, such as honesty, quality, employee satisfaction, humanity, philanthropy and preservation of the brand.

In the era of misinformation and a trust deficit, with the definition of reputation outlined in Chapter 1, there are nine aspects that underpin the creation of a positive reputation. They are:

1   A clear purpose

2   Values that are reinforced

3   Development of effective relationships

4   Engaged and supported employees

5   Effective leadership

6   Risk management and crisis preparedness

7   Financial stability

8   Cultural intelligence

9   Communication operating strategically

Underpinning every business should be a clear purpose for what it does, who it does it for and what it means for individuals and society. If this is not understood, then it can cause problems for staff who are not clear what they should do and what the priorities are for the business. It is also an issue for the public who will find it difficult to gauge the business on any firm foundation. This can mean that any reputation that is created is built on a flimsy foundation that can buckle at any moment. People create their views of what the business is about from the commentary of others in lieu of any concrete positioning from the organization. Clarity of purpose has a strong position within all business frameworks.

Building a positive reputation requires values to be in place that are reinforced within the business. The values should support the purpose of the business and need to be reflected in the decisions that are made and the actions that are taken. They should also be within the scope of accepted norms for the society and the moment in time. There are some values that are critical to establishing a positive reputation and these include being trusted, demonstrating operating with honesty and valuing people, whether it is customers, staff or others. A value that has become increasingly important, particularly with the proliferation of fake news and the development of artificial intelligence, is authenticity. It has become a way to judge businesses and has put pressure on those organizations who have relied on PR alone to develop their reputation. If PR activity is not an authentic representation of the business, it is viewed negatively as mentioned earlier.

Fundamental to all attempts to develop and establish a positive reputation are the relationships the business has and how they are managed. Developing relationships requires the business to understand other groups and individuals and what matters to them as well as how they view and assess developments. It is the investment in building connections and as part of that the trust within the business that can be maximized for promotional purposes and if a problem develops. The relationships that are created within the organization will support the employee experience and how engaged they are with the purpose. It breaks down the silos and helps build a unified workforce. It can also help to reinforce the values and create a desirable culture. A positive reputation requires the employee experience to be positive, with the ability to highlight concerns and know they will be heard. This removes the need for employees to raise concerns publicly that they feel the organization has failed to acknowledge internally. Staff need to be heard and feel able to support the development of the business and ultimately its positive reputation.

Leadership that operates ethically and effectively is a critical element to developing a positive reputation. The role of the CEO will be detailed later in this chapter. But the leadership needs to listen, be accountable, make effective decisions, understand the business developments that are required, see areas for innovation, and effectively advocate for the business. It is important to establish a legitimacy for the business to operate and exist. What they say and what they do needs to be rooted in honesty and integrity. It is important for the C-suite to drive the establishment of a strong organization that works holistically.

While businesses hope they have put enough measures in place to avoid the emergence of a problem or crisis, this is not always possible. All organizations need to be prepared for an issue or incident developing that may have a negative impact. There are two critical structures that need to be in place, understood and tested regularly. The first is a risk management framework that identifies potential problems before they happen and allows mitigation to be put in place and early alert monitoring systems to be developed. The second is to have robust crisis management plans that allow the business to move quickly and take the necessary action when a situation has developed. Communication professionals must be closely involved in the development of both risk and crisis management plans. They should help to inform risk management with details of the reputational risks they may be dealing with, and play a vital role in supporting the crisis response with effective communication.

It is not the only way to build a positive reputation, but communication has an important part to play. The focus needs to be on developing strategic communication that assists in the development of a strong business. It requires expert communication advice being given to the C-suite and the CEO, and influencing business decisions, as well as identifying opportunities to build relationships. The senior communication professional must have the ear of those at the top of the business to be truly effective. Financial stability is an important factor that should be in place for the development of a positive reputation. Any business that is perceived to be unable to effectively manage its finances will struggle to put itself in a positive position. For example, public sector bodies that are perceived as wasteful with funds or that may require cuts in services to balance the books will lack credibility. Any business that has to increase prices or that has to secure additional funding from shareholders or others to continue operation will also be perceived as unreliable. Finally, cultural intelligence is an important factor in a changing and diverse world where employees and customers may be from very different backgrounds. A business that has high levels of cultural intelligence will be more able to recruit and retain a diverse workforce and recognize changes to markets quickly.

The role of the CEO

As mentioned earlier, the role of the C-suite is essential in building the business that has the opportunity and ability to establish a positive reputation.

It is not down to the C-suite alone but without them it is not going to be possible to secure a good reputation. The CEO establishes the purpose and ways of operating as well as the accepted norms and behaviours within the business. Ultimately, the CEO can proactively develop the culture of the business or allow it to emerge unchecked or without involvement. The latter is a risky position to be allowed to develop. In the post-Covid era, the culture that exists within organizations and businesses has come under the spotlight like never before. (See the case studies at the end of Chapter 1.) Whatever the CEO does or does not do will have an impact on the way the business develops and how it is viewed by others including employees, shareholders, stakeholders and customers. It is important for those at the top of the business to do more than just run it, making the necessary decisions and ensuring it is financially viable. They are a figurehead and whether they seek publicity or not, the way they behave and what they do will be seen as a reflection on the reputation of the business. If they are seen as untrustworthy and lack the support of shareholders, they may quickly plunge the business into a crisis where new leadership is sought.

Leaders need to have an interest in the way the business is perceived and in its reputation, particularly among identified key groups. Systems and processes need to be focused not just on building a strong product but ensuring that there is trust and confidence in the operation of the organization. Structures have to be put in place to support the creation of a positive reputation and to allow the ongoing monitoring and evaluation of it. What leaders focus on is seen to be what is valued within the business, so they have a central role to ensure others also value the reputation of the business. Leaders must also establish a shared language and understanding of reputation throughout the business.

A strong organization needs to be open to challenge. Strong leaders should encourage employees to challenge what the business is doing, how it operates and what the future plans may be. The opportunity to challenge supports the internal feedback that is essential for a robust business and allows employees to be heard. Openness, trust and respect within an organization are values to be promoted and appreciated if they are in place. They support the development of a positive reputation and help to prevent internal problems escalating. In addition, a leader that allows communication and PR to operate with some delegated authority will allow the effective management of issues as well as allow opportunities to promote the business to be taken. Given the fact that CEOs may face personal damage if problems occur, they need to be confident in the ability of the PR and communication team and that they are able to identify and manage risks and issues.

Is corporate social responsibility important to reputation?

Corporate social responsibility (CSR) is often seen as a key part of the way an organization manages its reputation. It is the way a company contributes to communities and society by focusing on measures and actions often linked to environmental or social issues. CSR over the years has had an impact on how organizations are viewed, particularly when it was in the early stages of development and recognition. But in the modern world, CSR has little impact if it is not linked to the business' purpose and values, its wider operation and its behaviour. People are more interested in the credentials of a business in relation to the issues of the day. For example, when the Me Too and Black Lives Matter campaigns came into people's awareness, businesses needed to have a view on how they related to them. The same can happen with any significant world event including conflicts, disasters and social campaigns. With the increasing globalization, establishing an approach to CSR that has an internationally acceptable impact is a huge challenge. There are many societal norms that differ across the world and for a business, the approach to CSR can lack a universal applicability. The damage from this may be limited if the business operates in a local marketplace but for a multinational, the approach to CSR would need to take account of differences between countries.

CSR needs to link to the purpose, values and be rooted in the reality of the business or organization. In that way it can support the development of a positive reputation, but it can also be damaging if the approach operates in isolation or lacks authenticity. With the rise of concerns about climate change and the impact businesses and organizations have on the environment there was a rush for them to demonstrate their green credentials. This led to many examples of greenwashing, where misleading information is presented to exaggerate the business' green credentials. This problem is not confined to the impact of the business on the environment and washing can occur in other aspects of the areas of CSR. The communicator has a key role to play in challenging leadership that may attempt forms of washing in a bid to improve the organization's reputation. This will be discussed in Chapter 8.

So, is CSR dead? Over the years, CSR has often been an activity or approach that is promoted in a bid to improve the reputation of the business. This tokenistic operation of CSR should be relegated to the past. Businesses are now being questioned on a deeper level about their purpose and values, and how they impact on societies. This impacts on the reputation. The access to data and information has also allowed people to question and challenge what a company says about what they are doing. This came to attention when businesses supporting International Women's Day found a bot outing their gender pay gap details. The Gender Pay Gap Bot posts the details as an immediate response to key phrases in posts about International Women's Day.[4] CSR is no longer a way to support the development of a positive reputation unless it is rooted in the values and day-to-day operation of the business.

Finding where the business sits

In establishing and maintaining a positive reputation it is important to identify the quadrant that the business is located within. This is based on two elements: the level of interest in the management of the reputation and the preparedness to respond to any threats or challenges to the business. Understanding this will assist in developing the approach and considering where the strengths and weaknesses are. It can also support the review and monitoring of the impact of any changes.

FIGURE 2.1   Reputation management matrix

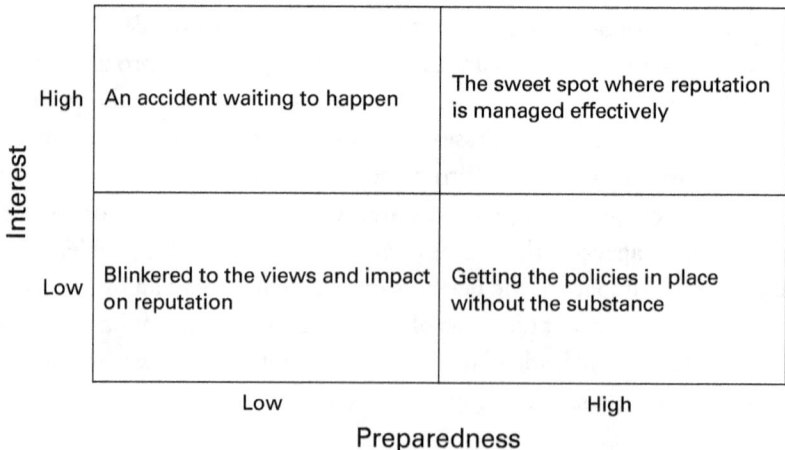

Interest

	Low Preparedness	High Preparedness
High	An accident waiting to happen	The sweet spot where reputation is managed effectively
Low	Blinkered to the views and impact on reputation	Getting the policies in place without the substance

Preparedness

The aim is to be in the top right quadrant of the chart where the business understands the importance of a good reputation and it is woven into everything that it does. There are strong risk management and crisis response processes in place that ensure issues are dealt with at the earliest opportunity avoiding reputational damage. But if the business is prepared without a focus on the reputation and how it impacts on departments and teams, it will be a theoretical process where policies are in place, but they lack the substance to make an impact on the reputation of the business. In the top left-hand quadrant are businesses that are aware of the work that is required to establish a positive reputation and may take steps towards introducing them. However, they are not prepared to deal with any challenges that emerge, making them an accident waiting to happen. They are likely to sustain significant damage when they are faced with problems or crises and will take longer to recover. Finally, businesses that are both low in interest and preparedness are in a state of ignorance. They are blinkered to the comments, views and perceptions that are in place and will be buffered on the rough seas of any reputational crises that may hit them.

Plotting the position of the business requires consideration of internal intelligence about both the operational strategy and preparedness both for innovation and change and to address turbulent times and problems that may lie ahead. In order for the business to build a positive reputation it must first understand the strengths and weaknesses that exist. Charting the position on the quadrant requires consideration of the elements needed for a strong business and the eight points for a positive reputation.

Challenges to a positive reputation

There are a number of challenges that a business may face in attempting to establish a positive reputation. This may cause progress to stall or require a new approach to be considered to address the issues. Challenges are developed from the internal approach that is taken as well as the external factors that may affect the business:

- *Overconfidence* – the business may have an unrealistic view of their own reputation and feel secure in their position. This confidence, if unjustified, can mean the business faces problems that are not being identified. It may also lead to the dismissal of problems as the implications are not fully understood. A leader that is overconfident in the position of the business may make poor decisions or fail to recognize the decisions that need to be taken.

- *Disinterest* – a business that is not interested in its reputation may continue to operate while there are no problems. But if the reputation comes under pressure or is threatened, they will not identify it and ultimately will be slow to act. At some point the impact of the reputation and people's perceptions of the business will hit and require it to be addressed.

- *Complacency* – in organizations where they have considered the impact of reputation and of what perceptions of the business may mean, they may also experience challenges. There may be complacency that they have systems in place and will be able to spot problems and address them quickly. But if this is not tested and reviewed it can be storing up issues for the future.

- *Inaccuracy* – providing information or perspectives that are not true representations of the business or attempting forms of washing, as mentioned earlier, can also be a challenge to the development of a positive reputation. It can undermine trust and confidence in the business if it is found to be manipulating and attempting to spin the situation to develop a positive reputation. Honesty is an essential part of building a good reputation.

- *Blinkered* – the business may have a fixed view of what is required and lack the ability to adapt to a changing environment. This may mean a narrow approach to managing the reputation, such as focusing only on the PR and communication activity. The leaders within the business may also fail to listen to different views and perspectives meaning they are slow to develop or respond to situations.

- *Ticking the box* – if reputation is perceived as a list of actions that need to be achieved, it can mean important developments are not considered and alternative actions not undertaken. This approach can fail to develop and mean those involved are not connected to the importance of developing a positive reputation. It can also fail to consider the impact of the actions that are taken, as the focus is on doing things rather than the impact that they have.

- *Internal challenges* – the views of the employees can create problems in recognizing the importance of a positive reputation and what goes into developing it. If the staff are not invested in the vision and purpose of the business and are not aware of how they can impact on reputation, it can restrict the ability to build a positive reputation. It may also lead to additional challenges from internal criticisms, staff behaviour and whistleblowers.

- *No action* – the approach requires more than words; it requires action to be taken. A positive reputation that stands the test of time and can withstand and respond to challenges cannot be created by communication alone. The business needs to ensure the required actions are in place including effective customer service, innovation and product developments, employee engagement and financial stability.

- *Third party actions and external events* – even if the business has a strong understanding of the actions required to establish a positive reputation, it can still be put under pressure by the actions of others. For example, if a supplier is plunged into a crisis because of something that has happened it can reflect on the business that works with them. Similar situations can occur when a business works with an influencer who then is connected to inappropriate activity. It reflects on the business with questions about whether they used due diligence in assessing the relationship. External events can also put pressure on a business, such as when the industry is the subject of a crisis. For example, in 2012–13 the food industry was put under the spotlight after horse DNA was detected in some frozen and ready meals.[5] Businesses involved in the manufacture and trade of meat and ready meals were put under pressure with questions about how they operated.

- *Old perceptions* – any business that has been in operation for a number of years will go through changes and developments. If they have been involved in some form of crisis or scandal in the past it may be that views of the reputation continue to be clouded by former events. Even when there has been a significant change in the leadership or the way the business operates it can still take time to impact on the perceptions that people have of it.

Being aware of the potential problems and recognizing them before they impact on the business is an important step towards building a positive reputation. Understanding the risks is a critical part of the plans that are put in place.

Where PR and communication can provide support

Having established that PR and communication is not the only element required to build a positive reputation, it is important to understand the role that it can play. Communication needs to be operating at a strategic level where it can advise about the impact of business decisions, changes and can bring external views into the operation. This will allow reputational issues and impact to be considered alongside operational demands. The communicator can push consideration of other courses of action or approaches if they are expected to benefit the business' reputation. In the same way policies and decisions are considered in relation to the impact it may have on equality, diversity and inclusion, it should also be checked for the potential impact on reputation. If communication is just tactical it can push information out, but will not be able to make a fundamental impact on developing a positive reputation. The work may support the development of a positive reputation, but it will be built on shaky foundations.

Monitoring, evaluating and assessing reputation is activity that PR and communication professionals can lead. They can identify the key factors that are important for the business to develop to achieve a positive reputation. This includes considering the weighting of each of the elements and identifying the key audiences and relationships. Putting evaluation in place on a regular basis will ensure that the impact of actions, events and decisions on views of the business can be understood. In some situations it is only with the data and information that those leading the business will recognize the importance of developing and maintaining a good reputation.

There are many ways that the day-to-day activities undertaken by the PR and communication team can impact on reputation and support building a positive reputation. Each of these can be part of a comprehensive communication approach to assist the overall influencing and management of reputation:

1 **Online reputation**

 Establishing a positive online reputation is a critical part of strategic reputation management. It is often mistaken as the only part of reputation management since the arrival of social media. However, it is important to have mechanisms in place that will manage the social media presence, search engine optimization and to maximize content marketing. What the social media accounts do and say can impact on the reputation of the business. Getting things wrong on social media is one of the quickest ways to a reputational crisis so having the right approach, strategy and staff involved is essential. Social media posts also remain in place unless deleted and can be searched or reposted at any point in the future. Once they are published, they can continue to impact on the reputation of the business unless methods of management are in place. The starting point has to be to understand what people think about the business and where they are sharing views or commenting. Social listening is critical to developing the online reputation as it opens eyes to what is happening. The management of social media also requires communicators to support the development of social media policies for employees. Staff need to be provided with boundaries rather than blockers, and having training and a playbook on social media can support reputation management.

2 Search engine optimization (SEO)

SEO is about making changes to your online presence, website and what you post to move the business up the search rankings. It is challenging to achieve as algorithms are often amended and developed, which can impact on rankings. But building reputation can be supported by an effective approach to SEO. When people Google or search for the business, what appears? Are there historical media reports or reviews about problems? Does it appear among the top businesses in the sector? The work to develop SEO to support building a positive reputation is about ensuring that people who search leave with a positive impression of the business. Specialists working in this area can help to ensure that the business' values are brought to the forefront and that it is seen as trustworthy with expertise in the sector. SEO also assists when an organization is under pressure, or a crisis is looming. If you have a strong position and rank highly in searches then your actions, comments and position in relation to the crisis will have a higher profile. It also has a role to play in rebuilding after a crisis and moving into recovery, which will be covered in later chapters.

3 Content marketing

Content marketing is defined by the Content Marketing Institute as 'a strategic marketing approach focused on creating and distributing valuable, relevant, and consistent content to attract and retain a clearly defined audience – and, ultimately, to drive profitable customer action.'[6] At the centre of the activity is developing content with impact, whether it is email and social media marketing, digital marketing or PR work. If the content is able to reinforce the purpose of the business and its brand values, then it can move beyond interesting to become influential to the development of a positive reputation. Content needs to be honest and be supported by the way the business operates. The ethical approach that is necessary to build a good reputation is also important to the way content is developed and distributed.

4 Media relationships

The mainstream media still has an important role to play in the way people view businesses and organizations. Despite the growth of social media and the impact of online activity, there is still a significant impact that media reporting can have on a business. PR and communication professionals need to ensure that they are investing in building relationships with key journalists and media outlets. When there is something positive to highlight, the media can amplify and more widely distribute the message. In moments when problems have emerged, the media will scrutinize the response from a business and being able to explain the position and action that is being taken can assist in managing the impact. Building relationships with the media should not be overlooked in a technological world.

5 Stakeholder engagement

Another element of the important building of relationships to support developing the reputation of the business is to prioritize stakeholder engagement. Understanding who your key connections are and what they are interested in helps to keep them informed about the business developments. It is also a critical part of any crisis response, keeping them informed of the situation and what the business is doing to respond to it. The view that stakeholders have of the business can, as mentioned in Chapter 1, impact on investment, product and service development and the future of the business. Communicators have a key role to play within this work even if the responsibility lies within another part of the business.

6 Employee relations

Building a positive reputation is not all about the communication that takes place outside the business. It is essential to ensure effective internal communication and engagement with employees. They need to be connected to the purpose of the business and be clear about the expectations and boundaries that they need to work within. It is also critical that this internal communication is two-way, and that management are listening to the issues and points raised from the frontline. Communicators should be leading, or involved in, the development of the relationship the business has with employees. This work was given a priority during the Covid-19 pandemic as it became critical for staff to understand the impact of restrictions, and on what they need to do. This is about more than effective systems and processes though, as employee engagement needs to be about engaging both hearts and minds.

7 Brand positioning

As well as brand management it is important to establish the brand's position. It sets the business apart from its competitors and makes a clear connection to its values and purpose. Establishing it means recognizing your unique selling proposition and what differentiates the business from others providing the same products or services. The brand is not the reputation but is a part of what comprises the reputation. The position that your brand has in the minds of consumers can be both positive and negative. Once the brand's position has been defined it can be used to inform the marketing, PR and communication activity, and help to build a positive reputation.

8 Advertising

Organizations need to be aware of the issues around the reputation of the business when they are developing advertising campaigns. There are many examples of where reputations have been challenged because of advertising campaigns that do not take account of issues taking place in the world, or within the business. For example, Pepsi had to withdraw an advert that was criticized for 'trivializing the Black Lives Matter movement'.[7] Building a positive reputation needs to ensure that the advertising approach is in line with the brand, the values and the position that the business wants to have both within the sector and on a world stage. Putting in place checks on the approach taken to advertising, gathering feedback and understanding community differences can help to avoid problems and ensure consistency with the reputational position.

9 Customer relations

One of the most important elements of building a positive reputation is the experience that customers have when they engage with the business. This can be where a positive reputation is built, even if there is a problem being experienced. Dealing effectively with complaints is a critical part of preventing problems developing into crises that impact on reputation. Communicators need to have a close working relationship with those who are responsible for managing customer relations. This will include understanding the themes, trends and issues that are emerging and what they mean for the business, and ensuring those dealing with customers are the first to receive details of internal developments and any changes. In the event of a serious or critical situation developing, the customer service team should be among the first to be given details of what has happened, how the business is responding and what to say to customers. They are a priority when developing internal communication plans for crisis management.

10 Crisis preparedness

The impact of crises on the reputation of the business can be significant and will be discussed in a later chapter. Being crisis-prepared is a vital part of business development and operation. First there needs to be an understanding of the biggest risks, the ones that have the potential to derail the business and the ones that are the most likely to occur. This will allow the most serious problems to be considered in detail. Plans need to be in place to respond effectively and swiftly to emerging issues, and communication is a critical part of that response. When a crisis happens, the way it is managed will reflect either positively or negatively on the reputation of the business. The preparedness needs to provide a comprehensive communication response considering all the key audiences and ensuring that feedback about views of the business is being tracked and understood.

Creating a reputation management plan

The first consideration is whether you need a reputation management plan and to understand what it could bring to the business. It is more appropriate to focus on influencing reputation rather than managing it, as per the definition in Chapter 1. However, bringing the important factors together, along with the actions and a way to track the impact can be beneficial when building a positive reputation. A reputation management plan is not a communication plan, as it will involve many parts of the business and will consider actions that are important to the development of the business.

The starting point is to understand and have evaluated the current reputational position, and to know what it is within the key audiences that you have identified. It is important to understand this so it can be tracked and monitored for any changes. An audit of the business operation needs to be undertaken alongside assessing the external perspectives. All the factors that contribute to a positive reputation that are outlined in Chapter 1 should be considered. Are there effective systems in place? What is the staff feedback and how does employee engagement work? Is there a strong risk management and crisis response process in place? It may assist the business to bring in an external specialist to assess the systems and processes and review the culture and leadership within the business. The feedback from this assessment will identify the key areas for development and how to outline longer term improvements to support the business.

Once this data has been gathered, details of the short-, medium- and long-term actions can then be outlined to address issues that have been raised. Considering external factors that may impact on the reputation of the business is also a critical element to include within the plan. For example, is there a report on the sector that is due to be published, has another competitor been hit by a crisis, or are there new regulations or legislation that may be introduced and impact on the business? All these external developments have the potential to impact on the reputation of a business, which is why the reputation management plan needs to include detailed horizon scanning.

The final stage is to ensure the plan is shared across the business and that it is understood by all who have a part to play in delivering against it. Systems and processes need to be in place to monitor, review and update the plan as changes happen, either externally or within the business. A reputation management plan needs to be in place as part of the suite of business documents that support the business operation and development. Putting a plan in place raises the importance of building a positive reputation based on more than communication and promotion.

CASE STUDY
LEGO

Background

One business that is continually at the top when considering the 'best reputation' is the toy manufacturer LEGO. The monitoring company RepTrak rates the Denmark-based company as within the 'strong' category for their reputation. They were ranked as number 1 in 2020, 2021 and 2023.[8] The RepTrak assessment uses a range of data points in relation to businesses and outlining how this operates, the 2023 report states: 'Through a combination of machine learning (ML), AI, and natural language processing (NLP), our reputation intelligence platform combines and analyses millions of perception and sentiment data points from online surveys, mainstream media, social media, business data, and additional third party sources.'[9]

There are some requirements for a business or organization to feature in the annual assessment. It must have a global revenue above $2 billion, have a global 'familiarity threshold' above 20 per cent across the 14 countries measured and have a RepTrak score above 67.3. This means the research limits the number of brands it tracks.

What does LEGO do?

LEGO is an educational toy for children and evokes positive memories for adults as well, who will have used it as children and potentially with their own children. So there is a positive starting point when developing the reputation. There is a clear purpose throughout what they do including the more newly established products targeted at adults. They have a strong employee offer with 26 weeks family leave for all staff, and 41 per cent of leadership roles are filled by women.

In reflecting on the position as most reputable company, LEGO Group CEO Niels B. Christiansen highlights that children are the role models and inspiration for the business' choices made towards establishing a better world. This is seen in not only LEGO play but the ways the business pushes to make a positive impact on the environment and society. The product is reuseable but also faces challenges in relation to the use of plastics in a world that is becoming increasingly environmentally aware. However, they have seen a reduction in the amount of waste product that goes to landfill. It will be an area of further challenge for the brand in the coming years.

An additional area that impacts positively on reputation is the Build To Give campaign, which has seen more than 2 million children given LEGO sets. They work with charities to arrange the distribution and it has been a campaign run since 2017. The campaign states: 'In connection with the #BuildtoGive 2023 Holiday Activation, the LEGO Group will donate one LEGO set to charity for every gift that is built with LEGO bricks and shared on social media with #BuildtoGive.'[10] This supports the purpose of focusing on children and having a positive impact as well as encouraging user-generated content on social networks promoting LEGO products.

LEGO is a very recognizable product and there is a strong brand identity across all content and communication activity. The brand also benefits from the development of the online products and LEGO movie franchise. Two points that have been highlighted as having a significant positive impact at a time of global uncertainty are the familiarity and novelty of the LEGO brand and product.[11] This is not something that all brands, businesses and organizations can have, but LEGO clearly has an approach to reputation that includes the nine points highlighted on page 29. There is a clear purpose and values that are reinforced across the business. It has developed effective relationships including with the charities involved in the Build To Give campaign. There is a strong employee offer and remuneration package focused on families, play days, health support and volunteering.

In 2014, LEGO was targeted by Greenpeace who were campaigning against a relationship the toy manufacturer had with Royal Dutch Shell. The relationship had been in place for 50 years and LEGO did not respond to all the steps taken by Greenpeace to target them but did decide not to renew the partnership when it concluded. From the position LEGO has almost a decade later, it is clear the impact on the reputation from the Greenpeace campaign was not significant.[12] Communication is operating at a strategic level and roles exist across the world so can take account of cultural differences. Finally, LEGO is financially stable and saw a rise of 1 per cent in revenue in the first six months of 2023 reaching 27.4 billion Danish Krone.[13] All these elements are identified as key to develop a positive reputation, which may be why LEGO remains top of the most reputable brands.

Reputation lessons

- Develop the business' purpose and values and be clear about what they are and how they drive the operation.
- Take care with the relationships that are developed. Working with other businesses and organizations, and influencers should be treated with care and due diligence needs to be carried out. This should also assess the potential impact on reputation from the connection.
- Building the brand identify over time can support the business and how it is perceived but has to be backed up by the reality of the work that is undertaken.
- Be ready to act when a problem emerges and this can mean changing the way the business operates, what it does and who it involves.

Conclusion

Building a positive reputation first requires an understanding of how interested the business is in it and how prepared it is to address challenges. This can shine a light on the actions that may be needed to create the right conditions to undertake the work required. The business needs to be working towards operational effectiveness in a number of key areas. Establishing it with a clear legitimacy to operate provides a strong foundation for the further work to develop the business and its communication.

Communicators have an extensive range of tools and approaches that can be taken to build and boost reputation. From online positioning through to branding there are lots of opportunities to position the business and build its reputation. All the elements of PR, communication, marketing and advertising need to be working together to achieve the maximum impact from their work. The consistency and clarity will be fundamental to significantly affect how people view and perceive the business and its operation.

Ultimately reputation management or influencing should not be an afterthought. It should not happen as an accidental by-product of other systems and processes. It requires careful thought and consideration as a strategic element of the business' operation. This is where a reputation management plan and framework are beneficial, bringing all the relevant aspects of the business together with a purpose, milestones and clear activities that will be undertaken. But before that can be developed it requires measurement and evaluation. Knowing the figures that matter to the business and how it is viewed and where it stands reputationally among key groups and against competitors is a critical starting point. The evaluation and measurement of reputation will be considered in Chapter 3.

References

1   A Zavyalova, M P Ferrer and R Reger. Celebrity and infamy? The consequences of media narratives about organisational identity, *Academy of Management Review*, 2017, 42 (3) 461–80, www.terry.uga.edu/wp-content/uploads/Celebrity_and_Infamy_AMR_2017.pdf (archived at https://perma.cc/8K82-EAUW)

2   P Jansen van Vuuren. The theoretical framework of the study and the relationship with the systems theory, Study notes of research methodology, University of Pretoria, 2002, www.docsity.com/en/the-theoretical-framework-of-the-study-and-the-relationship-with-the-systems-theory/8410191 (archived at https://perma.cc/E45D-SHGK)

3   T Langham (2019) *Reputation Management: The future of corporate communications and public relations*, Emerald Publishing, Bingley

4   Pay Gap App. Hello, hello, #IWD2023 is nearly here, and so are companies' cut-and-paste platitudes. And once again we're bringing you the data to see whose support for #InternationalWomensDay is genuine, and who's still got work to do, 6 March 2023, X, https://x.com/PayGapApp/status/1632727861537693696 (archived at https://perma.cc/9H8Z-ZVZ7)

5   F Lawrence. Horsemeat scandal: The essential guide, *The Guardian*, 15 February 2013, www.theguardian.com/uk/2013/feb/15/horsemeat-scandal-the-essential-guide (archived at https://perma.cc/E99R-FDMM)

6   Content Marketing Institute. What is content marketing? https://contentmarketinginstitute.com/what-is-content-marketing/ (archived at https://perma.cc/JF4V-PJEB)

7   D Victor. Pepsi pulls ad accused of trivializing Black Lives Matter, *New York Times*, 5 April 2017, www.nytimes.com/2017/04/05/business/kendall-jenner-pepsi-ad.html (archived at https://perma.cc/EBJ5-W88P)

8   RepTrak. The Global RepTrak 100 2024, 11 April 2024, www.reptrak.com/globalreptrak (archived at https://perma.cc/ZJ32-2AKC)

9   RepTrak. The Global RepTrak 100 2024, 11 April 2024, www.reptrak.com/globalreptrak (archived at https://perma.cc/ZJ32-2AKC)

10 LEGO. Build to Give: Build a heart, share the joy, www.lego.com/en-gb/build-to-give?age-gate=grown_up (archived at https://perma.cc/339W-E8XS)

11 RepTrak, The Global RepTrak 100 2023, What made LEGO #1, www.reptrak.com/globalreptrak/ (archived at https://perma.cc/R3LV-CJDP)

12 M Schulz. An analysis of LEGO's response to an attack on its partnership with Royal Dutch Shell, *Elon Journal of Undergraduate Research in Communications*, 2016, 7 (1) Spring, https://eloncdn.blob.core.windows.net/eu3/sites/153/2017/06/07_MaryClaire_Schulz.pdf (archived at https://perma.cc/L7KW-EH2M)

13 S Whitten. LEGO sales increase while other toy makers struggle, CNBC, 30 August 2023, www.cnbc.com/2023/08/30/lego-earnings-revenue-rises-in-first-half.html (archived at https://perma.cc/5TSU-7C9N)

3

Improving a reputation that is under threat

Introduction

Whether a business has a strong reputation or not there will be moments when it is under pressure and there may be a threat to how the business is perceived. It is important to be ready and able to respond to these moments, as well as to have invested in developing a positive reputation. The starting point is understanding the nature of the threat and to rate it as high, medium or low risk based on the likelihood of it happening and the extent of the impact that it could have on the business. As part of the effective governance of a business this risk management process should be in place to understand potential issues and to be ready for them. Having a process that considers both operational and reputational risks is critical to having an effective process. In addition, this risk management process supports the development of detailed response plans based on the scenarios that have been considered. For example, a significant business risk could be a cyberattack and the risk process should put actions in place that will prevent this occurring and develop a plan that can be used if the measures do not work. The plans should consider both the potential operational and reputational impact of an attack taking place.

When considering the nature of the threat to the business the most important factor to address is who the situation may impact on. This means considering what impact it will have on customers, the wider public, people living near key business locations, stakeholders, shareholders, regulators and others. The same process must also be undertaken when considering the internal impact: who within the business will be affected by the situation or who will be required to take action. The details of who may be affected will be necessary to ensure that the actions, both from the organization and in communication, are targeted at those who are most affected by the situation as it develops. Remember, the human impact of events will be a key factor in determining how severe the situation is and in analysing the impact on reputation. This will be discussed later in this chapter.

Assessing the potential impact on the business from a problem or difficult situation needs to consider the business operation, the financial implications, the staffing implications and any governance concerns. All these can help to inform a consideration of the reputational impact of the situation. The challenge for businesses is to be able to agree on a way to quantify reputation and evaluate what it is, both when it is not under pressure and when there is a critical incident or crisis that has occurred. Also, is it possible to quantify any loss to the business that may come from a threat or significant situation? To assist in doing this it is important to go back to the agreed definition of reputation and the weighting that elements have to the business.

Understanding your reputation

Before being able to effectively measure and evaluate the reputation of a business, the first thing is to be clear on the nine elements required for a positive reputation and consider which involve risks and which are the most critical to the operation of the business. Consider if there is a clear purpose and values that people both inside and outside the business understand. Are there effective relationships in place and if so, who are these with? Stakeholder mapping is critical to understanding the relationships and levels of importance. Are employees engaged and do they feel supported? Are internal relationships positive or under pressure? What is the position of leadership within the business? This means being clear if the CEO and C-suite have the support of their employees and whether trust exists within the business. If there has been a recent change in leadership this may impact the reputation of the business, which in turn could increase the possible damage from the situation that is developing. Understanding the financial position of the business also needs to be assessed. What is it now, what has it been and how has the profit been distributed in recent years? Is the business culturally aware and able to respond accordingly? The importance of each of these aspects to the way people view the business needs to be detailed so the situation that is developing can be assessed. For example, if the situation that is emerging is a financial irregularity and the business has had previous problems or may have lost a CEO because of issues in the past, then there will be a potentially more damaging impact on the reputation of the business.

As highlighted in Chapter 2, it is important to understand what matters to the business and how it is viewed by key audiences. Weighting should be given to each of the elements so that the priorities are clear. Weighting is a project management technique that is used to help in decision-making and prioritizing action. There are ways of using the mathematics to assist in adding weighting to scoring but in the case of reputation management it is the principle that can provide support. For each of the key elements to the reputation, consider outlining how critical they are to the overall reputation of the business. Start with a 100 per cent figure and assign a percentage of importance to the reputation. For example, if the financial operation is fundamental because it is a charity managing funding, or it is a financial institution, then it may be that financial stability is a critical factor so you assign a 50 per cent weighting to it; but that purpose is clearly understood due to being established for many years so the weighting may be lower at 10 per cent.

Deciding how to weight the different factors should be part of a discussion that involves managers from across the business and should also take account of external views. In considering the weighting, the purpose and values that the business has should be kept at the forefront of decisions. This work should provide the basis for the future reputation management approach including any reputation management plan, as well as how developments are prioritized for the future.

Quantifying reputation

Developing measurements for the reputation of the business is not an easy piece of work but it is essential if you are going to effectively influence it. It may feel that reputation is intangible or is comprised of a number of different elements making it problematic to quantify. But as mentioned earlier, it is vital that there is a way of quantifying reputation, so that improvements can be made, the impact of a challenge can be understood and to act as an early warning system of a problem that may be emerging. Reputation can be a fragile thing, particularly in the world of instant news and social media where damage can be done at the touch of a button, and people can join together to mount a targeted attack.

A significant challenge to developing the measurement is potential disagreements within the business. For example, a CEO will be focused on the profitability of the business and the bottom line to satisfy shareholders and Board members, but this may have less impact than its ethical operation and how it is viewed by customers. Professor Anne Gregory[1] explains how to use a spidergram to assess whether the values of an organization are being lived in the round and not just in one particular area.[2] In discussion, she said:

> You do a radar chart, a spidergram. For example, these are your five values: honesty, integrity etc. You ask various stakeholders to measure you and rank you from 1 to 10 on all those values. It then means you can come to a judgement about whether you are living them and address the situation.[3]

Professor Gregory explained that using this method will allow a focus on aspects beyond just the business performance, such as leadership, profitability and financial performance. But which elements are the most important to the business? Professor Gregory explained:

> I would say the traditional reputation indicators are what you do, you lead, you are innovative, you know, you are dynamic, etc. The other bit is how you do it, so they're inextricably linked. But if you ask for a ranking, I will say it has to be the values-based ones are coming first, because they then tell you how you go about the what.[4]

There are two aspects that need to be considered together: the performance of the business, and the character of the organization. Both need to have an importance when considering how to assess reputation. As Professor Gregory has highlighted, the weighting should be in favour of those spidergram value-based metrics rather than the business operation, but both need to be considered together.

Creating a suite of metrics across the business and supporting the two aspects will assist in quantifying reputation. Ultimately it is about identifying the attributes that are important to the operation of the business and the perceptions people have of it. Evaluating these attributes and progress over time will help to determine whether there is an emerging problem or issue that is impacting on them. The business operation will require assessment of the financial performance, value for money, the cost of the product or service, and investment in developments. But it also should be evaluating the effectiveness of leadership within the organization and particularly of the CEO and Chair of any Board or Trustees. Further measurements will consider the performance of the business, such as delivery times, customer services management and investment in the business. Staffing measurements, including employee recruitment and retention, also need to be considered as well as disciplinary information and professional standards data. As Professor Gregory highlighted, this is only part of the story and cannot on its own be the reputation measurement.[5]

The character of the business also needs to be evaluated. This includes understanding what people feel about the business and how they view it. Is it considered to be a 'good business' in terms of its purpose, operation and ethical standards? Does it reflect the values across the business from the top to the frontline operation? Is it trustworthy and reliable in what it does? Does it operate in support of, or recognition of current societal norms? This builds a legitimacy to operate that is a fundamental element of reputation. Simply measuring the communication and PR activity, using social media data, media coverage, sentiment or similar communication measures is not enough to determine reputation. It merely gives an indication of how many people have been exposed to the information provided by the business and whether they have responded in some way. Such elements may give an indication of the effectiveness of your PR and communication but not of reputation.

The cost of damage to reputation is often sought as an indicator and a way to explain the importance of reputation to senior leaders. Putting a figure on this could be linked to the loss of sales or a dip in trust levels that lead to a loss of sales, or in a public sector context it could be an increase in customer complaints. The amount of time taken in dealing with an increase in complaints could be financial qualified to give an indication of the financial loss. Being able to financially quantify the potential impact of a loss of reputation or a challenge to reputation helps to bring the two aspects of business operation and character together. One example of quantifying the impact of reputational damage is the impact of the Horizon IT Post Office scandal in the UK where an IT system failed, and subpostmasters were wrongly prosecuted and convicted of fraud and false accounting. The situation impacted on more than 3,000 people, a figure that is continuing to grow, and took place over two decades. The IT system was provided by Fujitsu and following an appearance of the European Director at a UK Government committee discussing the subject, the value of the company dropped by \$1 billion with shares down by 4 per cent.[6] This clearly demonstrates the cost of the reputational damage caused by the poor business processes being discussed at a public inquiry. This may identify the cost of the impact of a crisis, but it also highlights the significance of a good reputation to the valuation of a business.

Measuring reputation

Establishing the approach to measuring the elements within a business' reputation will require consideration of the composition of the business. If the business operates on a local level only and provides services in a defined area the measures need to be focused in those areas. For example, if you are a gym operating in a specific geographic area the views of the clients in the catchment area will be critical to you even if there is a misstep that draws media attention. However, if you are a multinational business that is seen on high streets around the world, then any issues can very quickly have an impact on the global reputation of the business.

Measuring reputation needs to be part of the organization's business framework and this requires a clear time frame for how frequently the reputation data is assessed. Some of the data detailed above may be available on a monthly basis and could assist an understanding of any changes or fluctuations. However, gathering views about the purpose, trust in the business and perceptions of the organization requires an investment of time and money, particularly if it has not been undertaken before. This should not be a barrier to undertaking the work as gathering the information is essential to really understand what is happening and whether the reputation is in a positive position.

Feedback from people is a critical part of understanding views, perceptions and changes over time. This requires gathering information and data from key groups that are the most significant to the business. Categorizing key stakeholders, customers, groups and interested parties is required so the views of a representative sample can be accessed. Involving the external perspective on the business is essential to effective measurement and quantifying of reputation. Focus groups, user panels, customer service email lists, surveys and feedback forms can all be utilized to support compiling an external perspective.

The starting point for the measurement needs to be what matters to the business, to its values, to its operation and to its legitimacy to operate. If this has been detailed as part of the work to understand the elements that comprise the good reputation, identifying the measures will be connected to them. This can be used to create a dashboard that will provide a regular view of the operation and reputation of the business. It is important to add details from the horizon scanning that may impact on the business. Any changes in the business and perceptions of it over time will be identified, as will the potential threats that may damage the reputation. As will be seen in later chapters, being able to move quickly to limit the damage from a problem or a crisis is essential, so this evaluation and measurement is a key part of managing challenges.

In addition, those elements that have the most impact on views and perspectives of the business should have a higher weighting in any assessment. Each business will have a range of metrics that it considers and not all of them are of equal importance. The values and purpose of the business have the biggest impact on perceptions. Does the business live and breathe what it identifies as important to it? Does it operate counter to what it highlights as a priority? For example, if you are a business that provides environmentally friendly products then your credentials as a green business will be more significant. If this business is found to be greenwashing or operating against those environmental priorities, then its reputation will be more significantly damaged than a business that operated in a different sector and was found to have been involved in exaggerating its green credentials.

The importance of inclusivity

A critical factor to reputation and the way a business is perceived is how it responds to all people. It is more than just having an equality, diversity and inclusion strategy. The way the organization operates, reflects inclusivity in its values and lives its values will all be the subject of intense scrutiny. This is where businesses with cultural intelligence can respond more effectively to the changes in society. Poor behaviour or failing in this area has the potential to be detrimental to the reputation of an organization or business. It is not enough to have the EDI plan, or to have it reflected in the values of the business; there needs to be action and an authenticity to the approach. It is an important element in the integrity index; the spidergram highlighted by Professor Gregory. If the approach to inclusivity is merely seen as a tick-box exercise, that in itself will be a challenge to the reputation of an organization.

In evaluating reputation, getting feedback that will help to define the position, whether using the integrity spidergram or any other system, is essential. This means listening to a range of diverse voices is critical for the measurement to be meaningful. As a public sector organization that is in place to provide services to everyone, it is vital to understand what perceptions exist among all communities. It means knowing which audiences and groups you regularly connect with, and those where relationships do not exist. For businesses, the priority has been on key stakeholders, shareholders and existing customers. This needs to be expanded, as when there is a threat to the reputation of the business it can come from any part of the community. Listening to feedback and views from differing voices will act as an alert to any threat to the business, and also can provide a clear picture of the business' reputation.

Cultural intelligence is a vital part of an effective business. It is more than having an equality, diversity and inclusion policy or trying to develop a culture that is inclusive. It is about an organization, how it operates, its people and the business it does and how it connects to and understands diverse cultural experiences, backgrounds and situations. A business may be culturally diverse but can overlook the existence of other views, perceptions and experiences. This creates internal challenges but can also prevent the company from seeing those differences externally, and how they relate to its reputation.[7] A business that is taking a positive approach to its reputation will be striving to ensure it is culturally intelligent.

The ability to hear from diverse groups becomes essential when a crisis is affecting a business or organization. People will be taking information from a range of sources and the priority is for the business to become the trusted source of the updates about what has happened and what is being done to address it. This requires a clear understanding of who is affected, the extent of the impact of the crisis and where it may damage the reputation of the business. As Amanda Coleman stated in *Crisis Communication Strategies*: 'Gathering alternative perspectives and listening to different voices about the crisis, the impact of it and what it means for different communities is essential insight to gather as soon as practicable.'[8] If work has been undertaken to listen to the views of diverse groups in relation to the evaluation of reputation it will be able to support the crisis communication response. Situations may disproportionately affect certain groups or communities, and understanding this is critical within the response and communication. This was highlighted during the response to the Covid-19 pandemic in 2020–21. Governments and authorities in countries including the UK and US did not consider the impact of the pandemic on diverse communities. During a session of the UK Covid-19 Inquiry, a former senior civil servant said that a lack of diversity within key meetings led to overlooking the impact of decisions being made on women.[9] This has also been identified in research into the impact of Covid-19; one paper on the issue said the UK national lockdown 'rules, policies and communications' did not 'adequately include the increased risks faced by ethnic minority groups'.[10]

Equality, diversity and inclusion feature among the values for many organizations with an increased recognition of previous failings. However, it has to be integrated throughout all the business processes, approach and operation, which can then support the development of a good reputation. Inclusivity is a social value that is growing in importance and requires businesses and organizations to ensure they are doing more than just putting a policy in place.

Developing engagement and building influence

When a business' reputation is under pressure the customer outreach and community engagement become critical. Working with those staff who lead customer relationship management or who connect with those who use the service can identify when problems are starting to develop. This could be a failure in a product or service, or concern about a business decision. Interrogating the data and information that is received by these frontline staff is an important way to recognize an emerging problem and attempt to address it at the earliest opportunity. These relationships are also essential when managing a problem and responding to a potential crisis. Being able to reach out to people with details of the approach and activity can limit the impact on the reputation of an organization facing a threat.

As well as the importance of bringing outside voices into the organization so they can be heard, it is also important to understand within the relationships where supporters and influencers exist. Influencers are those groups and individuals who are listened to by others and whose views are trusted. They can support the development of a positive reputation or have a significant detrimental impact. Stakeholder mapping, which would include the influencers, remains an important part of all PR and communication activity. It can be used to support the measurement of reputation, help build a positive reputation, and assist when responding to a crisis or critical incident. Supporters are those who may not have influence but are loyal to the brand or business. The views they share may lack the reach influencers have but can provide a boost to a business and help to amplify the communication and messages that are shared. Building relationships and networks is fundamental to reputation and boosting a reputation that may be under threat. Businesses working to establish and maintain a positive reputation cannot neglect their relationships.

Reputation being affected by others

Challenges to a business' reputation do not always come from what it does and how people view it. Reputation can be manhandled, misrepresented or damaged by others connected to the business. Views and perceptions of the business can be shared quickly in a highly connected world and when these are inaccurate it creates a significant challenge to any brand. Being ready and able to respond to these situations is critical and will be discussed in Chapter 7. If these views or comments come from a notable third party the damage is increased. People and organizations that have influence and are trusted can leave lasting damage if they criticize a business. Monitoring and identifying these issues early are vital if the business is going to respond quickly and limit the potential damage. When negative comments are being made and shared, failing to respond and hoping the situation will disappear is not an acceptable approach. Only the global power brands such as Amazon, Apple, Facebook and Microsoft can ignore such situations. The characteristics they possess of providing a service that is easy to use, gives quick results, makes lives easier and is convenient mean they have grown to have global domination in their marketplace. People will continue to use them even when they dislike what they do and how they do it. This is not the situation for smaller brands, those operating in crowded markets or who are trying to establish themselves. In some cases the negative commentary around a brand can be used in a positive way, such as Ryanair, which is considered in the case study later in this chapter.

The relationships and connections that a business has are also points of risk where issues or problems involving the third party could be contagious to those around them. It is vital that due diligence is practised with every high-profile connection that is made. Suppliers and those involved in the supply chain can be affected by their own damaging situations. Damage from these situations has the potential to be felt by the rest of the businesses in that chain. Attempting to lessen the impact of this on the reputation of the business is challenging as there is a lack of direct involvement in the response and management of the issue. Within the PR and communication activity, influencers can be problematic, and their actions may lead to a reputational challenge to the business. This has to work within the regulations that are in place and ensure that any influencer marketing is clearly labelled. Identifying the right influencer to connect with is essential as is establishing a clear understanding of the actions to be taken and the boundaries to work within. For example, if a lifestyle influencer was being paid to support a new healthy food supplement, but was then found to criticize it in other online posts, this can put pressure on the business. A similar situation could emerge if that same influencer was then found to be promoting excessive weight loss and encouraging eating disorders. The actions of the third party have the potential to damage the reputation of the business.

Stakeholders play a key role in working with organizations and businesses. The views and comments that they share in relation to the business can either enhance or damage the reputation. This is why stakeholder engagement and building effective relationships is a critical function for every business. Through these relationships, details of positive developments can be shared to keep stakeholders informed so they can share with others and possibly endorse the business. But it is also essential when any threat to the business is identified as it keeps them informed and can answer any questions or concerns. When a business is under threat, sharing information with third parties outside can feel challenging. In risk-averse organizations this may be avoided. However, as will be discussed later, the benefits of building these relationships both in good and bad times outweighs the threats.

Stakeholder, influencer and third-party connections should be mapped so that issues are identified early, and any risks can be proactively managed. This includes developing a stakeholder plan that can build trust and confidence in the business among those third parties. This information can be used to redefine and reshape a reputation management plan and should be subject to continued review and updating. It can also assist with horizon scanning and recognizing challenging situations at an early point to allow action or mitigation to be put in place. The whole business needs to be engaged in developing these documents so it can be a true reflection of the connections that exist and identify where they need to be developed. Managers across the business also have a responsibility to develop the relationships in line with the outlined plan, and to identify new stakeholders that need to be included. Reputation management is about more than the internal systems and processes that need to be in place. It also requires effective horizon scanning to highlight issues that could impact not just on the business but on those connected to it.

Step-by-step actions to help boost reputation

There are steps that can be taken to boost the reputation of a business which may be anticipating a future threat or challenge. It is important to ensure ahead of taking these steps there is an understanding of how the reputation of the business rates, as well as the nature of the threat or issues that may be on the horizon. This may require a focus on some of the steps, but others may be of less importance. However, all these steps should be considered in a situation where there is pressure on the reputation of the business or organization:

1   **Understand the data and insight**
    Start with the information that exists about the business and its operation. What does that data show about the products and services? What does the customer feedback show? What are the trends within the industry? All this information is important to give an understanding of what is working and where problems may exist. This allows planning and activity to focus on the areas of weakness and ensures that threats and risks are identified so further action can be taken. Without this detail there will be a lack of clarity and the potential to focus effort in the wrong areas.

2   **Governance**
    In order to boost the reputation of the business the internal processes and structures need to be effective. Review the governance that exists within the business. Ensure that decisions are made at the right level and that there is oversight and scrutiny of the operation and the decision-making within the business. Define a process that allows this scrutiny to be undertaken quickly if necessary.

3 External perspectives

Listening to external voices and gathering perspectives from outside the business is critical. As mentioned earlier, this is a key factor to effectively evaluating and measuring the reputation of the business. Perspectives from customers, service users, stakeholders and other groups that matter to the business need to be collected. Views on the potential threat to the reputation of the business can also be assessed and understood even before any impact is felt.

4 Clarify audiences

It is critical to understand the audiences that are the most important to the business or organization. When you are looking at limiting the damage of a threat on the horizon it is important to start looking at who will be affected, who will have something to say about it, who has influence and which of the business' stakeholders are most important. This can then assist in ensuring that the communication and engagement activity is focused on the way that will have the biggest impact.

5 Review stakeholder mapping

Building on understanding the audiences, the next step is to look at any stakeholder mapping that exists. Is it relevant for the situation or issue that is on the horizon? Is it up to date with any new or emerging stakeholders? The mapping is not just about recognizing who are the most influential groups and individuals but also what aspects of the business they are most interested in. Keeping in touch with stakeholders and updating them with developments within the business will strengthen relationships for the moment a problem or crisis emerges.

6 Create a reputation management plan

It is easy for a business to review and manage its financial operation because there are systems and processes in place to monitor the income and expenditure and to take action if things are not balancing. The same needs to be introduced to manage the reputation of the business. This means having the right measurement and evaluation system in place to support an understanding of what is happening, together with effective horizon scanning. This can inform the action that is taken to boost and influence the reputation of the business. Having a plan helps the business to keep focused on what matters and the actions that are needed by everyone and not just the PR, communication and marketing function.

7 Review PR and communication, and refresh content marketing

The approach that is being taken to PR, communication and marketing should be kept under constant review to ensure it is in line with the business' values and takes account of societal changes. Being able to effectively influence the reputation of the business requires the ability to move quickly to adapt and refine the approach that is being taken. This includes the SEO and content marketing that takes place. Attitudes, views and opinions can turn quickly with the online commentary and influence and while it should not push the business away from its values it will require careful communication management.

8 Create a positive internal culture

The internal operation of the business needs to be working effectively as was highlighted at point 2, focusing on governance. A positive internal culture where staff feel able to raise issues and concerns and feel that this will be listened to will limit the requirement for them to become whistleblowers or communicate their issues externally. This is not about silencing people from talking publicly but about giving them the confidence that they will be listened to, and action taken or an explanation of why no change is made about an issue of concern. This positive internal culture is recognized as important to establishing a positive reputation. It can also support the development of cultural intelligence.

9 Issues management and crisis response

Being ready to address issues at an early stage, and effectively managing a crisis response can assist in building a positive reputation. Where problems are tackled swiftly, and people feel they have had redress for their complaint, it will be viewed positively. For example, if a train is delayed the passengers will want to be heard about the problems it created and be given compensation where appropriate. Where this happens and they receive a swift apology in some form, it will avoid negative social media commentary and external criticism. Every service failure chips away at the positive reputation the business is attempting to build. Reputational crises are as damaging to the business as operational ones. As mentioned earlier the IT company Fujitsu lost $1 billion linked to the reputational damage of the Post Office Horizon IT scandal.[11] The communication response to crises will be discussed in Chapter 7.

10 Take an ethical position

Every day the business and its leaders need to be operating ethically and in line with societal norms. Where they are seen to be operating with a disregard to ethics it can be damaging to the reputation. Building a positive reputation needs senior leaders to be aware every day of the reputational impact from the way they speak, act and behave. This was highlighted by Marc Whitt, PR author, who explained that leaders needed to have strong ethical roots. He said: 'If the roots are deep with the tree, then it will be able to withstand the winds.'[12] If the business is built on an ethical approach, then crises should have less impact on them and their future viability.

When reputation is under threat, all the prior work to influence reputation and place it into the operation of the business becomes central to how it responds. Having a plan to address the situation and looking to boost the reputation of the business is important. But the starting point needs to be an awareness and understanding of the reputation of the business among key groups, stakeholders and audiences. Without any monitoring the early warning signs of a reputational challenge may be missed, and without measurement the impact of challenges cannot be quantified. Keeping a regular check on the way people view the business or organization, and the way those critical groups view it, should be in place.

CASE STUDY

Ryanair

The budget airline has long been seen as having a terrible reputation within the sector and among travellers, and yet it continues to be financially viable. A quick Google search of news about Ryanair will include a list of complaints and problems that customers have raised with the media. In 2013, it was voted the least popular short-haul airline in Europe and a dedicated 'I Hate Ryanair' website was created. In addition, the head of Ryanair regularly makes controversial and sometimes outrageous comments to the media attracting a lot of attention. CEO Michael O'Leary in his dealings with the media reinforces the values of the budget airline with a no nonsense approach. The business has continued to grow and is a big name in airline travel.

The reputation has been viewed negatively due to complaints about customer service, hidden fees hitting passengers and a depersonalizing approach to passengers. Ryanair maintained the same approach until 2013 when profit forecasts had to be revised twice in two months. There was a loss of £28.7 million in the final quarter of the year.[13] It led to a change in approach with a recognition that the reputation needed to be developed and that gaining returning customers was important.

O'Leary himself stated that they needed to stop annoying passengers and they made changes that allowed a free second carry-on bag, reducing high fees for issues such as not having printed a boarding pass, as well as introducing family discounts. At the same time the communication was overhauled focusing on the customer experience not just the low-cost approach. Investment in the website made it easier for people to do business online.[14]

Professor Anne Gregory explains that people understand what to expect if they fly with Ryanair[15]. She said: 'Some businesses accept that they have a bad reputation. With Ryanair people know what to expect when they fly with them. It is in the deal or contract, and it is good to know what that deal is.' This means that Ryanair continues to operate in a way that people expect even though that may be at a low level. If their values and approach were about providing luxury travel or excellent customer service, then the discord with the experience would have a more serious impact.

Ryanair continues to own its approach and position within the travel industry. Customers have low expectations and will continue to use them if they accept the approach and what goes along with it. The business appears to be developing its offering and is trying to address some of the negative perceptions, but it may take some time before that is achieved. The budget offering is now firmly connected with people's perceptions and ultimately is how the reputation is assessed.

Reputation lessons

- Managing the expectations of the customers and service users has an impact on building the reputation.
- When perceptions are negative it can be overlooked for the convenience and cost benefits of using the service or business.
- Attempting to develop and adapt the business can be challenging when it has become well known for a particular approach, and it may take a significant period of time to address the long-held views and perceptions.
- Any business that accepts the negative reputation that has been established will need to have a tough skin and a robust approach to issues and crisis management.

Conclusion

Evaluating and measuring reputation needs an investment of time and resources. There is no quick fix, but it can be achieved by any business. Use the information about the important groups to the business and speak to them. Even if this is not using technology or a third-party company to undertake the work, simple systems to get customers to rate the business in key areas will provide insight. Other data related to the operation of the business including recruitment and retention rates in relation to staffing, or complaint statistics and the length of time it takes to bring them to a conclusion are also essential information. Reputation management needs a suite of statistics, data and insight that the business can use to give it a position and allow it to chart any improvements or reductions.

However, it is important to recognize that this is not a static measure. Developments within the business, changes in the world and the actions of third parties can all have an impact on the way a business is viewed. Analysis needs to consider these elements when determining the relative position of the business. There are a few global brands that command a different position due to their all-encompassing approach and relevance to lives. They can withstand significant challenges and reputational pressure. We will discuss in Chapter 9 whether there is anything other businesses can learn from how they operate.

Without an understanding of where the business is, it is almost impossible to be able to see how situations are either boosting or damaging reputation. In the same way PR and communication has to evaluate to ensure that the action is having an impact and achieving results, a business has to be able to measure its reputation to identify where changes need to be made or where it is being successful. This is a strategy for a positive future and there are steps to take to boost a reputation and to rescue a bad reputation, which will be considered in Chapter 4.

References

1 Author interview with Professor Anne Gregory, 15 January 2024
2 A Gregory and P Willis (2013) *Strategic Public Relations Leadership*, Routledge, Oxon
3 Author interview with Professor Anne Gregory, 15 January 2024
4 Author interview with Professor Anne Gregory, 15 January 2024
5 Author interview with Professor Anne Gregory, 15 January 2024
6 J Harris and M Negishi. Horizon Post Office Scandal: Fujitsu shares take $1 billion knock, *Bloomberg*, 17 January 2024, www.bloomberg.com/news/articles/2024-01-17/fujitsu-takes-1-billion-knock-as-post-office-scandal-escalates (archived at https://perma.cc/WP4Z-SEG9)

7 Author interview with Professor Anne Gregory, 15 January 2024

8 A Coleman (2023) *Crisis Communication Strategies: Prepare, respond and recover effectively in unpredictable and urgent situations*, 2nd edition, Kogan Page, London

9 B Quinn and A Adu. Lack of diversity in No 10 led to women's deaths in lockdown, Covid inquiry told, *The Guardian*, 1 November 2023, www.theguardian.com/uk-news/2023/nov/01/boris-johnson-unbelievably-bullish-over-covid-top-civil-servant-tells-inquiry (archived at https://perma.cc/6F7E-Q36D)

10 R Mathur, L Bear, K Khunti and R Eggo. Urgent actions and policies needed to address COVID-19 among UK ethnic minorities, *The Lancet*, 19 November 2020, www.thelancet.com/journals/lancet/article/PIIS0140-6736(20)32465-X/fulltext (archived at https://perma.cc/4ETR-FK49)

11 J Harris and M Negishi. Horizon Post Office Scandal: Fujitsu shares take $1 billion knock, *Bloomberg*, 17 January 2024, www.bloomberg.com/news/articles/2024-01-17/fujitsu-takes-1-billion-knock-as-post-office-scandal-escalates (archived at https://perma.cc/WP4Z-SEG9)

12 Author interview with Marc Whitt, 31 January 2024

13 L French, Ryanair's reputation recovery takes off, European CEO, nd, www.europeanceo.com/business-and-management/ryanairs-reputation-recovery-takes-off/ (archived at https://perma.cc/74B4-9VLY)

14 L French. Ryanair's reputation recovery takes off, European CEO, nd, www.europeanceo.com/business-and-management/ryanairs-reputation-recovery-takes-off/ (archived at https://perma.cc/74B4-9VLY)

15 Author interview with Professor Anne Gregory, 15 January 2024

4

Can you rescue a bad reputation?

Introduction

Is a bad reputation something a brand will have to live with? In short, there is always an opportunity to reform and redevelop a business' reputation. But the ability to do this depends on a variety of factors including how bad the damage is, how widely the impact has hit the business, and the reasons why the business is perceived as bad. Importantly, a key question is whether the damage is caused by a recent situation or has the reputation been deteriorating over a long period of time. A full understanding of what has led to the business having a bad reputation is required. This means a careful review or audit of the business position and operation should take place. Most businesses will be aware that their reputation has been damaged or that they are no longer seen as reputable. The problem is that many will not act until the reputation has reached a significant position where it may be threatening to derail the business, future operation and investments.

The first question is how bad the reputation is and what is the extent of the damage that has been done to it. Remember that reputation will change over time and among different groups. If evaluation and monitoring is in place as outlined in Chapter 3, then this should be relatively easy to arrange, and it can be done quickly. However, if the business has not put systems in place, then some urgent evaluation and listening to views and understanding why the reputation is diminishing is required. This can be achieved by looking at connecting with those key audiences that are seen as the most critical and influential. Different groups will have different perspectives, and understanding stakeholders and the audience views is vital. In the case of a global business the views may vary between markets. But it is important to remember that the global marketplace has shrunk and due to technology and developments, a problem in one geographic location can quickly spread. Auditing the current position needs to address not just the reputation and why it is bad but also the way the business is operating in the key areas outlined in Chapter 1. A poor reputation, as discussed earlier, will be created because of failings in the way the business is run and operated and not just from any PR and communication activity.

It is vital to fully understand what has led to the poor reputation. Was it due to past behaviour? Is it due to a product failure? Has it been created by lack of response to complaints and concerns? Could the business have prevented the problem or situation? Could you have made changes earlier? Or is it, as likely, due to a combination of issues. The information is required before starting to consider how to respond to the situation. It can be supported by a severity assessment that details the issues and the extent of the damage to the business and its reputation. Taking urgent action without understanding what has caused it and how it is impacting on the business can lead to inappropriate actions being taken which make the situation worse. This is not a crisis situation that requires swift and immediate action to be taken. It is time for the business to reflect on what has happened, where they are and importantly, where they want to be.

Undertaking a severity assessment

A severity assessment is a formalized way of reviewing the impact that something has, or will have, on an organization or business. It is used mainly as part of the risk assessment and management process to consider which risks will have the biggest impact on the business. There are many severity assessment processes that exist to deal with specific problems: such as assessing the impact of a health challenge, or of a health and safety risk. But it is beneficial to take a similar approach when considering existing challenges or issues, particularly when linked to a loss of reputation. A severity assessment provides a way of understanding the problem that is being faced, which can then support the development of the approach to address it.

There are four phases to a severity assessment about a challenge to reputation:

- Stage 1 – Understand the issue or issues that have impacted on the business. What is it? Who does it impact on? How widespread is it? What are the consequences of the situation?

- Stage 2 – Assess the impact of the issue or situation. Has it affected people and how detrimental has it been? Are staff affected by it and how severely are they affected? Is it a localized issue or does it have global impact?

- Stage 3 – Assess the legacy of the situation. Is it going to have a limited life span? Could the damage be so severe that it will be in place for many months? Will the situation get worse, and could it affect key groups and audiences?

- Stage 4 – Review the actions that have been taken to date and plan the next phase by focusing on the areas most affected. What has been done to attempt to address the issue? What has been done to communicate about the response to the situation? Who has taken the action? This phase will also bring the previous stages together to help develop the assessment, which can inform an action plan to address the cause of the bad reputation.

Carrying out a severity assessment needs to be done with an understanding of the purpose and values of the business, and the factors that have been identified as critical to its reputation. This is crucial to the consideration of the impact and legacy issues.

The same four-step assessment can be undertaken for the situations that have not yet happened. It is linked to the risk assessment process. In such situations you would also consider the likelihood of the situation emerging. The severity assessment is used to help manage a situation when the problem has already happened. When conducting a severity assessment people from across the organization need to be involved in the discussion and review of the situation. It is important to use data and insight to support the conversation and also reflect the external views and perspectives. Remember the important groups and audiences and consider the impact on them and the legacy of it.

Once the business is starting to move forward, implementing the action plan, and addressing the reputational challenge, the factors highlighted in the severity assessment should be considered in the ongoing risk management process.

Reputation and change over time

Situations do not stay the same and the views and perceptions of an organization will change over time. Reputation will change over time, so this makes it essential to understand what has led to the bad reputation and whether it is a new or a long-term problem. People will make judgements related to experiences, views or situations that they observe or learn about from others. Attitudes towards the business and actions from the business need to be examined to understand the triggers leading to a poor view of it. People may have short memories, but the media are not likely to forget or ignore transgressions from the business. Monitoring the perception of the business over time is critical to being in a position to respond when needed and avoid an overreaction to a reputational blip. The internal reputation should also be considered and assessed for changes over time. Are there frustrations, anger or negativity from employees? If so, what is it related to and how has it developed? Listening to staff is an important factor in an effectively run organization. It highlights problem issues before they develop and can give an indication of where the internal reputation is under pressure. But this has to be followed by a response and some form of action to improve the situation and ultimately the reputation among employees.

There is a scale of views in relation to businesses and organizations that ranges from hate to love. The majority of people will be in the middle ground where their views can be positively or negatively influenced. It is this group that should be the focus of the action that is taken. How can the poor reputation be improved and how can positive views be reinforced? Being aware of those who hate the business is important when working to prevent becoming a toxic brand, but the impact of the action will be less among those with wholly negative views.

What is moral, legal and acceptable from the business needs to be clear to prevent reputational damage. This analysis has to be rooted in the societal norms and values, both at that point in time and in that geographic location. A business that breaks the law in its operation will face criticism and the potential for long-term court cases linked to the breach that will add to negative perceptions. A business that lacks a moral compass will face a backlash from customers, people on social media and potentially, from staff. The lack of morality may be linked to prioritizing money over people, or a lack of transparency in the way a business operates. In addition, there are acceptable ways to operate and act which may be contravened. A business that promotes itself in a way that is not seen as appropriate could damage its reputation. For example, Balenciaga ran an advertising campaign that involved a child model holding a bondage teddy bear, which was criticized for being inappropriate and unacceptable.[1]

If a crisis has emerged there will be an impact on the reputation of the business which could be either positive or negative. If there is a level of culpability where the business has a responsibility directly for a situation that has occurred, then damage to their reputation is likely to be increased. This is also the case where there is a refusal to apologize for the situation or acknowledge that it is connected to the business. This will be discussed in Chapter 7, considering the strategies for when there is a crisis in a business' reputation.

Ten principles to turn negative situations around

In each approach to try to manage and improve reputation when it is under pressure or has been through some negative experience, there are 10 principles to inform the approach. Developing the activity, both operational within the business and involving PR and communication, should ensure these are adhered to:

1 Honesty
Being honest about what the situation is and what impact it is having, or has had, on people in the business and outside is essential. There should be no attempt to brush over the problem or to cover it up. The action that is taken to respond to the challenges must be delivered in an open and truthful way. Building or rebuilding trust in a business or brand is vital. Attempts to turn things around will fail unless there is a truth to the action that is taken and how it is talked about.

2 Adaptability
A business must be ready to listen to the issues that people are raising and to act on them. This includes changing and developing to improve the

systems, processes and way they operate. If a negative situation is going to be addressed, it requires some acceptance of the views and perceptions that people hold regardless of whether they are accurate or not. Being flexible and open to change is an important way to regain trust.

3 Humility

For businesses to be able to accept that change is necessary there has to be humility, particularly among the C-suite. They need to acknowledge that they may not have all the answers about how to improve and listening to the views of others is critical. Any arrogance about the way things are done, the knowledge within the business, and the approach that is taken will further damage the reputation.

4 Openness

Once a business is under pressure there is a tendency to be risk averse and to try to limit the information that is given. But this is the time when openness and transparency is required about what is being done to address the situation and how the business is responding. Building trust and confidence cannot be achieved without accepting there is a problem and addressing it in a positive way. This can be through talking with key groups or stakeholders or sharing internally with employees.

5 Value driven

The values of the business need to be central to any action to manage an issue or problem. If the action taken goes against the stated purpose and approach it will damage confidence in the response. Dealing with a challenge provides an opportunity to use the response to reinforce those values both among employees and those outside the business. For example, if the business wants to be ethical and sustainable then it should be reflected in the actions that are taken. This would mean avoiding senior executives flying long distance unnecessarily or prioritizing profit above people.

6 Visibility

Many businesses will try to stay out of the spotlight when a problem has emerged. Saying nothing or limiting public exposure will be at the heart of a risk-averse approach to the situation. Damage to the reputation will be intensified with people talking and commenting on the situation and the business. This is the point where the business needs to be involved in the conversation to address misinformation and to explain the response. Being visible, listening, responding and learning from the situation is critical.

7 Accountability

Accepting responsibility for what has happened is often counselled against by legal representatives. But if the reputation has been damaged because of something the business is responsible for, and that has had a detrimental effect on people, failing to recognize that will be called out by others. Attempting to address the damage to reputation needs to be grasped by the business making an apology or demonstrating some contrition for the situation.

8 Ownership

A business needs to own its narrative and story about the situation. Leaving others to make comment or fill in the gaps will increase the possibility of misinformation and further damage to the reputation. This links closely with visibility and accountability. Together they support the honesty that is required when attempting to rebuild reputation and turn things around. Without dynamic intervention, the situation can grow and develop leaving more lasting damage to the reputation of the business.

9 Commitment

Demonstrating a determination to address the problem, situation or impact is essential. If there is a perception of apathy, dismissiveness or downplaying the issue this will exacerbate the damage to the business' reputation. It may not seem a significant problem for the business, but if it is causing concern the potential for further damage to the reputation is substantial. Turning things around needs a recognition of the situation, the views or the perceptions and action taken to address it.

10 Competence

The final principle should be at the heart of the action and communication that is undertaken, and that is to demonstrate competence. As mentioned earlier, businesses need a legitimacy to operate and that comes from people trusting and having confidence in what they do. This needs to be reinforced so that the market position is secured. When damage has been done to the reputation of the business, the response must reinforce the capability it has to address the situation and bring it to a satisfactory outcome. What constitutes a satisfactory outcome will vary between groups and stakeholders, so it is important to reflect on the data and information about their views. Having identified the most influential groups and stakeholders this needs to be considered in prioritizing the response and activity.

Brands that can brush off challenges

There are some brands and businesses that are able to continue to operate despite facing damaging criticism, challenges to what they do and poor reputation among certain groups. Customers continue to use the products and services despite negative views about many aspects of how these brands behave. There is only a small group of brands that command this position. They are large and have significant influence in the global marketplace. They operate in most countries and amass huge profits that put them in a position of domination. Amazon reported net income of $30.4 billion in 2023[2] and its net worth is greater than many countries. In a 2021 report, Amazon was compared to the gross domestic product (GDP) of a number of countries and it was worth more than Australia, Spain and Mexico.[3] Similarly, an assessment of Apple highlighted a net worth that was greater than Canada, Russia, Italy and Brazil.[4] Microsoft, Alphabet (Google), Tesla and Facebook were all in the same group of businesses with a huge impact on modern life.

The size of these businesses gives them global recognition and a significant amount of influence on life and politically. People continue to use these businesses and products despite concerns about how much influence they have, and how they treat staff and damage other businesses. Amazon provides a quick and convenient shopping experience where people can order and receive items the same day without leaving the house. Apple, Microsoft and Google offer products that make life easier and this allows people to compartmentalize their views. The product and the business can be separated. This phenomenon of such global influential businesses has not been seen before and while they have an operating model that has allowed them to continue with little impact from public perceptions and concern there is no understanding of what may happen. In the coming years the situation may change, and as modern life develops, they will need to ensure they remain relevant.

But these brands and businesses are few in number. Most businesses and organizations are not able to operate with a disregard to emerging challenges and negative perceptions. Where Amazon is little impacted by a minor protest against it, a smaller business would be affected more significantly. All the elements required for a positive reputation are still in place for these giant brands, but it would take a colossal event for it to have a detrimental impact. A tornado that hit an Amazon warehouse in Illinois, US, in December 2021 'raised concerns' about employee safety.[5] Six people died and there were allegations that staff were threatened with termination if they left to move to a place of safety. Even that significant crisis appears to have had little impact on the profits of the business. But the treatment of staff by Amazon remains an ongoing challenge to the business. In coming years, changes in society, politics and economics may yet have an impact on these global behemoths.

Toxic brands

A toxic brand is one that continues to fail to demonstrate the elements that comprise a good business. The business operates without those factors being demonstrated and this attracts consistent damaging media coverage and online commentary. If there is one very significant event, it can have a similarly significant impact on the business' reputation. For example, OceanGate was a company providing crewed submersibles that suspended operations following an incident when a submersible that was journeying to the wreck of the Titanic imploded killing five people on board, including one of the founders Stockton Rush. The significance of this tragedy and the high profile it received had a devastating impact on the OceanGate business.[6] See the case study at the end of this chapter. If there is a continued failure to improve perceptions of the business and how it operates it can build to create a toxicity around the business. For example, the way Ryanair operates creates damage that it is attempting to address.[7] In some situations, businesses become toxic because they are out of step with societal norms and attitudes; for example, tobacco companies now compared to when they operated in the 1940s and 1950s.

In the same way that reputation will be viewed differently by different groups and cultures this can be seen in which brands are labelled as toxic. What is acceptable business practice in the US, Canada and UK may be viewed as unacceptable and even toxic in other parts of the world. This is a further reminder of the role of cultural intelligence within reputation and how it is influenced.

How does a business become toxic? In short, it continues to allow failings to persist over time and does not take account of perceptions that exist. It puts reputation low down on the list of priorities and trusts in people continuing to purchase the product or to use the service. The failings will, over time, lead to the bad reputation growing and ultimately it will create significant damage. As mentioned in Chapter 3, this can be quantified in changes to share price and profitability. Ultimately, in the worst cases, the bad reputation can lead to the end of the business. For example, in 1992, comments from the then Chairman of Ratners jewellery chain described its products as 'total cr*p', which dealt a near fatal blow to the business. There was a sales slump and a £122.3 million deficit.[8] In many cases, where there is a crisis in the reputation the business resorts to a rebrand or changing its name in an attempt to create distance.

Toxic brands can redefine themselves and make changes that ensure they operate and are profitable. This is not an easy road and takes time, consistent effort and a determination to change and address the problems that have been identified. People do move on, and with a consistent approach to redesign and improve the areas that led to the reputational damage, and after a certain amount of time, the former toxic brands can continue, re-emerge and become profitable again.

The impact of polarization

The world is becoming increasingly polarized and through media and social media, businesses and organizations are labelled as heroes or villains when a problem emerges. This can have significant damage on reputation when a crisis happens and also when attempting to boost and improve a reputation. Polarization is often discussed in relation to political views and the growth of the extreme political positions linked to ideologies. However, it is relevant to emerging societal issues and the way the media reports issues. This often drives the public narrative and opinions that things are either good or bad, so those involved with them are either good or bad. The impact of the heroes and villains narrative can be seen in many media reports of situations and particularly where a brand, business or global organization has acted in a way that has a significant impact on individuals. People are keen to find someone to blame who is culpable when something has happened, or where there is a crisis. This is followed by a demand for action from those considered responsible for the situation.

It can also be seen with the social media echo chambers, where people are exposed to views that support their approach to the world and events. In a 2021 review of research on echo chambers, the problem was not just about exposure to like-minded individuals. Rosa Borge and Ludovic Terren found '... the problem not only lies with users communicating with like-minded others on social media but also (and perhaps even more importantly) with users – often passively – consuming and being exposed mostly or solely to attitude-reinforcing content (cf. metaphor of the filter bubble).'[9] Despite the ability through technology to access perspectives from around the world, it has in many cases led to a narrowing of views about issues.

Polarization of views increases the challenge of attempting to improve a reputation that is damaged or under pressure. A business that has been the subject of criticism from the public will be labelled as a villain and it will take a plan of consistent activity to move to a neutral position. This extends the time taken to recovery from a reputational crisis. The actions required will involve the whole of the organization that needs to address the reason why the business has a bad reputation, and this can then be supported by a programme of communication. It is important for businesses and organizations to avoid trying to talk of themselves as the heroes in a situation. This increases the possibility of polarization affecting them, and they may find they are moved to the villain position at some point. A business that promotes itself as the saviour of an emergency situation will appear to be motivated by improving its reputation rather than addressing the problem at hand. Categorizing your own business as a hero is incredibly damaging, but it can be as problematic if the media or those on social media do the same. Remain focused on addressing the situation that has emerged, whether it is a problem, a change that is needed or an improvement that is required.

How to identify a fatal or near-fatal blow to a business

Being able to address a reputation that is under pressure requires being able to spot when the situation is so serious that it demands a significant response. With significant damage to a business' reputation people will no longer want to use the goods and services. They will not want to work for the business, and in a public sector context they will not trust you and want to be connected to you. This can also impact on the level of investment that is made in the business. This significant damage to the reputation will impact on the C-suite as well as the wider business. For example, when Yorkshire County Cricket Club was criticized in an independent review that investigated allegations of racism, it led to the entire coaching staff leaving, the club Chairman and Chief Executive resigning, a number of brands withdrawing sponsorship and the club being suspended from hosting international cricket. Lord Kamlesh Patel, who was brought in as Chairman, said: 'Significant change is required at Yorkshire County Cricket Club and we are committed to taking whatever action is necessary to regain trust.'[10] Without confidence that the club had addressed the issues and was changing and developing, brands would not want to be associated with it and players would look to other clubs. If law enforcement loses public confidence people will not come forward with information and will avoid contacting the organization for help. This is outlined in the case study in Chapter 1.

It is also important to understand what has caused the deterioration and whether there is a lack of action, level of dishonesty or some other element of chaos that has prompted the negative perceptions. Gathering the information and ensuring a detailed understanding is essential before considering the action to take. It is important to avoid making a knee-jerk response that is based on flawed information as, at worst, this can cause the situation to deteriorate further.

The potential impact should be assessed by reviewing the way people have been affected. Who has had their lives changed by the situation that has developed? How far has the situation spread? What is the perception of the business in relation to the situation? And importantly, what are the perceptions among those who have been affected? If a situation is potentially going to be fatal or near fatal to a business it is going to be driven by a lack of humanity, a failure to understand the impact on people, and a lack of empathy in the response.

Consider the internal damage that the situation may leave. When an organization is under the most intense pressure it can threaten the future of the CEO and the wider C-suite. They can become directly connected to the crisis situation and when it is a reputational crisis, they will be expected to take responsibility for the culture and behaviour that exists within the business. Ultimately, they will be expected to manage the situation to a satisfactory conclusion, unless they are so damaged by the events that there is a loss of confidence in them. In these situations, the potentially fatal damage can be avoided by removing them and replacing them with someone that has, or can gain, the confidence to manage the response. For an organization under pressure, this can be a problem for the staff who may feel unsettled by the action that has been taken and the change that will be required. It reinforces the importance of staff engagement as part of the activity to influence the reputation of a business. Ensuring the internal stability of a business that is in chaos will help in the positive response and building for the future.

Considering long-term implications of a bad reputation

The 10 principles mentioned earlier are essential in addressing any damage to the reputation. But when the situation has been allowed to persist for some time it will require a carefully constructed plan that takes things a step at a time. Action in these situations is critical but it needs to be the right action, at the right time and affecting the right people. If opportunities have been missed and then these have had a further impact on the negative perceptions about the business this will require a longer-term plan. It also means the C-suite need to accept the time taken to move forward and build a positive reputation will be much longer. A business that is under pressure and facing a reputational challenge needs to develop a consistent and comprehensive approach to address the situation. In using the monitoring and evaluation discussed in Chapter 3, it also needs to take care to review the changes over time. What has made the situation worse? When did it deteriorate rapidly?

The reputation improvement plan needs to cover the whole business and should have actions that range from changing policies and procedures through to revising marketing material. As identified in Chapter 1, reviewing those elements that comprise the reputation of the business should be the starting point. Attempting to address the situation and the longer-term implications by pushing out a lot of positive stories will backfire. It will not make the required improvements to the business. It will not change the internal culture, and it will not demonstrate listening to the views and perceptions that have been highlighted. For example, if the reputation is linked to a problem that then is subjected to a cover-up, such as the UK Post Office Horizon IT scandal,[11] it requires a significant package of actions in the long term to demonstrate that the business is changing. The reputational impact of crisis, issues and poor handling of problems cannot be underestimated.

Senior managers and leaders in organizations will want to put the situation behind them and move forward as quickly as possible. However, people's views and perceptions can persist for a long time and change can be slow. Trying to turn things around using PR and communication alone will not address the fundamental problems that exist. Approaches that look at renaming the business to create distance with the damaged brand, to cut out the problematic part of the business, or to plough on with positive PR regardless of external factors will lead to further damage to the reputation. The focus needs to be on reshaping and revising the business approach, and considering the change in culture that may be necessary. Building a plan will need to take a 12-to-24-month approach and consider the threats and risks that may lead to setbacks along the way.

Building for the future

A bad reputation does not have to be accepted as part of the way a business or organization is viewed. In most cases, if action is taken then the situation can, over time, be rescued and returned to a neutral position before potentially building a positive reputation from the ashes of the previous situation. It requires a recognition of the importance of addressing the challenges, which for some businesses may itself be a challenge even if they are financially viable. While the business may be profitable now, there is no guarantee that position will be maintained in the future. Unchecked and poor reputation that is not addressed can lead to a position where the only way forward is to clear out the senior management, or to cease trading and redesign itself.

To create firm foundations for the future, there need to be no empty promises, or attempts to use PR and communication alone to turn things around. The action needs to follow the 10 principles when considering the way forward and importantly, the tangible action that the business is going to undertake to address the issues and concerns.

In some cases, the bad reputation may not be based in any facts but in unfounded views and perceptions that may have gone undetected or unchallenged. Perceptions are people's reality and addressing this requires careful management. Be clear that there is no problem that has not been recognized and consider the situation from other people's perspectives. Businesses can use open and transparent communication to address the perceptions. This situation demonstrates there are areas to change and develop; areas of the business including promotion, stakeholder management, and staff engagement. Whenever there is an issue or problem related to the reputation of the business, it requires review, change and improvements to be made.

Businesses need to take steps to work within regulatory, ethical and societal norms, as well as exercise cultural intelligence to avoid problems occurring in the first place. Being aware of how the business operates, where there are risks and how views of them among key audiences and stakeholders may be influenced over time provides a strong foundation to address issues of concern. Once a reputation is under threat or has been damaged it takes a concerted effort and potentially a significant amount of time to turn things around. This is time that can be spent on business development and successful promotion if there is an effective issues management process in place. This will be discussed in Chapter 5.

CASE STUDY
OceanGate tragedy

Background

OceanGate was founded in 2009 by Stockton Rush, providing manned submersibles that are used in diving expeditions. The work had included assisting universities to carry out underwater studies and research. In 2017 the company announced that it would start to offer manned dives to the wreck of the Titanic, and that these would be open to private individuals at a high price. There were a series of delays to the expedition. But in 2020, OceanGate announced it had raised $18 million to fund its fleet of submersibles and publicized a new date of 2021 for the dives to the Titanic to begin. The first dive to the Titanic is reported to have happened in July 2021. A further dive took place in 2022, and there were media reports that 60 paying customers and 15–20 researchers had been taken on the submersibles to view the high-profile wreck.[12]

On 18 June 2023, the Titan submersible started its descent of 12,500 feet to the wreck on the bed of the North Atlantic Ocean. The trip was expected to take two hours to reach the wreck, but 90 minutes into the dive communication between the submersible and the surface was lost. It then failed to reappear at the time it was expected to resurface. On 22 June 2023, debris was found, and it was announced that those on board the Titan were lost, which was likely to be the result of a catastrophic implosion. A few days later, pieces of the Titan submersible were brought back to the shore to be examined. On 2 July 2023, OceanGate announced that it would be ceasing operations.[13] It was also reported that shortly after that social media sites for the business were deleted[14] and the website was closed with just a short message in its place saying: 'OceanGate Expeditions has suspended all exploration and commercial operations.'[15]

In the days that followed there were reports that safety concerns about the submersible had been raised five years before the ill-fated dive to the Titanic. This was detailed in a letter from the Marine Technology Society to the operators concerned that they had not gone through the recognized certification process for the vessel.[16]

At the centre of this situation was the tragic loss of five lives and the impact on their families and friends.

Reputation lessons

In the situation that OceanGate found itself, could it have continued operating? This is one situation where the severity of the crisis, alongside the loss of life in a high-profile way would make it unlikely that it could continue to operate. The reputational damage was extensive, and the event raised questions about the way the business operated.

- Address issues of concern about the operation of the business at an early opportunity.

- If the business operates outside of recognized guidelines and approval mechanisms it needs to be able to justify why and demonstrate it is fit to operate. The legitimacy to operate is a key part of reputation.

- Recognize where the situation is so critical and damaging that it is unlikely that the business can continue to operate and make the necessary decisions to cease operation.

- Explain why the decision has been taken if there are any plans for those in senior positions to move to other businesses and organizations. They need to be able to address the concerns about their personal involvement if they are going to move forward.

- If this situation had not been so catastrophic, the business could have continued if there was a willingness to review how it operated and to address the concerns raised by others working in the same industry. But it would have taken a significant period of time to rebuild the lost confidence in the submersible and the expeditions.

Conclusion

A business or brand does not have to accept that it has a bad reputation. It can do something about it and look to make a change that will help to increase trust and confidence. The business first needs to act quickly to address a problem that is starting to cause deterioration in the reputation. Ongoing monitoring of trust, confidence and reputation can assist with this and make it easier to identify problems at an early stage. Tackling the situation also requires a good understanding of what is causing the bad reputation and the extent of the damage it has done and may do if it continues unchecked. The use of severity assessments is common in risk management, but can be used to support reputation management. Within this assessment is a need to understand whether the impact could be a fatal or near fatal attack on the business. If this is identified it can help the prioritization of resources, and the undertaking of action to turn things around as the business recognizes it is under extreme pressure.

When a business acts or is perceived to act against moral, legal and acceptable societal norms it will increase the potential for negative views, and a strong emotional response from audiences, customers and staff. The 10 principles outlined should be used to support the response and limit the potential for significant reputational damage. The most important one of the 10 identified is honesty, which should underpin all aspects of the response. It supports an ethical approach to reputation management, which will be considered in Chapter 8.

There are both toxic brands and those who appear to be immune from reputational damage when issues or incidents occur. A brand that is labelled as toxic will have failed to recognize and respond to either a significant reputational threat, or a series of reputational problems. It is the end of the road for a business labelled in that way. There is a final chance to challenge the perception and take action to turn things around, and this will need to be significant change. But for a lucky few this is not a problem they face as they appear to be immune to reputational challenge. Brands such as Amazon and Google can withstand reputational damage due to their size and the benefits to customers. This is a relatively new phenomenon linked to technology developments and globalization, so the potential for long-term damage remains unknown. An additional challenge to reputation management comes from social media echo chambers and the polarization of societal norms. This needs to be considered when developing plans to respond to the bad reputation.

A business that is facing a bad reputation needs to develop a long-term plan to turn things around over time. There is no quick fix when a business has seen a slump, and this is when a reputation improvement plan can assist. The plan will bring together all the actions that the business is going to undertake to impact on the views people have of the business. It is not just about improving perceptions through communication and requires business changes to be put in place. There are challenges to being able to turn around the negative reputation and these will be detailed in Chapter 5.

References

1 C Ritschel, P Hirwani, M Clark and J Whitehead. Balenciaga scandal: Brand issues new statement, drops lawsuit as creative director responds to backlash, *The Independent*, 3 December 2022, www.independent.co.uk/life-style/balenciaga-scandal-ad-child-campaign-news-b2237949.html (archived at https://perma.cc/83CU-TRVA)

2 Statista. Annual net income of Amazon.com from 2004 to 2023, May 2024, www.statista.com/statistics/266288/annual-et-income-of-amazoncom/ (archived at https://perma.cc/A8TH-ZNFN)

3 P Dughi. Apple, Amazon are wealthier than 92% of the countries in the world. *Stronger Content*, 29 March 2021, https://strongercontent.com/apple-amazon-are-wealthier-than-92-of-the-countries-in-the-world/ (archived at https://perma.cc/DNU4-7YCA)

4 P Dughi. Apple, Amazon are wealthier than 92% of the countries in the world. *Stronger Content*, 29 March 2021, https://strongercontent.com/apple-amazon-are-wealthier-than-92-of-the-countries-in-the-world/ (archived at https://perma.cc/DNU4-7YCA)

5 C Tebor. Feds have 'concerns', but no punishment, for Amazon after deadly warehouse collapse in tornado, *USA Today*, 26 April 2022, https://eu.usatoday.com/story/news/nation/2022/04/26/amazon-illinois-warehouse-collapse-osha-punishment/9545707002/ (archived at https://perma.cc/3EMT-CF6H)

6 J Nye. OceanGate will suspend all exploration and business operations following death of Titanic five in 'catastrophic implosion' during $250,000 mission to wreck of liner, *Mail Online*, 6 July 2023, www.dailymail.co.uk/news/article-12272101/OceanGate-SUSPEND-exploration-business-operations-following-death-Titanic-Five.html (archived at https://perma.cc/ZZ5Q-RMVT)

7 L French. Ryanair's reputation recovery takes off, European CEO, nd, www.europeanceo.com/business-and-management/ryanairs-reputation-recovery-takes-off/ (archived at https://perma.cc/74B4-9VLY)

8 L Buckingham and F Kane. From the archive, 22 August 1992: Gerald Ratner's 'crap' comment haunts jewellery chain, *The Guardian*, 22 August 2014, www.theguardian.com/business/2014/aug/22/gerald-ratner-jewellery-total-crap-1992-archive (archived at https://perma.cc/W7TL-L6Y3)

9 L Terren and R Borge. Echo chambers on social media: A systematic review of the literature, *Review of Communication Research*, 2021, 9. 99–118, https://doi.org/10.12840/ISSN.2255-4165.028

10 S Burnton. Azeem Rafiq and Yorkshire: Timeline of a county cricket crisis, *The Guardian*, 31 March 2023, www.theguardian.com/sport/2023/mar/31/azeem-rafiq-and-yorkshire-timeline-of-a-county-cricket-crisis (archived at https://perma.cc/6S67-JRBF)

11 Post Office Horizon IT inquiry, www.postofficehorizoninquiry.org.uk/ (archived at https://perma.cc/K6F7-L67J)

12 A Kassam. 'A race against time': how shipwrecks hold clues to humanity's future, *The Guardian*, 9 January 2023, www.theguardian.com/environment/2023/jan/09/a-race-against-time-how-shipwrecks-hold-clues-to-humanitys-future (archived at https://perma.cc/3SRT-ALFD)

13 D Pulver. Patents, lawsuits, safety concerns – then tragedy. A timeline of OceanGate's Titan sub, *USA Today*, 22 June 2023, https://eu.usatoday.com/story/news/nation/2023/06/22/timeline-oceangate-founding-expedition-history/70344305007/ (archived at https://perma.cc/44G2-BKU9)

14 K Wei and K Tan. OceanGate tried to scrub the internet clean of traces that it ever existed, taking down its Facebook, Instagram, Twitter and LinkedIn pages, *Business Insider*, 14 July 2023, www.businessinsider.com/oceangate-take-down-website-social-media-suspend-commercial-operations-2023-7?r=US&IR=T (archived at https://perma.cc/M5V9-DCAF)

15 OceanGate Expeditions, https://oceangateexpeditions.com/ (archived at https://perma.cc/2FRX-FJBX)

16 D Trotta and B Brooks. Missing Titanic sub: experts raised safety concerns about OceanGate Titan in 2018, *Reuters*, 22 June 2023, www.reuters.com/world/us/missing-titanic-sub-experts-raised-safety-concerns-about-oceangate-titan-2018-2023-06-21/ (archived at https://perma.cc/XQZ8-893D)

5

What are the challenges to effective reputation management?

Introduction

The main problems when considering how to introduce effective reputation management all relate to people. The way people behave, their attitudes from the frontline through to the top of the organization and the CEO, all can present issues when working to improve the reputation of a business. Poor behaviour and culture are a significant threat to the perceptions of any business. Organizations can become out of step with societal norms or fail to move with the times. Beyond the business, the perceptions and feelings that others have, needs to be understood so it can be addressed. Customers, service users and stakeholders can all present a challenge by reinforcing negative perceptions or by sharing misinformation. But the challenges are not just from the views and perceptions; the actions and operation of the business can present a problem when trying to tackle issues and take opportunities.

In Chapter 2, the elements of an effective business were outlined. They are:

- A clear purpose
- Values that are reinforced
- Development of effective relationships
- Engaged and supported employees
- Effective leadership
- Risk management and crisis preparedness

- Financial stability
- Communication operating strategically
- Cultural intelligence

If a business is failing in any one or multiples of these, it risks derailing the reputation and presenting barriers to moving forward. These issues cannot be addressed by PR and communication, and will require the business to confront the problem that exists. If it is weak leadership then the board will need to consider whether those in senior roles have the right approach for the business to develop. If there are problems with staff feeling undervalued and lacking support, then HR and personnel processes may need to be reformed, and the reward and recognition systems overhauled. If the organization does not understand its risks, then time needs to be invested to ensure there is awareness and appropriate systems are in place.

Effective reputation management requires the business to have a clear understanding of the elements that comprise a positive business and reputation. This places them in a position of being able to confront failings as well as demonstrating this, to attempt to improve on negative perceptions. At the centre of understanding this is ensuring there is an effective risk management process in place, which will highlight areas of challenge or that require further monitoring, research or improvement. Getting ahead of any problems is vital to reputation management so negative situations don't happen and if they develop, action can be quickly taken to limit the impact. Effective risk management needs to involve the whole of the business so that both operational and business risks, as well as the reputational risks that may be faced, can be identified.

What are classified as risks?

Risks are anything that has the potential to seriously impact on the business and its operation. There will be a long list of possible threats, and being able to identify those with the biggest impact and the most likelihood of occurring is critical. Existing risk management processes and the development of risk registers within businesses usually focus on threats that could prevent the operation of the business. For example, the supply chain collapses, or the IT fails, damaging sales. But these are not the only risks that could be detrimental to the business; reputational risks should be part of the risk management process. The recognition of reputational risks is vital in a globalized world where there are many potential online challenges. The vital element of effective risk management is identifying those possible situations before they happen, putting steps in place to mitigate wherever possible and being ready to respond if it occurs. Understanding threats to the business and where they may emerge from should be part of the risk management process. This process has to take account of reputational issues if it is to be effective.

Reputational risks can include damaging comments from senior leaders, customer services failures, inappropriate staff behaviour and PR/campaigns. They are likely to be identified first by PR and communication teams who are monitoring views and perceptions of the business. If these teams have the evaluation in place that was outlined in Chapter 3, any deterioration in the reputation will be identified. Reputation management requires the problems and threats to be understood and to be subjected to the same organizational processes as operational challenges. Assessments will need to consider previous reputational crises and issues, internal risks, and those external problems that may be highlighted through horizon scanning.

> Review your risk management processes and consider whether they are looking at all areas where threats may exist. Are reputational risks given the same focus as operational areas of concern? Does the risk register or documentation detail reputational problems that may need mitigation, attention, or plans to be developed?

What are the risks to effective reputation management?

Reputations can be affected by a whole range of different problems. Effectively, wherever a problem occurs it has the potential to impact on the way people view the business. Where the business responds poorly to situations, fails to live up to the purpose, values and expectations that people have, or is affected by sector-wide challenges, these are all risks to reputation. Identifying the main problem areas where those risks may emerge and linking them to the requirements of an effective business requires understanding internal and external risks to reputation. The former should be more easily identified by the business and there is a greater ability to have a direct impact through the response. However, external risks should also be considered with appropriate plans and actions put in place.

Internal risks

- *Disconnected staff* – if staff are not linked to the purpose and values of the business, it can leave them disinterested in the issues that impact on reputation and can lead to poor behaviour and a challenging culture. It is vital to engage staff with the purpose and priorities of the business. This risk can impact on the ability to recruit and retain staff. A lack of boundaries and clear expectations can allow poor behaviour to develop. Employees need to be able to raise issues and concerns and those at the top of the business need to demonstrate active listening.

- *Lack of purpose* – a business that lacks a clear direction and purpose will find it difficult to clearly understand what the reputation is and what they want it to be. This can lead to problems developing unchecked and without a satisfactory response. Employees will be unclear of the expectations the business and the customers have of them. It can lead to staff focusing on areas of business that inhibit growth or moving into work that does not support the core operation.

- *Silo working* – if the parts of the business work independently and there is a lack of sharing between teams, this can impact on the reputation. There will be a lack of clarity about the factors of importance to the reputation of the business and slow and unco-ordinated responses to issues, problems and ultimately crises. There may be a lack of a risk process that brings together leaders from across the organization and this could mean significant issues are overlooked. Silo working leads to the duplication of work and gaps in delivery, which may allow reputational issues to develop unchecked. The business will also be unlikely to identify trends and changes that are happening within the business and around them.

- *Poor culture* – an organization that has a problematic internal culture will lack cultural intelligence and will not be listening to feedback about them. A culture is not related to one person at the top of the business, but to the way the leadership team or C-suite operate and what behaviour is allowed and what is rewarded. If unethical practices are not challenged or inappropriate behaviour is not addressed, it will lead to the development of a poor internal culture. The expectation the business has of its staff needs to align to those the public and society have of the business and its employees. Poor culture is a sign of weak leadership, and that staff are not aligned to a clear purpose.

- *Ineffective leaders* – being able to focus on reputation management needs to have the support of those at the top of the business. What leaders are interested in will drive how the business operates and what is seen as important. If leaders are not open to feedback, are only interested in the bottom line, or fail to put clear boundaries in place, it will block effective reputation management. Ineffective leaders can allow unethical and inappropriate behaviour to continue and will face a challenge to their integrity.

- *Operational failing* – if the business is not operating effectively, has problems in its systems and processes that are unchecked, or experiences a significant failure, it has the potential to negatively impact on the reputation. Competency and the legitimacy to operate will be challenged by a significant failure or ongoing problems. Customers, service users and stakeholders expect more from the business, and will want to see change. Where there are internal failings there will be a lack of investment and innovation, and negative feedback may develop unchecked.

- *Weak governance* – when staff are not clear where the roles and responsibilities lie within a business it will impact on effective decision-making. There will be a lack of accountability and decisions will be made without oversight and challenge, if necessary. This is a significant threat to developing effective reputation management. There needs to be clarity about where decisions are made, who has delegated authority and for what decisions, and who can act. If decisions are made and action taken outside of agreed processes, they will be risky and could lead to reputational damage.

- *Inappropriate behaviour* – any actions of staff, particularly those at a senior level, which is out of alignment with the stated purpose and values, or that causes offence, anger and even outrage is a significant risk. There needs to be clear expectations of employees and sanctions that are put in place when these are transgressed. Creating the positive culture that is part of a strong and effective business is critical to reducing the likelihood of inappropriate actions occurring, and not being challenged if they do occur.

- *Bullish or blinkered operation* – a business that is not prepared to listen, is convinced of its approach, and bulldozes through any feedback that it dislikes, will be unlikely to value the reputation of the business. Such a business will not be listening to feedback and will likely face significant damage, possibly even fatal to the business, before it recognizes the poor reputation it has and takes steps to address it.

External risks

- *Misinformation and disinformation* – the reputation of a business can quickly be derailed or damaged by people sharing inaccurate information. This can be problematic when it is misinformation and is not intentionally inaccurate, as corrections can be made. However, when this information is left unchecked, it can become difficult to change. Disinformation is much more challenging as it is information that is deliberately shared with a view to creating damage and upset. There is a growth in the use of deepfakes where the image or video can appear to be from a high-profile person or individual when it has in fact been artificially generated. Crisis and risk planning needs to take account of this and identify how these situations can be addressed quickly and continuously. A good example of the challenge came in March 2023, when photographs of the Pope emerged wearing a puffer coat, which were shared extensively before it was identified as a fake.[1]

- *Regulatory frameworks* – the legal and regulatory frameworks around businesses can restrict what information is shared and at what point it can happen. This can present significant challenges when attempting to improve a reputation, or to manage possible damaging situations. For example, listed companies have restrictions on how and when to release information and these have been developed to reduce the opportunity for insider trading or other actions. In such cases, information will need to be released publicly before it is shared with staff and stakeholders, which puts additional pressures on the communication team. The General Data Protection Regulation (GDPR) restrict the sharing of personal details, and public sector organizations can be subject to Freedom of Information requirements to share documents and information. Individuals can make Data Subject Access Requests (DSAR) allowing them access to all information that an organization holds on them. There may be issues where internal documentation, emails and online messages that are potentially derogatory about the person are then shared through a DSAR. This presents a huge risk on how the internal information and data is managed, and how communication systems are used. In addition, a duty of candour is in place in some organizations that have a legal requirement to be open and honest in their response when something has gone wrong. This is evident in the health sector with requests that it extends further across the public sector.

- *Data overwhelm* – where businesses or organizations have a significant amount of data available to access it can be difficult to identify the information that really matters. People can potentially focus on data that may not be the most beneficial to developing a positive reputation. They can face paralysis as they are unsure and unclear about what the information shows and the trends that it may point towards. Gathering data without a purpose can also be a risk as there can be challenges that the business was aware of, but where it failed to act. The use of artificial intelligence systems to manage data and provide insights is developing quickly and should assist in preventing people being overwhelmed with information.

- *Media scrutiny* – the mainstream media continue to play an important role within society, even with the development of social media. Operating 24 hours a day, seven days a week, there is a global speed of information. Issues move from local to global within hours or even minutes. They are responsible for sharing both facts and commentary but are given a position of authority. In the UK, the Office of Communication (Ofcom) identified that there was still a role for the mainstream media for where people accessed news.[2] The media scrutinize the operation of businesses and where there is damage to a reputation, or a reputation that is under threat, they will pay even closer attention. Effective relationships with the media are still an important part of PR and communication work.

- *Social media attacks* – the proliferation of social media channels and the development of echo chambers,[3] where the space can magnify messages and restrict rebuttals or corrections being available, are a significant challenge to developing a positive reputation. Groups can become difficult to access or connect with, and misinformation and disinformation can grow unchecked. In addition, negativity and criticism can grow and become a social media pile-on, where people come together to attack someone or something. The possibility of trolls, keyboard warriors and bad actors using social media to attack a business is high. Businesses are not in a position to control the situation but can attempt to manage it by addressing the rumours, false statements and inaccuracies. The growth of TikTok as a method of news has created additional pressures, as has the way algorithms share information to users. There is also a risk from the dark web and how it operates out of sight. Some data monitoring tools can provide details of comments that are made on the dark web, and this can assist in understanding the hidden risks.

- *Trust deficit* – there is a significant lack of trust in institutions, organizations and establishment figures in the post-Covid pandemic world. Research in the UK has shown trust with politicians, journalists, estate agents and police officers are among the lowest levels for many years.[4] This presents a risk to organizations that are attempting to improve their reputation, as it may be affected by a lack of trust. If the business is an estate agent in the UK, it would need a more carefully planned and detailed plan to overcome the lack of trust. A critical part of addressing the trust deficit is to demonstrate integrity and to ensure authenticity in all communication and activity. The lack of trust can spread, and the perception grow quickly, if it is not addressed.

- *Uncertainty in geopolitics* – even when an organization has developed a positive reputation and is establishing its position, there are events that happen outside their control that can have an impact. Changes and actions around the world will affect businesses. Geopolitical events can put pressure on supply chains and can restrict trade if sanctions are placed upon working with a specific country or regime. A business that fails to take account of and respond to events around the world could be damaging its reputation. Businesses will be expected to express views about world events and with polarization, a lack of comment will allow people to assign a position whether it is accurate or not.

- *Changing societal norms* – the definition of acceptable behaviour is continually changing and developing. Actions and behaviour that was acceptable a decade ago may be reputationally damaging today. This requires businesses are aware of, and adapting to, the circumstances around them. It can be further complicated for multinational businesses that have multiple societies to consider when they are developing plans and communication.

- *Artificial intelligence* – whether it is viewed as an enabler or a threat, artificial intelligence is a risk to a business and its reputation development.

If it is moving too quickly and integrating artificial intelligence into systems more quickly than people can accept, it will be potentially damaging. But if it is moving too slowly and failing to utilize the developing technology, it will also be criticized. Those responsible for developing innovation within businesses need to work closely with communication teams and those monitoring societal changes to ensure progress at an acceptable speed.

How to understand risks and where to find them

Understanding the situations that have the potential to negatively impact the business is critical and for PR and communication it means recognizing the areas of reputational damage. Ultimately, these problems can emerge from anywhere, but there are six main areas to consider when identifying risks:

1 People

2 Product

3 Policies

4 Perceptions

5 Finance

6 Environment

The way people behave, internal culture and attitudes, and the actions that employees take are a risk to the business. Having strong employee policies and procedures and a positive culture that is reinforced by visible leadership can all help to reduce those risks. Products and services can also be problematic with failures, recalls and a lack of customer services; all areas where risks can develop that can impact on reputation. Policies are often overlooked as a source of risks and particularly, reputational risks. But in the same way policies are subject to equality impact assessments, they should be reviewed for reputational impact if they are not adhered to or if something goes wrong. Perceptions are fundamental reputational risks. People have views that can impact on the business, its operation and reputation. This was discussed in Chapter 1. Finances can be a source of possible risks from where money is spent, through to how it is invested and what pay is given to senior executives. Finally, the world around a business can be a source of possible threats both to operational activity and the reputation. There may be an issue with a supply chain or with logistics and distribution. There may be an event that changes perceptions and attitudes towards an industry or a product. There may be a product contamination with a source product. There may be political discussions around the sector the business is within. All these are external events in the environment around the business that can threaten its operation and reputation.

Gathering information about risks can be lengthy and time consuming. It requires the assessment of data from the past and present operation of the business to help identify and predict problems that could occur in the future. Historically, identifying and understanding risks has been something linked to data gathering, understanding insight and systems to bring together senior leaders from across the business. It could be time consuming and involve a level of subjective assessment linked to those reviewing the risks. Developments in artificial intelligence (AI) can make a big impact on risk assessments and the identification of threats. This is not restricted to the operational risks but given the abilities of AI, can assist in identifying and analysing reputational risks.

AI can analyse text information from social media, customer feedback and news articles around particular areas of concern. The systems can look for sentiment and areas of biggest risks. This can also be supported by a review of historic data to support predictive analytics to understand the future threats that may emerge. The modelling of risks can also be developed using AI so that the impact and likelihood of situations can be estimated, to support identification and recognition of the biggest areas of concern.[5] This can be achieved using AI systems that are developed within the business to avoid the risks from using publicly available systems. The use of AI requires access to relevant, appropriate and accurate data that can then inform assessment and modelling. This work cannot be totally given over to AI and technology. It still requires the oversight of the organization and the review to ensure it is functioning appropriately and taking account of the reputational threats.

The role of boards, trustees and investors is also significant when considering risks and the management of them. There are rules and regulations about the way boards, trustees and investors operate and these should be understood by people taking up those positions. The relationship should be developed so that they can support with reputation management as well as the development of the business. Individuals in these roles also need to understand the impact that they can have when acting or commenting on difficult and challenging situations. Communication and PR teams need to develop relationships with board members, trustees and investors so that information is shared and can limit the potential risks from disagreements with these groups.

The risk management system

A system to manage risks needs to be in place regardless of whether AI is being used to support the work. There are four areas that need to be covered by the risk management process that exists within a business:

1 **Risk identification**
Using a paper-based assessment of the business and reputational risks, or maximizing the opportunities of AI, there needs to be a system for the identification of threats. This should be looking at the past events, present concerns, as well as problems in horizon scanning. Identifying the top risks that are the most likely to happen and could have the biggest impact will allow the business to be ready and prepared. It may include plans to mitigate problems before they happen, or to be able to respond quickly if situations develop. The quality of the work in this phase, and the investment at this stage, is essential to effective risk management.

2 **Governance**
The identification is the first step of the risk management process. The second element needs to be a structure and governance that is in place. This could be through a regular meeting to discuss the risks, mitigation approaches and plans. An online process may be used to gather the feedback and information from across the business. The key in whatever approach is put in place is to ensure that there is an understanding and involvement in risk management throughout the business. Each leader and department head needs to understand what they are required to do and how they contribute to the process.

3 **Roles and responsibilities**
Every member of the business should understand the responsibility they have in highlighting problems and areas of concern at the earliest opportunity. Getting ahead of problems can only happen in an open

culture where employees feel comfortable raising issues and discussing failures. If there is a culture where people are concerned about highlighting problems, then issues will develop, and cover-ups will take place. A training and education programme needs to be in place to ensure that everyone understands the role they are expected to play and what it means to them.

4 Review

Every risk management process needs to be subject to regular review and evaluation. It is important to understand if the system is working or where improvements could be made. For example, are the right people involved in the process, are threats being identified early enough, and does the governance structure work? Time to reflect on what is being highlighted and what it means for the wider development of the business beyond the immediate risk process is critical. After every incident, problem or crisis that occurs, the business should reflect on the learning from the situation and what may need to be developed within the risk management process.

The impact of political interference

Every business will have to work within a political framework for the countries within which they are working. This will set legislation, regulations and the boundaries that are in place in those business sectors. The connection between organizations and politicians is, for the most part, one that continues without any areas of concern. But at times of elections, or where there is a situation that is attracting a lot of attention, there could be political interference. These are moments when those in political positions intervene or get involved in situations when they are not adding value. A business that is responding to a damaging situation may find politicians making comments about the business, the situation, the response and the future. All these comments have the potential to impact on views of the business and ultimately on its reputation.

Political commentary can happen locally, nationally and internationally. The involvement will be a response in line with the party politics of the politician or political group. This means that it is likely to be focused on what is best for the political position rather than for the business or more importantly for the people involved in the response to the situation. Stakeholder management and processes have a crucial role to play in working with politicians and ensuring they are aware of situations and understand the impact of their commentary or involvement. Where this is not in place or does not work, a business can find itself becoming a political football; that is, being kicked around by different political parties.

The politicians will be involved for many reasons including that as it is a situation that involves constituents it is seen as a vote-winning situation to become involved with, they may be following party directives, or it may be virtue signalling. Virtue signalling is when individuals express a viewpoint or align themselves with a position of social conscience or morality with the aim of improving their own position. Investing in stakeholder management and having processes in place is an important element for the effective operation of a business. Businesses will benefit when they maintain a balance across political parties, as they need to be able to operate within political systems.

In countries where there is no democratic system in place, political interference will be a regular occurrence and it can have a significant impact. This may mean the ruling group demand certain actions are undertaken, or that the business behaves in a particular way. It restricts the ability to be able to proactively manage the reputation of the business as the power rests with another group or individual. What that group or individual say about the business and how it operates will drive the prevailing reputation.

Lobbying is part of public relations activity and is when the communication activity is designed to influence and inform decision makers on matters of policy and law. Many businesses will be involved in lobbying in relation to their industry and the way it operates. There are increasing ethical requirements on the way lobbying is conducted and more regulation may be in place in coming years. If lobbying is conducted in a negative way, uses unethical approaches, and fails to adhere to guidance, it has the potential to impact on the reputation of a business. Maintaining an honest and open approach to communication is essential when considering lobbying. Being open about the way lobbying is conducted can minimize the potential for reputational damage or risks to emerge. When lobbying works well it can inform and assist societal and regulatory developments and changes. But when it is negative it can be seen as an attempt to negatively influence those in power for business gains. Communication and PR teams need to understand the business' approach to lobbying and monitor the impact it is having on reputation. Building effective stakeholder engagement with key groups, individuals and politicians is essential.

Dealing with outrage

When a public outrage situation emerges it has a significant impact on the reputation of the business or organization that may be at the centre of it. Outrage can be caused by people, decisions or actions that are taken. This usually manifests itself in relation to some form of moral outrage where norms and conventions are felt to have been breached. It provokes strong responses from people including repulsion, disgust, hatred and anger. This strength of feeling can in turn lead to forms of action being taken and protest both online and in person. It highlights the importance of businesses and brands understanding the normative frameworks and accepted behaviour within different societies to avoid sparking outrage.

According to Daniel Diermeier there are five main sources of outrage: perceptions of norm violations, intuitive judgements driven by emotions, a desire for punishment, violation of trust, and the malleability of perceptions.[6] The important elements are the societal boundaries that are felt to have been breached and the damage to trust. If a business finds itself involved in a situation of outrage, there will be demands for retribution and penance which can often manifest itself as a demand for the most senior person or Chief Executive to be sacked. Responding to such situations will require significant action from the business and will need to acknowledge and show due consideration and apology for the transgression.

Outrages can occur when there is a failure to prioritize people above profits and property. They are also more likely to impact on businesses and organizations that have a purpose and societal standing. Public sector organizations that are considered to have stepped outside acceptable standards can find they are at the heart of outrage. For example, the murder of Sarah Everard in the UK in 2021 by an off-duty serving police officer sparked significant outrage and led to protests and vigils. The emotion was evident in the vigils and police clashed with those attending.[7] The case had a significant impact on the levels of trust in policing. In the months that followed, surveys revealed half of the women involved in the surveys had less trust in policing.[8] Cases of outrage have a significant detrimental impact on the reputation of the business, brand or organization involved.

Sustained and deliberate reputational attacks

Whenever there is a sustained and deliberate attack on the reputation of a business, it is vital to understand what is driving it. If there are strong emotions involved, or an outrage, the impact on the business will happen over weeks, months or even years. Protest groups and individual campaigners can also be provoked because of frustrations with a lack of acceptance that there is an area of concern. The perceptions that a business is not interested or is failing to recognize the area of concern can be treated as facts if there is a lack of action. The importance of acting and responding to these situations is clear.

When there is inaccurate information or perceptions of the business that are circulating and fuelling the attacks, a response plan needs to be developed. The facts of the situation need to be shared consistently and without becoming defensive. Any response needs to take account of the views and emotions that are evident. In such cases, internal communication becomes a central part of the response as employees will become frustrated and even angry at the consistent attacks on the business. Effective reputation management will be put under pressure in these long-term situations. It requires detailed planning and appropriate resourcing to be in place. Approaching sustained attacks as a crisis using the frameworks, process and plans for crisis response is the most effective way forward. The responses to long-term situations of reputational attack and damage will be detailed in Chapter 7.

The communication response

There are many challenges and risks to the communication response developed to address reputational issues. This can start with a lack of a clear approach and direction to the communication which fails to address the identified problems. Responding to a threat or reputational damage requires careful consideration and a plan that is developed from reviewing the feedback, data and other insight. The details of the responses that can be made will be covered in detail in Chapter 7. Clarity and transparency are needed in the development of the communication plan. Failing to develop a plan in the hope that the situation will disappear or blow over in time will leave others to decide the future of the business. Influencing the perceptions of the business needs to be developed in a deliberate and strategic manner. A 'no comment' approach to an emerging problem is unhelpful when trying to develop a positive reputation. It lacks transparency and honesty and leaves the way open for inaccuracies and fake news.

A business that acts in a way that contradicts the communication it is providing is creating a significant risk. There needs to be a consistent approach and the actions and words must be aligned to address negative perceptions and build trust and confidence. It is important to remember the elements that impact on the views people have of the business and involve them all in the development of the response. In addition, a decision on whether to apologize or not for a situation that has emerged is also a risk to repairing or building a positive reputation. Legal representatives will often advise against any form of apology as it may link to culpability of the business. But there are many ways apologies can be made that can support building a positive reputation, even when there has been a crisis or negative issue. If the business is responsible for the problem, it builds confidence when this is acknowledged at an early stage and where a positive plan to address the failing is in place.

A positive communication response is built on having access to the right information and ensuring that it has been fact-checked. PR and communication teams need to be able to understand what has happened, what the issues are, what is being done and how things are developing. They should be in a position to challenge the information they are given and to ensure there is open access to the details. This can ensure that confusion is avoided, and clarity is provided.

Communicators can find their ethics under pressure when reputational problems emerge, or threats develop. There may be attempts to downplay the problem, to avoid addressing it or to withhold vital information. This can present a huge issue to reputation management and effectively building a positive reputation and dealing with challenges. Establishing a reputation management framework which involves the whole business and is supported by an open culture can limit the potential for these issues to happen. This will be covered in detail in Chapter 8.

Ten steps to manage problematic issues

Effective reputation management relies on understanding and taking action to address problems and issues when they emerge. The longer an issue goes unresolved the more likely it is to grow, develop and become a significant challenge. The following 10 steps[9] need to be in place to ensure that effective issues-management strategies can be put in place:

1 **Ensure early indication of the emerging problem**
   Being able to spot situations quickly and develop a response plan is essential in the fast-paced modern world. Situations can quickly move from being a local to an international issue. Involve the whole business in the

identification of issues, whether they are from customer complaints, supply chain delays or social media posts.

2 Understand the details of the situation
Once the issue is identified be clear about the details. Where has it come from? What does it involve? Is it a matter of perception or has there been a business failing that has prompted it? How could it impact on the business? Without an understanding of the details of the situation the initial actions could make the situation worse.

3 Consider how it may develop
Scenario planning is an important part of issues, risk and crisis management. Use the details of the situation to consider what happened in the past and how it could impact on the future. Consider worst-case scenarios and use knowledge of previous situations and their implications to assist the discussions.

4 Define those who are affected or could be affected
Map the groups and individuals who are, or could be, impacted by what is developing. Understand who the most affected are and how severe the impact could be. This will assist in considering the action that needs to be taken and where communication is needed the most.

5 Understand who in the business is involved in the issue
Issues rarely involve just one part of the business. They will impact on, and require the support of, many different departments and sections. Limiting the impact on the reputation of the business will need the involvement of the whole organization, not just the department that has identified the issues first. For example, issues are often quickly identified on social media, but the response will require more than the PR, communication and social media teams to be involved. It needs the department linked to the complaint and others to be involved.

6 Consider a range of interventions
Once a clear understanding of the issue and its impact is understood, the next step is to consider the interventions that could be undertaken. These can be anything from monitoring how it develops before responding through to an apology or more detailed intervention. Use scenario planning to consider the most appropriate course of action and develop an escalation plan for potential future developments.

7 Alert others to the situation and proposed response plan
An issues management structure and process should be in place for a business. This may use some of the structures that are used for a full

crisis response but on a smaller scale. Consider whether groups and individuals outside the business need to be made aware of the situation and response. This can assist in ensuring effective stakeholder management is in place.

8 Develop a whole business approach

Bring the business together to discuss the situation and its development. If the situation deteriorates, the whole business may need to be involved in the next stage of the response. Management of the issue may also mean other work, projects or initiatives need to be adapted, delayed or revised to prevent any impact on the effective response.

9 Create an issue management plan

The situation, the actions being put in place, and the potential further actions that may be taken if the situation deteriorates should all be detailed in an issue management plan. This can be anything from a one-page document for smaller issues that emerge, through to a detailed response plan for situations that have the potential to significantly damage the reputation of the business.

10 Monitor and review how things develop

An essential part of issues management is the ongoing monitoring of the situation to assess whether it has been alleviated or is getting worse. This information can be used to review the plan and approach, and take further action as required. Issues should never be ignored as they can be an early warning of potentially larger and more damaging problems.

CASE STUDY
P&O Ferries

Background

On 17 March 2022, 786 employees of P&O Ferries were sacked with immediate effect through a video message that was shared. P&O Ferries run a fleet of more than 20 ships that sail across the English Channel, North Sea and Irish Sea employing almost 2,000 people.[10] The move was widely criticized by politicians, media commentators and unions. The move was claimed to be a breach of UK employment law particularly in relation to a failure to consult in relation to collective redundancies, a failure to notify relevant government authorities and unfair dismissal.[11] In response to the news, some crew refused to leave the ships and had to be removed.[12] The business then replaced the former employees with foreign agency staff.

Politicians widely condemned the action that the company took. The UK's Prime Minister at the time Boris Johnson said that the company would not 'get away with it' and suggested that legal action may be taken.[13] In the House of Commons then Transport Minister Grant Shapps announced nine measures aimed at forcing the company to reconsider their decision.[14] They included new powers to protect maritime workers.

A week after the sackings took place, the Chief Executive Peter Hebblethwaite told a joint hearing of the UK Government transport and business committee that they had chosen not to consult, even though it was legally required. He added that he would make the same decision again to protect the business. During the hearing he said the action was necessary because unions would never have agreed to the proposals and focused on the compensation that was being given.[15]

In the months that followed the action and condemnation, the business struggled to regain the same customer numbers it had before the removal of the staff. There were delays in getting the ships running and operational following the transition to the new agency staff.[16] The decision was also reported to have had a significant impact on the brand and its reputation. YouGov's BrandIndex showed P&O Ferries dropped by 18 points from 14 to 20 March 2022, a drop from 13.9 to −4.1, and by April 2022 it was at −31.2. The score measured brand health, looking at value, quality, reputation, satisfaction and recommendation scores. But it slowly recovered back to −3.6 by December 2022. At the same time the parent company DP World saw no impact on the profits of the business with revenue growth reported at 60 per cent.[17]

There was further criticism of the government and a lack of action against the company in the years that followed. On the anniversary of the sackings, the media reported that there had been no sanction, no legal action and no reform that had taken place, and the company had been able to continue as a market leader.[18] But it also recognized that the brand had become linked to negative corporate operations.

Reputation lessons

The actions of P&O Ferries led to significant political involvement and commentary that continued for many months. While the removal of staff did spark condemnation that had an impact on the reputation of the business, it was able to continue to grow the business. The business operates on routes that are not serviced by others so there are few alternatives available. But the events of March 2022 are still being discussed and are forever linked to the reputation of the business.

- Consider the reputational impact of decisions that are going to be made about the operation of the business and challenge actions that may be significantly detrimental.

- A business decision that is outside of agreed boundaries and regulations will impact on the reputation and should be avoided or have plans put in place to limit the impact. The approach and actions could have been more focused on supporting staff to still achieve the same outcome.

- Situations that put profit above people, and breach societal norms can spark a moral outrage and possible longer-term damage.

- Prepare for the political commentary, actions and discussions about business decisions that are controversial. Such situations require careful stakeholder management before, during and after the action.

- Having a monopoly or unique service can ensure that a business remains profitable, but the reputational damage may not be easily identified. This could include challenges in recruitment and retention of staff, and customer service ratings.

Conclusion

Effective reputation management requires systems and processes to be in place that support issues management. Many businesses will look for those crises and significant threats but can ignore the issues, trends and complaints that can be an early warning to a bigger problem emerging. It is vital that there is a robust risk management process in place that will look at all those threats and areas of concern. Understand where those reputational risks may be lurking within the business. There are a number of internal and external risks to effective reputation management that all businesses and organizations should consider and be prepared to address.

Everyone in the business has a part to play in risk management in the same way they have a part to play in reputation management. The systems and processes that are put in place to support identification, governance, response and review should involve the widest group of employees. As they become involved and aware, they can influence the developments and actions taken bringing different perspectives.

Businesses should always consider the political reaction to issues they are managing and actions that they consider taking. Political involvement may support the action that is being taken, but political interference can threaten to intensify the damage to the reputation of the business. Stakeholder mapping and management processes have a critical role to play in limiting and managing the political challenges to effective reputation management. Developing a response to a situation that is reputationally damaging requires careful consideration, particularly where the action has sparked a moral outrage. Such situations are heavily rooted in emotional responses and agreed societal norms so require more than a practical response. The level of interest, commentary, emotional response and political interference in relation to a situation the business is managing can quickly escalate something from a minor issue to a full-blown crisis. Being able to recognize, identify and act on this will be discussed in Chapter 6.

References

1 S Ellery. Fake photos of Pope Francis in a puffer jacket go viral, highlighting the power and peril of AI, *CBS News*, 28 March 2023, www.cbsnews.com/news/pope-francis-puffer-jacket-fake-photos-deepfake-power-peril-of-ai/ (archived at https://perma.cc/GFZ7-HNSD)

2 Ofcom. News consumption in the UK: 2023, www.ofcom.org.uk/siteassets/resources/documents/research-and-data/tv-radio-and-on-demand-research/tv-research/news/news-consumption-2023/news-consumption-in-the-uk-2023/?v=329963 (archived at https://perma.cc/SB3H-HBQS)

3 A Arguedas, C Robertson, R Fletcher and R Nielsen. Echo chambers, filter bubbles, and polarisation: A literature review, *Reuters Institute for the Study of Journalism*, 19 January 2022, https://reutersinstitute.politics.ox.ac.uk/echo-chambers-filter-bubbles-and-polarisation-literature-review (archived at https://perma.cc/4BMC-C5AL)

4 Ipsos. Veracity Index 2023: Trust in politicians reaches its lowest score in 40 years, 14 December 2023, www.ipsos.com/en-uk/ipsos-trust-in-professions-veracity-index-2023 (archived at https://perma.cc/EE64-PA2H)

5 V Božić. The role of artificial intelligence in risk management [pre-print], April 2023, www.researchgate.net/publication/370005124_THE_ROLE_OF_ARTIFICIAL_INTELLIGENCE_IN_RISK_MANAGEMENT (archived at https://perma.cc/A7HA-3B5A)

6 D Diermeier (2011) *Reputation Rules: Strategies for building your company's most valuable asset*, McGraw-Hill, New York

7 E Graham-Harrison. Police clash with mourners at Sarah Everard vigil in London, *The Guardian*, 13 March 2021, www.theguardian.com/uk-news/2021/mar/13/as-the-sun-set-they-came-in-solidarity-and-to-pay-tribute-to-sarah-everard (archived at https://perma.cc/MU5X-F754)

8 L Sabin. Nearly half of women trust police less after Sarah Everard murder, survey suggests, *The Independent*, 18 November 2021, www.independent.co.uk/news/uk/home-news/women-police-trust-sarah-everard-b1959760.html (archived at https://perma.cc/BEN9-9Y3C)

9 A Coleman (2022) *Everyday Communication Strategies: Manage common issues to prevent a crisis and protect your brand*, Kogan Page, London

10 P&O Ferries. 'About us'. www.poferries.com/en/about (archived at https://perma.cc/QTW7-5CVG)

11 TUC. P&O Ferries mass sackings – one year on, 17 March 2023, www.tuc.org.uk/research-analysis/reports/po-ferries-mass-sackings-one-year (archived at https://perma.cc/6LXD-HEQS)

12 J Martin. Outrage and no ferries after mass P&O sackings, *BBC News*, 18 March 2022, www.bbc.co.uk/news/business-60779001 (archived at https://perma.cc/3SVK-HUFP)

13 A Forrest. Boris Johnson says P&O did break the law and government 'will take them to court' despite Grayling exemption, *The Independent*, 23 March 2022, www.independent.co.uk/news/uk/politics/boris-johnson-p-o-ferries-law-grayling-b2042132.html (archived at https://perma.cc/7K3V-FAGM)

14 Department for Transport, Maritime and Coastguard Agency. Oral statement to Parliament: P&O Ferries: new powers to protect maritime workers, House of Commons, 30 March 2022, www.gov.uk/government/speeches/po-ferries-new-powers-to-protect-maritime-workers (archived at https://perma.cc/6KW6-B8UB)

15 G Topham. P&O Ferries boss admits firm broke law by sacking staff without consultation, *The Guardian*, 24 March 2022, www.theguardian.com/business/2022/mar/24/po-ferries-boss-says-800-staff-were-sacked-because-no-union-would-accepts-its-plans (archived at https://perma.cc/374K-4NQL)

16 J Hills. Revealed: P&O Ferries struggles to win back customers 10 weeks after brutally sacking 800 crew, *ITV News*, 27 May 2022, www.itv.com/news/2022-05-27/p-and-o-ferries-struggles-to-win-back-customers-10-weeks-after-sacking-800-crew (archived at https://perma.cc/N8T2-MVFH)

17 M Innes. P&O Ferries' brand health continues to suffer 10 months after scandal, *Marketing Week*, 6 January 2023, www.marketingweek.com/p-and-o-brand-health-suffer-scandal/ (archived at https://perma.cc/9E3A-ANQU)

18 G Topham. One year on, has P&O Ferries got away with illegally sacking all its crew?, *The Guardian*, 17 March 2023, www.theguardian.com/business/2023/mar/17/one-year-on-has-po-ferries-got-away-with-illegally-sacking-all-its-crew (archived at https://perma.cc/TK7F-LP65)

6

Recognizing when an issue becomes a crisis

Introduction

Identifying an issue is the first step on the road to effective crisis management and communication. It is vital to understand what could possibly happen that could negatively affect the business and its reputation. As outlined in Chapter 5, issues management is essential to try to get ahead of a crisis and put measures in place that will prevent the situation escalating. The business should be continually monitoring for operational and reputational risks, as well as being able to see the trends and concerns. Reacting and responding to situations can mean the difference between an issue that is managed and brought to a satisfactory conclusion and one that grows to become a crisis.

An escalation plan is an essential part of the issues management process and supports proactive reputation management. It gives a framework to deciding on what elements will prompt a response, when to get publicly involved, and the points at which monitoring may be the best course of action. Managing an issue can feel like a game of chess where moves have to be decided depending on the action that is taken by the other party. But there are times when the situation has developed to such an extent that action has to be taken. When a reputational crisis has occurred there is no question of sitting back and waiting to see what happens. At these points, actions are required to prevent the situation deteriorating and to avoid significant damage to the perception of the business.

Effective reputation management, as outlined in Chapters 1 and 2, requires a responsive and comprehensive crisis management and communication

approach to be in place. When discussing crises it is important to understand that a crisis can come in many different forms but is a point where the
business is under significant and sustained pressure. It does not have to be a
severe weather event, cyberattack or damage to critical national infrastructure for a crisis to be declared. There are many situations where an event
may have no physical footprint but is a significant threat to the reputation
of the business. Developing the approach to issues and crisis management
starts by understanding what the difference is between the two.

What is an issue and what is a crisis?

Issues and incidents are linked to problems that have a negative impact on the
business. There are eight elements that may come together to create an issue
of concern. When they are connected together, rather like a circuit being
created, they lead to a situation that can damage the reputation of the
business. The eight elements are:

1 It is an unexpected situation for the brand or business

2 The situation is negatively impacting on the business' reputation

3 People and/or property are affected

4 The impact of it is seen or heard by someone

5 It is newsworthy

6 There is a misunderstanding

7 People may be concerned, upset or offended

8 There is a perceived injustice[1]

Acting at an early stage can prevent the situation escalating to become a
crisis. Assessing the severity of the situation that is developing can ensure
that a response is prepared and used to contain the damage. In contrast to
the eight points that come together to highlight an issue that needs to be
monitored, managed and addressed, there are five elements[2] that are identified when a crisis is confronting the business:

1 It is a time of intense difficulty or at the worst, extreme danger. This is
   why the severity assessment that has been outlined in Chapter 4 becomes
   important to the business and communication response.

2 It requires action to be taken. Unlike when dealing with an issue and monitoring may be the best way forward, when a crisis has occurred it needs some proactive action to be put in place. Without this intervention the situation will escalate, and the impact will be more serious.

3 It must be a negative position, potentially negative position or a negative change in the prevailing position of the company. There is no crisis that brings a positive position for the business in the initial stages. But opportunities to develop the reputation and the trust and confidence in the business can come through the response.

4 It develops abruptly. Whereas an issue may develop slowly with a range of issues coming together to cause a problem for the business, a crisis hits a point in time where the impact is so serious that critical urgent action is needed.

5 The situation must have an impact on people. Problems that emerge and have a direct impact on people will always be more likely to become crises. For example, a business that puts profits above people, which has a product recall, or has had a data breach will be facing a crisis with each of those situations being centred in a significant impact on employees, customers and other people connected to the business.

The definition of an issue or a crisis is the same for operational areas of concern and reputational challenges that may emerge.

The four As of issues management

The start of the issues and crisis response is based in the management of those initial areas of concern or threats to the business. Preparing an effective response can be assisted using the four As of issues management;[3] these are assess, analyse, articulate and act. Assess the situation and the impact it is already having once it has been identified. Use the scenario planning, mentioned in Chapter 5, to support the understanding of how the issue may develop in the coming hours, days and weeks. In the assess phase, ensure that environmental and social conditions and factors are being taken into consideration. Understand the impact of the issue on the key audiences that the business identifies within the elements that comprise the reputation of the business. There will be some groups whose views and perceptions have a more significant impact on the successful operation of the business. Understand how key audiences are perceiving the issue, and what they may expect from the response.

Once the information has been gathered, review exactly what it means for the approach that is being taken and may be developed in the future. Information should support effective management by assisting in understanding, rather than overwhelming, those setting the response in place. Decisions need to be made and actions taken to avoid being swept along with a growing problem. In coming years, the developments in artificial intelligence may assist in analysing this data to support core effective issues management.

Trying to restore balance, the reputation of the business and return to business as usual requires a clear plan to be in place. The approach is about more than effective communication and should involve key areas of the business. Even when the approach is to monitor the issue and wait until there is a trigger to take more action, it should be a proactive decision that is made rather than a failure to respond. Any issues management plan must consider the need to make changes to the business as well as the written and visual communication. Finally, after the first three As have been completed, then actions should be put in place. Implement the plan and ensure there is a process wrapped around it to allow decisions to act to be taken more quickly. If a crisis is to be avoided, consistent effort and focus needs to be in place in the early stages of a problem emerging.

Effective issues management also requires a business to be aware of the near misses or those moments when a problem was avoided. If these are overlooked, then trends and ongoing issues could be ignored making it more possible for a crisis to develop. For example, if there are a number of complaints about a product that are responded to on an individual basis, but they all relate to the same thing it could be highlighting a need to change and innovate that product. If this information is captured the business can act, thus preventing a crisis. Monitoring and identifying situations at the earliest opportunity is an important way to avoid challenges and problems developing. Puffin Books, the children's arm of Penguin Books, found themselves facing a reputational crisis when they announced plans to rewrite Roald Dahl's books. It sparked controversy and had it been identified earlier the extensive media coverage and discussion could have been avoided.[4]

Be prepared and have an issues management structure and framework. This includes monitoring processes, governance to manage the situations, processes to discuss developments, the right people involved and ultimately a plan in place.

The role of the escalation plan

The move between issue and crisis is fluid. There will be a point where the mitigation and attempts to manage the problem fail to work and it deteriorates. Every business should be clear about what the threshold is for when a situation is classified as a crisis. This will be linked to the level of risks that the business has to manage and its appetite for risk acceptance. It is essential that the designation of a crisis is understood by all the senior leaders in the business. At the point it is declared a crisis, there are a whole range of activities that should be triggered, and the crisis management and communication plans should be put in place.

Crises can occur from many areas. There are two main types of crises: operational and reputational. The crisis response from businesses is often geared towards managing a practical and operational crisis, but the threats from perceptions and reputational crises is real. There is also the real possibility that the response from the business to whatever has occurred is poor and that becomes an additional crisis in itself. Reputational crises should never be overlooked as the damage can be significant and sustained.

Being alert to the development of a crisis should be within the structure and operation of any business, brand or organization. This requires the development of an escalation plan that will consider the potential developments and look at the further action that may need to be taken to address the situation and minimize its impact. When an issue emerges, an escalation plan can provide some clarity on what needs to be done and who within the team is responsible for doing it. The plan will detail the many scenarios that could develop, looking at the ones that threaten to have the most impact and are most likely to happen. It should detail what actions will be taken to attempt to avoid the situation getting worse. Such plans should involve more than just the PR and communication team as the actions can involve any part of the business. For example, if there are complaints about failures in customer service, the plan may consider when to change the approach to customer relationship management, the point at which social media criticism would be addressed and when to undertake proactive media management. It requires a whole business approach to escalate the action that is needed to limit the damage from the situation. The plan should include details of the triggers that require further action to be taken, the questions to consider when reviewing the development, the actions that should be carried out or considered, and further areas of consideration. It can support the prioritization of activities and how to proactively manage the situation. When head of the Royal Spanish Football Federation (RFEF)

Luis Rubiales made headlines with his celebrations after the women's team won the World Cup in August 2023, an escalation plan could have assisted.[5] It would have outlined the actions to remove people from positions when there are accusations of inappropriate activity and considered the severity of transgressions.

The escalation process requires a structure and procedure that makes it easy for employees and senior leaders to understand their role and responsibilities in relation to it. This may be using the crisis response process, or the risk management process, to ensure that the right people are involved in the development of the response and are alerted to actions that may be required in the future. Accountability and the prioritization of work can take place using this structure. Building external views into the development of an escalation plan is good practice. This can be done before any problems have occurred by using existing consultation methods and systems. Meet with your key audiences identified as critical to the reputation management work and understand what matters to them, how they feel when issues emerge and the action that is required to maintain trust and confidence. This is a critical part of the work to limit the impact of issues and work to avoid crises developing. An escalation plan should closely link to the elements that have been identified as a priority to the reputation of the business. For example, if the support of investors and funding to innovation is a critical factor then the escalation plan must prioritize the action needed if the issue threatens that aspect of the business.

It is possible, in future, technology will be trained to assist in this escalation process. The use of existing data and insights could be reviewed using artificial intelligence to provide an overview of how to approach the escalation. Developments could remove some of the human interaction and biases that may diminish the importance of situations and events. But there are many variable factors to consider including the issues and events that have occurred in the wider world and in the industry surrounding the business.

An escalation plan should ask: is the situation impacting on the business? Is it affecting people and how significantly are they affected? Is it attracting significant commentary on social media? Are journalists following the problem or issue? Is there any high-profile individuals or institutions that are commenting on the situation? Are there any additional issues affecting the sector the business is in? Are there any wider external issues now or on the horizon that may increase the attention on the issue? How do people feel about the emerging issue? Who are the communities and groups that may be interested or affected? Does the issue have the potential to spark outrage? Does the situation breach societal or cultural norms?

What role does reputation management have when a crisis occurs?

Within the disaster management and emergency communication sector of crisis communication, reputation should not be the driving force. The focus needs to be on preserving and protecting lives and ensuring that vital safety information is shared as quickly as possible. If the focus becomes to protect the reputation of the organization involved, then in the worst case people may be severely affected by your focus. In such situations, if there is a challenge or threat to the reputation of the responding organization, then it should be considered separately and should not be allowed to interfere with the priority communication. For example, if a public body or emergency service is responding to a flooding incident but knows that it has failed to share early warning information to people, this should now be allowed to change the actions and messaging. It is still vitally important to share information that tells people how they can stay safe. The reputational damage because of the lack of early warning will still need to be addressed at some point and plans should be put in place once the threat has reduced.

In other crises situations, the focus on the reputation of the business is important but again should not be allowed to cloud the honest approach to events. Organizations and businesses can build a positive reputation, or limit the impact on their reputation, through the actions they undertake and how they respond to the situation. No amount of communication and positive words will effectively manage the crises without supporting actions that bring it under control and limit the impact on people. A crisis response that focuses on addressing the issue, minimizing the impact it has on people, and helping people to move forward will build confidence that supports the management of the business' reputation. When fast food company KFC ran out of chicken in 2018, they used it to apologize and speak to customers.[6] They didn't try to hide the problem in a bid to protect the reputation of the business.

When reputation is the only consideration for the business it can lead to unethical behaviour that looks to cover up, gaslight and be in denial to try to avoid damage. This has a huge impact on the reputation of the business. When a crisis happens the business needs to be demonstrating their legitimacy to both operate and be responsible for responding to the situation. Legitimacy is an important factor in building a positive reputation. This can be boosted by ensuring that external voices of key audiences are heard within the response to a crisis. Finding ways to carry out consultation and to engage with the key audiences the business has, helps to build a more effective response. It identifies challenging aspects of the crisis and the response, which may have negatively affected people. This understanding of the reputational impact can assist the response but should never be considered in isolation.

Crisis response roles and who should be involved

Every business needs to have a crisis response framework that will be used at the times when problems emerge. This identifies those key roles that need to be in place and involved in the response from the strategic level through to the tactical implementation of plans. Effective crisis management needs to involve all the key parts of the business in a coherent response. This core group needs to be able to work closely together to monitor the developments, consider the actions to take and ensure they are ready to respond at speed.

Communication is a key part of this crisis response but should operate at a strategic level advising on the actions to take, the impact on reputation and how to build confidence. A crisis response should be led by the CEO or another senior leader within the business. They will be the ultimate decision maker agreeing the plans that are put in place. Leaders can be risk averse and may be focused on the impact the crisis will have on their own career prospects. But they need to be open-minded and ready to listen to the advice and guidance from across the business. This is why having a range of specialists from across the business involved in the discussions is essential. Other departments that should be involved in outlining the actions to take are human resources, finance, operations, business development and there is also a role for Boards and trustees. Boards and trustees have an important role to play in holding the business leaders to account. The oversight and critical review that they can provide can help to build confidence in how the business is responding to events. All those involved are people who can affect change in the business, which is needed in responding to the problem. The role of human resources is critical as all issues and crises will impact on employees. Even in small businesses someone needs to be ready to take up this role and identify issues, consider the impact on staff and ensure steps are taken to support the well-being and morale of the workforce.

The communication lead is a critical role in the crisis response team. Communication in this case includes media, social media, stakeholder engagement, marketing campaigns and advertising. The communication lead should sit in the strategic meetings and discussions and work with public affairs colleagues or those responsible for stakeholder management. In some cases, stakeholder engagement can be undertaken by the communication team, but if it is a role for a different department they must work closely together. There may be other parts of the business that should be involved. The aim is to ensure the best information is available so that effective decisions can be made. The communication lead needs to be able to consider the operational actions that need to be undertaken and communicated, as well as discussing the short-, medium- and long-term reputational damage that may be caused by the crisis and the approach to the response. As mentioned in Chapter 3, there is a requirement to understand the reputation the business has among the key groups and audiences before any problem occurs. This should then be monitored as the crisis develops and the actions taken aim to bring it under control. PR and communication teams need to be able to influence decision makers, and to bring to the forefront the reputational challenges created by the crisis.

When the crisis is linked to a reputational problem within the business the involvement of the whole business remains critical. The same structure and framework that is used for the response to cyberattacks, power outages, product failures and other operational situations should be implemented to respond to a reputational crisis. Such situations are not a PR crisis, they are a business crisis that PR and communication can assist in managing. In all situations it is vital to have the right people from within the business involved in the response and the communication around it. In responding to the crisis the actions and communication need to take account of not just what has happened, but the history of the organization and the previous problems that may have been faced. It also requires the wider external factors to be considered. The business needs to consider what has happened in the world and the industry that the business is based in.

The opportunity within the crisis response

Difficult issues and problems are potentially damaging to a business and its reputation, but they are also times to learn, develop and change. The problem may be an indication of a change that is needed to the product or service, or how the business operates. Understanding the details about where the crisis has occurred and creating a proactive plan to manage it is an opportunity to develop. Where the response makes swift changes or takes actions, it can boost the reputation of the business at the centre. The opportunity to strengthen the reputation and increase trust and confidence arrives every time an issue becomes a crisis. This was what happened with the KFC situation, in 2018, mentioned earlier.

It is the learning and action that happens after a challenging situation that can strengthen the business for the future. Once the immediate actions that are required have been carried out there needs to be a stage of understanding what happened and why it happened. What caused the problem? Was it known about, or did it arrive without any prior knowledge? Who was affected? What lasting impact has it had? If the potential impact on the reputation of the business is going to be reduced it is vital to look at how to change. This could be changed to prevent the problem recurring in the future, or it could be a need to make improvements based on the situation.

Attempting to respond to the legacy impact of the problem by simply throwing out more positive stories and communication activity will not repair damage and rebuild confidence. It appears as a negative attempt to gaslight and steer the conversation in a different direction. It ignores the impact of what has happened and can appear to be insensitive to those who may have been affected. The crisis and issues management framework needs to include moving forward from the problem and what is required. This will be covered in more detail in Chapter 9, considering how to recover from the crisis.

Crisis response and communication principles

The heart of any crisis response has to be to support and assist the people who are affected. Actions should be taken in an attempt to limit the damage that is done to people because of the issue, crisis or problem. Demonstrating empathy and humanity are key principles to both the actions taken in the response and to be felt within the communication response. For example, when an accident happened at the Alton Towers theme park, in the UK, in 2015 the response and communication focused on supporting those who had been involved.[7] If this is at the centre of the plans, policies and procedures developed to respond to a crisis then it can boost the reputation of the business. But this all has to be done with authenticity and faking it with some sensitive words within the communication response will be uncovered.

Significant damage can be done to the reputation of an organization where the actions that they undertake are different to the words and message that they use to talk about the response. Demonstrating honesty and integrity in the crisis management are also important principles that need to be in place. They are essential elements in building and maintaining trust and confidence in the business, in its crisis response and in its operation. A loss of trust and confidence can happen quickly when a problem occurs and can take a long time to recover. Businesses with a positive reputation have to understand the damage that can be caused by actions that are perceived as dishonest, unethical, or self-serving. This does not mean the crisis response needs to manipulate or cover up what has happened but to recognize it, talk about it and take action to manage it. Reputation will be boosted or repaired by a business that can accept the problem it has and will demonstrate action to bring it to a conclusion.

Planning and preparing for tough times and challenging situations are essential. All businesses should have a plan and process to be implemented when a crisis occurs. They need to identify risks, as well as consider the scenarios that may be faced and the actions to take. Alongside this it is important to be flexible in the response and especially in the communication as a crisis occurs. A business cannot plan for every possible detail of a crisis that may happen and should have a framework that is flexible enough to be built upon. Communication and PR professionals must be able to consider the details and situation and develop plans that can address concerns and rebuild confidence. This is about more than posting information that the business wants to put out. It is vital to provide information that people need and to understand what is most concerning to them. The involvement of the media and the commentary on social media will spotlight elements of the issue and the response to it. Extra attention should be given to the aspects that have been highlighted as this will impact on the perceptions and views people have of the business and its response.

Another principle to consider during a crisis response is to ensure cultural intelligence is involved in developing the plans and communication activity. It is an important element involved in reputation development and management and has a key role when something has gone wrong. Culture may be involved in the situation that has developed and will be involved in the response. The business needs to adapt its response to take account of different norms, values and beliefs.[8] For example, a multinational that has experienced a significant supply chain failure will need to consider the impact this has on the business and look at communicating with cultural sensitivity in many countries. If there has been a reputational crisis linked to the behaviour of staff, or even the C-suite, it will be viewed in a variety of ways depending on the societal norms and culture. There needs to be clarity around this aspect to ensure that the communication plans are created with it in mind. This is not just about providing things in different languages but understanding how different cultures will view what has happened and the actions taken in response. Again, consultation has an important part to play in giving some insight to the business responding.

CASE STUDY
Air traffic disruption

Background

On 28 August 2023, a problem emerged with the UK National Air Traffic System (NATS) which led to chaos at airports. Nearly 1,600 flights were cancelled on the day and hundreds more on the following day. It took a number of days before the system returned to normal.[9] The incident happened on a bank holiday and an estimated quarter of a million passengers were affected as take-offs and landings were limited for four hours.[10] NATS apologized for the situation and the Chief Executive said the problem had been caused by some flight data that was received. It was said to be a single piece of data in a flight plan that was wrongly input by an unnamed airline.[11] In statements it was emphasized that this was not a cyberattack and was linked to normal operation of systems. Air controllers had to use manual systems while the systems were brought back online. The airline industry bodies were critical of the situation and the costs that airlines would face linked to the failure.

The situation affected a significant number of passengers and those included high-profile individuals and celebrities. Journalists and other celebrities were posting on social media and talking to the media about the problems that they were facing.[12] There were also many personal stories from families and individuals who had been affected by the cancellations and chaos of amended flights. The human impact of the technical problem was highlighted very quickly.

In the aftermath, the Civil Aviation Authority (CAA) classified what happened as 'extraordinary circumstances' and in that situation, passengers would not be entitled to compensation. The CAA called on airlines to ensure they kept passengers informed and offer them the chance to be re-routed or receive a refund.[13] While leading travel correspondent Simon Calder claimed there had been a vacuum in information that he had been trying to fill with some speculation on the situation.[14] In the aftermath, there were calls for more improved systems to be put in place to prevent a similar situation happening in the future.[15]

Reputation lessons

This was an example of where a small issue can escalate quickly and have a significant impact. The impact was practically on the many thousands of people who had to change travel arrangements or who were left stranded, as well as on the reputation of the business. It also threatened to impact on the reputation of other businesses, including the airlines who had to manage the frustrations of their passengers. Airlines and the air travel industry are used to facing crises and being prepared for emergencies. But this was not just an operational challenge but a reputational threat. It also involved many of the factors that would be identified in an escalation plan; from the amount of people that were impacted, the high-profile and celebrity commentary, financial challenges, and the failure of an internal process and system.

- Businesses need to prepare for system and process failures and consider where the weaknesses and threats lie so they can be addressed. In the aftermath of this situation there should have been a clear indication of the improvements that would be made and a willingness to listen to those who had been affected to start to rebuild trust and confidence.

- The support from airline operators is an essential part of the reputation of NATS. How they view the air traffic system and the confidence they have is critical. The communication between NATS and airline operators was critical as a key stakeholder.

- Communication to the frontline staff who were speaking to passengers and those affected should be a priority to try to limit the anger and frustration wherever possible. But this does not mean gaslighting people who were furious with the personal impact of events.

- Crisis management needs to involve strategic communication that can highlight the external views and perspectives as well as shine a light on the reputational damage from the response.

- Rebuilding trust and confidence in a system that has failed to such a serious degree will take time and there needs to be a recovery plan in place. This would identify the actions needed to improve the operational system as well as the communication that can assist in reconnecting with key individuals and groups. Crisis response structures need to be in place throughout the lifespan of the problem, issue or crisis.

- All risk and crisis plans and responses need to be focused on limiting the impact on people and supporting them through the situation. NATS were not directly involved in this, and the CAA were providing guidance to the airlines as the link to the passengers. This was a significant challenge as the reputation of NATS was being handed to other businesses and organizations. More proactive communication would have helped to rebuild the relationship with the airline operators and in turn, support those caught up in the chaos who were sharing their stories on social media and with the media.

Conclusion

Managing an issue before it becomes a crisis is essential to support effective reputation management. Whatever is occurring and however long it takes to address, it is critical to remember the goal of the response. This should be in place throughout the escalation plan, which details all those scenarios and developments that may happen. It can help to drive the business forward by managing tasks, defining actions and creating agreements about the way risks will be addressed. Any escalation plan has to include the whole business in the monitoring and response. It is possible that in the future, artificial intelligence will be able to support risk management and the development of escalation plans.

But regardless of the actions taken there are still occasions where the issue will develop into a crisis. This is a moment when decisive action is required and needs to be taken quickly. Businesses need to have a crisis management plan which identifies the key roles that will be involved in responding to the situation. There will be roles for all the key departments, and the CEO and C-suite need to be heavily involved. They are required to define the approach that will be taken and be ready to listen to specialist advice. Communicators have a key role to play as part of the response team, but this goes beyond the steps taken to address perceptions. They need to operate with a strong ethical position to ensure that the focus is not on reputation management as a priority but on supporting those who have been caught up in the crisis. Communication and PR is not effective in a crisis if it is just used as a way of posting out updates and information. It needs to operate strategically adhering to the principles and defining the actions required to build trust and confidence throughout the crisis.

Ensure there is clarity about what is an issue and when a crisis is taking place, particularly where this involves a reputational problem. A structure and framework are required for both, but the actions taken will depend on a range of factors outlined in the escalation plan. The response to both issues and crises needs to involve the whole business with roles for all in helping to limit the impact of the situation on the people, business and financial viability. Communication professionals have a key role to play in advising and developing the strategic response. They can provide insight into the reputational damage, potential or real, and the external perception of the issue and response. The aim of the response to both issues and crises should be to help people move forward and to learn from what happens. A positive reputation comes from what the business does and not from what it says, and prioritizing reputation can be damaging. Where the business attempts to move forward with reputation management alone, it makes poor decisions and may appear to be trying to cover up, gaslight or manipulate the situation.

Both issues and crises provide an opportunity to change. The recovery needs to involve actions to improve the way the business works, what it does, and whatever led to the problem developing. The group involved in the development of the response needs to still work together going forward and in recovering from the situation. The strategies taken to respond to damage to the reputation of the business need to be built on strong crisis principles including honesty and integrity. The steps and actions taken need to be robust ethically and supported by organizational change. The strategies that can be considered will be outlined in Chapter 7.

References

1   Coleman, A (2022) *Everyday Communication Strategies: Manage common issues to prevent a crisis and protect your brand*, Kogan Page, London

2   Coleman, A (2023) *Crisis Communication Strategies: Prepare, respond and recover effectively in unpredictable and urgent situations*, 2nd edition, Kogan Page, London

3   Coleman, A (2022) *Everyday Communication Strategies: Manage common issues to prevent a crisis and protect your brand*, Kogan Page, London

4   A Syed. Why rewrites to Roald Dahl's books are stirring controversy, *Time*, 21 February 2023, https://time.com/6256980/roald-dahl-censorship-debate/ (archived at https://perma.cc/8R6P-8Z3C)

5   M Delaney. Luis Rubiales is just the latest crisis in Spanish FA's dark history, *The Independent*, 31 August 2023, www.independent.co.uk/sport/football/rubiales-kiss-jorge-vilda-spanish-football-women-b2402458.html (archived at https://perma.cc/AK52-QPH3)

6   Newsbeat. KFC's apology for running out of chicken is pretty cheeky, *BBC News*, 23 February 2018, www.bbc.co.uk/news/newsbeat-43169625 (archived at https://perma.cc/4398-5D32)

7   Coleman, A (2023) *Crisis Communication Strategies: Prepare, respond and recover effectively in unpredictable and urgent situations*, 2nd edition, Kogan Page, London

8   I Gross. How cultural dexterity stops an incident becoming a crisis, *School Management Plus*, 5 July 2023, www.schoolmanagementplus.com/communications-pr/how-cultural-dexterity-stops-an-incident-becoming-a-crisis/ (archived at https://perma.cc/6YBM-RBTZ)

9   G Topham and J Grierson. Hundreds more flights cancelled in fallout from UK air traffic control failure, *The Guardian*, 29 August 2023, www.theguardian.com/world/2023/aug/29/air-passengers-face-further-delays-after-uk-air-traffic-control-failure (archived at https://perma.cc/HSP4-3768)

10 G Topham and J Grierson. Hundreds more flights cancelled in fallout from UK air traffic control failure, *The Guardian*, 29 August 2023, www.theguardian.com/world/2023/aug/29/air-passengers-face-further-delays-after-uk-air-traffic-control-failure (archived at https://perma.cc/HSP4-3768)

11 G Topham. UK air traffic control failure: what caused it and who will have to pay?, *The Guardian*, 30 August 2023, www.theguardian.com/world/2023/aug/30/uk-air-traffic-control-failure-what-caused-it-and-who-will-have-to-pay (archived at https://perma.cc/HJV8-T5AG)

12 C Moloney and M Banfield-Nwachi. Issue with UK air traffic control system 'identified and remedied' but thousands still face major delays after fault – as it happened, *The Guardian*, 28 August 2023, www.theguardian.com/world/live/2023/aug/28/air-traffic-control-uk-delays-airport-travel-live-latest-updates (archived at https://perma.cc/K5XB-F6U7)

13 Civil Aviation Authority. Guidance to industry – 30 August 2023, www.caa.co.uk/media/etrlbfw1/guidance-to-industry-atc-incident_.pdf (archived at https://perma.cc/UYA4-GVD7)

14 S Calder. What is causing the air traffic control chaos? The authorities have some explaining to do, *The Independent*, 29 August 2023, www.independent.co.uk/travel/news-and-advice/air-traffic-control-airports-flights-b2401157.html (archived at https://perma.cc/JPG9-JT8H)

15 *ITV News*. Traffic chaos caused by 'flight data received' by air traffic services, 6 September 2023. Available from www.itv.com/news/2023-08-28/travel-disruption-could-last-days-as-thousands-stranded-by-cancelled-flights (archived at https://perma.cc/KY59-PQ2Q)

7

Strategies and approaches to address a crisis in reputation

Introduction

When there is a serious problem that is facing a business, then it is time to make sure that action is being taken and that communication is in place to provide support. This has been outlined in Chapter 6, which considered the importance of being able to spot problems before they develop into crises. At the point the crisis is affecting the reputation there needs to be a crisis response system in place, a crisis communication plan developed and a framework that is being used to ensure both business and communication actions have been detailed. The time and effort to develop the plans and processes will pay off when a situation develops, and they can be used to address what is happening. But these plans need to consider the specific circumstances that have occurred and be adapted depending on what has happened.

It is vital that the communicator understands the background to what has happened and the details of the circumstances. How did it emerge and when was the situation first noticed? How did it develop and were there any actions that were taken to try to bring the situation under control earlier? And importantly, who is affected by the situation that has been identified? When considering the impact it has on the business' reputation, it is important to consider what are the most important groups. The weighting of the elements of reputation that were outlined in Chapter 3 need to be used to help frame and drive the response. It will assist in focusing the work on the priority areas and the audiences where perceptions are most critical to the future of the business. In addition, understand the purpose and values of the wider business so that the impact of the situation can be quantified. This information will also help to prioritize the actions that will be taken to address the problem.

Whether the impact is caused by the facts of a situation or the perceptions that exist around the business needs to be clarified. It will change the approach and impact on the planning and actions being taken. As has been outlined earlier, a reputational crisis that is linked to perceptions around the business, or something it has done, is more challenging to address. Perceptions are people's reality and attempting to use facts to challenge perceptions will fail to deal with the underlying views. The communication approach needs to be more sophisticated and consider how, over time, the perception can be challenged and confidence in the business rebuilt. Where those perceptions are being shared intentionally to try to discredit or damage an organization it requires an approach to tackling disinformation. Fake news is not something that only impacts on governments and major brands. It is a problem that can affect any organization and at any time, including when they are attempting to turn around a poor reputation. In planning and preparation the steps needed to address disinformation should be clearly laid out.

A whole business approach

When a crisis in reputation is identified it requires more than PR and communication to be involved and developing the response. The framework that is available for a crisis response should be in place to help understand the impact of the problem and define the tangible, as well as communication, actions. It needs the approach to involve the right people who have decision-making powers so that the crisis response group can work together to create the response. For example, the damage to the reputation may be linked to the development of a new project or service. This may have been greeted with concern or consternation. In such cases, the business needs to look at why the views have emerged and what that means for future development. A communication approach that just keeps telling people they have not understood the new product or service will have limited impact. In addition, an approach of telling people they are wrong and have not understood the situation is gaslighting. How the business demonstrates the benefits of the new product or service will be critical. The ethical considerations of the responses to reputational crises will be considered in Chapter 8, but it is a crucial part of any successful crisis response. Whatever actions are put in place and communication is developed, it needs to have integrity, as without trust the business faces an uphill struggle.

A crisis response system needs to bring decision makers together as well as be clear on the roles and responsibilities throughout the business. In the same way that it is used for emergencies and business continuity, it can be introduced to address the reputational crisis. In emergency response, there is a Gold, Silver, Bronze approach which provides clarity about who is doing what as part of the response, and where lines of accountability exist. The same approach can be introduced to support the response to a reputational crisis. The Gold Commander is the ultimate decision maker within the business, which is likely to be the CEO or equivalent. Around them they will have a Gold group, which includes the key parts of the business as outlined in Chapter 6. Communication and PR is a crucial participant in those meetings and discussions. The communication lead needs to be able to explain the situation and the challenges it presents so that operational actions can be identified. They also have to be able to provide a strategic approach to the communication that will be developed. The Silver role is to lead in each of those sections of the business that are involved in the discussions at a Gold level. The Bronze level is those involved in the tactical delivery of the actions needed. From a communication perspective, Gold liaison will be the most senior communication and PR employee within the business, Silver will be the person overseeing the whole implementation of the plan, which is often a second in command. The Bronze will be those given the responsibility to oversee aspects of the response such as employee communication, stakeholder management and media liaison.

The approach requires processes to be in place that support the response to the crisis. This can include the risk management approach that needs to be directly linked to the crisis response framework. Other processes that need to be in place are the connections between the communication team and the customer services team. The two areas of the business need to work closely together when a crisis develops, and the silos of normal business operations need to be broken down. There may also be a need to establish processes for sharing information with employees efficiently and effectively when the crisis response team is being brought together. In developing the crisis communication strategy and plan, key processes can be identified and addressed.

Finally, there will be policies that need to be established to support the crisis response. This may be within the operational activity of the business.

For example, there may need to be a policy about who calls the crisis response team together and what circumstances need to be in place for that to happen. It may also detail elements of the financial approach, customer services approach or other critical functions within the business. There are two ways to develop this. First, there can be details of the crisis activity within the wider policies on financial matters etc. Second, these can feature within a crisis response policy. The approach to take will vary depending on the way the business operates and how it develops and manages policies.

Within the communication and PR world there are policies needed to assist in the management of social media, the media, stakeholders and internal communication. Social media presents a significant challenge to any business on a day-to-day basis and when a crisis emerges this is exacerbated. The social media policy should consider who is able to post, what they can post and the consequences of stepping outside of the policy. A media policy will need to consider who speaks to the media, what information is able to be released to the media, and how relationships are managed. Similarly, any internal communication policy will need to document how employees will receive critical information, who will have the responsibility of sharing that information and the details of how employees are required to support the response. Policies are relevant to the whole workforce and business and as such need to detail the critical elements of a response, who it relates to and what is required.

Being prepared for any type of crisis that may emerge is critical to every business. It requires the business to have the right culture in place where there are clear expectations on managers to participate in the crisis response. Staff need to have clear expectations of what is required from them, as well as to understand the consequences of their actions. Underpinning effective reputation management is having standards, values and purpose of the business that run through the risk and crisis framework.

Considering approaches to a crisis

When a business' reputation is facing a crisis, there are two main approaches that can be taken: to be proactive in managing it, or to be reactive. The difference is that where a business is proactive it will be planning and implementing both business changes and communication activity. Where problems are identified there will be a swift response in an attempt to get ahead of the issue. The proactive approach involves acting at an early stage. A business that decides to be reactive to the challenge to its reputation will wait to see how the situation unfolds and will rely on an escalation plan. The escalation plan gives some clarity on when to take some form of action either operationally or in communication. Whatever approach is taken there is a requirement for a business to be adaptable and flexible in its response.

The approach should be decided by considering a number of factors. First, is it an issue that has emerged or has it become a crisis? As outlined in Chapter 6, a crisis requires action to be taken, whereas a more reactive approach can be taken to an issue. Understand the details of the situation and how serious it has become at the point it has been identified. Is it factual or linked to rumours and perceptions of the business and the situation? In addition to understanding the situation that has arisen, the second factor is to recognize how it appears to other people and particularly the key audiences for the business. What are the elements of it that matter to people and what is causing the biggest concern? Third, consider what the impact may be in the future. This should be undertaken with scenario planning. Scenario planning lays out all the potential developments that could happen in relation to the situation. This can help to define the actions that may need to be taken and whether to make an early decision to be proactive. Consider the future in relation to the business operation, employees, financial impact and the reputation.

In reality, most situations will involve a mix of both proactive and reactive actions in relation to managing a crisis in the reputation of a business. Their challenge will be to identify the right action at the right moment in time. This requires careful consideration of the situation.

SIX STEPS TO ASSESS THE SITUATION

There are six questions to consider when trying to understand the details and the impact of the situation that has occurred. This will provide a firm foundation for the plans that are developed to respond:

1 **How severe is the impact on the business and its reputation? And how widespread is the impact it is having?**
   Where there is a huge impact that is affecting many people and is looking as though it is spreading and impacting on many more people, then a proactive response will be preferable. Quantifying the impact of the situation on both the business operation and its reputation is essential. If a business

waits, reviewing the situation and considering what steps it may take, then criticism is likely to follow as a lack of action is taken as disinterest or insensitivity.

2 **How significant is the issue to the key audiences and stakeholders for the business?**
Assessing the level of impact should be considered against the elements that are important to the reputation of the business. When the impact is significantly affecting audiences and stakeholders that are critical to the business, then some form of proactive action and communication will be required. If key audiences become aware of the problem or issue from a third party, it will damage trust in the business.

3 **Is the issue related to a factual and real situation, or is it rooted in perceptions of the business, its operations and actions?**
Understanding whether there is an operational issue that needs to be addressed, or if the issue is based in an incorrect perception of the business is critical. The physical manifestation of a problem will require action to be taken so that it is addressed, limited or prevented from deteriorating further. But where the situation is based in perceptions that people have of the business, then there needs to be careful consideration of how this can be addressed. How can the business show the perceptions are inaccurate without appearing to dismiss people's views? It will require long-term action to be taken.

4 **Does the business have some culpability in the situation that has developed? Is there some responsibility that it bears for the problem that has occurred?**
Where a business is responsible for the negative situation that has developed, it needs to recognize this and take a positive position in addressing what has happened. The reputation can be positively impacted if there is an open and honest response to the situation that does not attempt to hide or dismiss the situation and people's concerns. In the early stages of a problem developing it is sometimes unclear if there is any culpability, but this should be kept under continuous review while the response takes place.

5 **How does the situation impact on the values and purpose of the business?**
If the situation conflicts with the purpose and principles of the operation of the business, then the impact on its reputation will be more significant. Where it contradicts its own values, the damage can be intensified. For

example, in 2020, nut milk producer Oatly came under pressure when it sold shares to a company that was considered to be in contradiction with its environmental values.[1] The company came under intense scrutiny over its business dealings and whether they were aligned with its stated purpose and principles. It is not always the way the business operates that can increase the pressure it faces. Senior leaders, C-suite or the CEO may make comments that are not aligned to the values and purpose of the business.

6 **Does this link to any other issues or any previous crises or negative situations involving the business?**
Reputational damage can be significantly increased where it is a reoccurrence of a previous problem, or where it can be connected to other failings, or perceived failings. Challenging situations are often viewed and responded to in isolation. Reputation is built over time and the damage to it can also have been done over time. A previous situation may not have been appropriately addressed or the business may be caught up in a wider problem affecting the whole industry.

The questions can help to frame whether a proactive or reactive approach is required in relation to the crisis that is affecting the reputation. In reality, the response will usually require a mix of both proactive and reactive communication activity. But where there is significant reputational damage, the threat of significant reputational damage, or it is having widespread negative impact on people, a move to proactive communication and direct action by the business will be the more effective approach.

Approaches to managing a reputational crisis

Proactive

Many organizations will avoid taking a proactive approach to a reputational crisis, preferring to step back and hope the situation dissipates. There is a significant challenge from risk aversion affecting the response to crises. But using the six steps to assess the situation, as well as gathering information from case studies, can be used to influence senior leaders and develop a proactive approach. Underpinning all proactive communication to respond to a crisis is showing that the business cares and is concerned about the situation or the perceptions that exist:

1 Recognize the issue and the views that people have of it, particularly those who are critical to the business. Speed is a priority when aiming to be proactive in the response to a challenging situation. There is a 20-minute window where the business can grasp the issue and demonstrate a competent approach to addressing it. This is being driven by the impact of social media where people will be discussing the issue and will fill in any gaps with speculation, rumour and assumption. Identifying there is a problem must happen first and then the business can step in to own it and the response to it. In this initial stage, identify there is a crisis and then understand the impact it is having on audiences that are important to the business' reputation. In the UK, the report into the police handling of the hunt for missing person Nicola Bulley highlighted how a failure to communicate quickly about key aspects of the investigation had led to extensive rumour and speculation. This created significant problems and impacted on her family.[2]

2 Create a plan to address the issue and the perceptions people have of it. A proactive response needs to have a focused approach where there is ongoing communication to promote the business and the action that has been taken. The plan should consider the purpose of the business and how it has been affected and prioritize the communication to key audiences. Prioritize the communication to those who are critical to the business and its reputation. The plan can drive proactive communication and ensure that business changes are made as necessary.

3 Move quickly to put actions in place, identify organizational changes that are needed and communicate about the work that has been, or is being, undertaken. A proactive response needs to centre around actions that the business will undertake to address the problem that has occurred. This can also address perceptions by making tangible changes to the work, products and services that will challenge those views. Communication can then follow to explain the action that has been taken and demonstrate the newly developed position for the business.

4 Accept responsibility if necessary and make an early apology if there is culpability. This may be unclear when the situation emerges, but if it becomes clear that the business has created the problem then an apology

may be appropriate. It is often part of a stealing thunder approach, where information that is damaging is released by the business before it is uncovered. It is the most proactive position to take and requires an acceptance of the risk that the situation may be escalated by the action. But it allows the business to demonstrate it is open and honest and, in a situation where there is a responsibility for what has occurred, can positively impact on the reputation. The best example of accepting responsibility early was in 2015, when Alton Towers amusement park admitted responsibility quickly for the Smiler accident that caused significant injuries to five people.[3]

5 Review the communication activity linked to the business. When there is a serious problem and something that is impacting on the reputation of the business, all communication should be reassessed. If there are advertising campaigns or marketing activity that is taking place, this should be reconsidered in light of the issue and its implications. Consider what people may be seeing and hearing from the business and assess it against the problem and the views it has elicited from people. Halt activity or make amendments as necessary to PR, SEO, advertising, marketing or other activities.

6 Implement a detailed plan to address online comments and fake news. Social media has a crucial role to play in crisis management and requires careful consideration of how it will be used. This starts with effective monitoring of systems being in place. The business must then be aware of the commentary and consider how to triage so that replies are provided where necessary. Responses online can be taken offline when it involves personal situations, but there should be a public comment to ensure the business is seen by others as reacting. The proactive social media response can also help to address both misinformation and disinformation, proactively providing accurate information, correcting inaccuracies and building a clear narrative about the situation. In 2024, details of how a photograph of the Princess of Wales was Photoshopped created widespread concern and fuelled rumours and speculation online.[4] Being proactive in managing this swiftly would have curtailed some of the misinformation being circulated.

7 Maximize relationships and look for third-party endorsements. When the business is under pressure it should invest time in servicing the relationships that matter. Stakeholders are an important part of the response to a challenging situation. They should be told what is happening and what the business is doing to respond, and be provided with updates about the situation on a regular basis. Stakeholder mapping should be used to identify who to speak to, when and who in the business should make the connection. This approach can also help secure third-party endorsements for the business which, when authentically provided, may boost the reputation and legitimacy of the business.

8 Consult on the impact the situation has had and on the actions that are being taken. A truly proactive approach to a crisis in a business' reputation will be listening to the voices of those individuals and groups that matter. Their views and opinions should help to shape both the business and the communication response. Using consultation panels, customer feedback groups and others can quantify the impact the situation has had on the reputation of the business. It will identify whether the communication has been effective or if further action is required.

9 Keep the actions and approach under continuous monitoring and review. If the approach is going to be proactive it needs to recognize developments or further implications before they occur. Scenario planning is an important part of the proactive response where the possible developments are identified so action can be taken. Reviewing the actions and the impact they have had on the situation will also allow the operational and communication response to be revised, as necessary.

10 Consider a long-term plan to address the legacy impact of the issue. Finally, when there has been damage to a business' reputation from a problem that occurs it is essential to identify the long-term problems that it may elicit. There will be aspects of the issue and the response that can have an impact for many months or years to come. This can be proactively addressed through long-term planning and considering what changes may need to happen for both operational and communication activity. A reputation management plan that is in place needs to be updated or could be developed to support the business as it moves forward.

Reactive

Many businesses will want to look to a reactive approach to managing a crisis that is affecting the reputation. This is linked to being risk averse and hoping to wait until the situation blows over. But there are ways to ensure, even when taking a reactive approach, the business can be prepared and ready to move at an appropriate time. The reactive approaches include:

1 Establish an escalation plan to support the consideration of when and how to intervene. This would identify the scenarios and situations that may emerge and the trigger points that would lead to action needing to be taken. This can include both operational and communication activity. For example, if there are criticisms about a product it may need a significant level of complaints to be reached before action is taken, either to review the product or to make some comment about it publicly. Monitoring the discussion and development of situations is critical for this approach to be valid.

2 Avoid making any public comment and provide a 'no comment' response if approached by the media or on social media. This is a dangerous and potentially damaging approach to take. This approach is used where there is a potential for a situation to disappear or for the problem to be limited and contained. But where this is implemented, and a situation deteriorates rapidly, it can increase the reputational damage. Failing to address a situation that has emerged will also allow rumour and specula- tion to increase, which allows the conditions for misinformation and disinformation to be experienced. This approach is also part of the 'wait and see' plan and as such requires careful and efficient monitoring to be in place.

3 Gather internal and external views to indicate when action needs to be taken. Even when the business is waiting to see how situations develop before putting communication in place, it can gather views about the issue. How are people viewing the situation and the response to it? This information can help to refine the escalation plan and may highlight when action needs to be taken and communicated. Views from staff are important as they are at the frontline of the business. External views are fundamental to be able to operate quickly and put a proactive response in place.

4 Use customer services and other frontline staff to address complaints or concerns in a limited way. Where the problem or issue is restricted to certain groups or individuals it may be possible to communicate directly with them and avoid widespread interest in the situation. The action could be taken in a localized way, and this includes the communication that may be required. Customer service staff would be the frontline to

identify those affected and speak to them directly. However, there is no guarantee that it would contain the situation, as affected people may post and discuss the situation online.

5 Identify the key problem areas and take limited action, being ready to then issue communication. The business may want to make changes to its operation linked to the emerging problem before it makes any public comment about the situation. Again, this can be a risky approach to take. But it would allow any information and messaging to focus on the action that had been taken. It can also support the escalation plan by recognizing the triggers for internal changes that may allow proactive communication to take place.

6 Prepare the CEO and C-suite to be ready to step in and communicate when necessary. Even when the business is taking a reactive approach it can use the time to ensure it is ready to operate effectively when required. Communication and media training for the CEO and other spokespeople can ensure they are ready to step in and know the communication that may be required once the plan is activated. This preparation should not be only restricted to media training, as the CEO and C-suite may need to communicate with stakeholders, employees, shareholders and investors. They may also need to speak at public meetings with those affected by the problem.

7 Outline the stakeholder engagement that may be required. Mapping groups that may be affected and detailing who will speak to them, when, how often and what about, is important to responding even in a reactive way. This approach will also allow proactive stakeholder management when the business is attempting a 'wait and see' approach to the communication around the issue. Having a stakeholder engagement plan in place will be necessary to explain the reactive approach when it becomes public.

8 Develop statements to be used with the media or on social media when necessary. Whatever happens the plan should include a range of statements that can be used as action is taken. This can be linked to the escalation plan and the scenarios identified within it. The statements should consider what people will want to know, not just what the business wants to say. The narrative needs to explain the action being taken and why the business waited before making people aware of what is happening. The focus has to be on maintaining trust and confidence and ensuring this is supported through the messaging. The move into proactive communication

and activity that is evident publicly will happen quickly and will be easier to manage when planning and preparation has been carried out.

Decision-making on the approach to take

When considering the approach to be taken to the reputational crisis, the six steps identified earlier can assist in really understanding what has occurred and how things may develop. The following are important to any escalation plan: who is affected and how severely have they been affected? Is it going to have a life-changing effect on people involved in the situation? Are there significant implications for the whole sector that the business works within? For example, if there is a loss of trust and confidence in one business could it have an impact on how other businesses in the same sector are viewed? How widespread will the impact be? Is there significant discussion of the situation on social media? For example, is it trending, or is it being extensively discussed in key groups that matter to the business? Is there local, national or international media interest? International media coverage does not demand action to be taken, as it matters more if the interest or concern is among key groups that matter to the business and its reputation, such as customers or investors.

It is vital that the business and the communicators take stock of the situation and how it is developing before making decisions on the approach. A business can then focus its effort where it is needed the most to limit the damage to its reputation. This is also important to reconnect with the business' purpose and values. Are they still being upheld? Are they damaged by the situation that has developed? Does the business need to publicly demonstrate that it is reconnecting and reinforcing those values? Reputational damage can be significantly increased when a business acts against, or outside of, its purpose and values. It is also important to review this and consider the future direction of the business. How is it planning to develop and what does this problem mean to those plans? It may require further action to be taken and this can inform which approach to take. Horizon scanning is an essential part of the decision-making process.

Whatever the situation, always ensure that the impact on people is put above anything else, including finances, damage to the business and investment. Managing the impact that a problem has on people – whether customers, employees or others – should be the driving force to address the crisis. If this is done sympathetically with genuine empathy, then it can limit the reputational damage or even increase the business' positive reputation. There are many occasions where this is overlooked for a focus on the financial implications of a situation which, while important to the business, will be viewed negatively by others. For example, in April 2020, and following Covid-19 restrictions being introduced, British Airways Chief Executive at the time Alex Cruz told staff they were going to have to change approach and make significant redundancies. In the letter to staff, the financial implications were the primary focus with the impact on staff being relegated to the end of the statement.[5] This was a very difficult time, as the pandemic swept across the world, but the support to staff and a recognition of the human impact should have been central to the statement.

Visual representations of the problem and the business

For many years, the response to a crisis has focused on developing statements and messages that can be used. This is still important as a part of being crisis ready. But with the development of the digital world and social media, what people see and hear when a problem emerges is of more importance. Images on social media go viral when a problem or crisis emerges. Monitoring social media for the images and understanding what it says about the business and its response is essential. Words and hashtags are not the only elements of the social media commentary that should be assessed and considered. The images that are provided can be read in many different ways depending on people's understanding of what has happened. This can lead to the image being interpreted or misinterpreted.[6] This means effective communication at a time of crisis, and in preparing for any potential problem, needs to consider how visual information can be shared by the business.

Before any crisis has occurred, the signs and symbols linked to the business need to be understood. What do the photographs and images that are released say about the business, its values and what matters to it? Understanding this can highlight what images are able to boost the reputation and which can be damaging. In addition to any statements and messages that are used there needs to be a consideration of the images the business can provide to put the situation into context, limit the damage and attempt to boost the reputation. It is easy to get too focused on the words alone and this will limit the effectiveness of the crisis response.

Understand what the business assets are, how visual they are and whether there is anything to see from the situation and its impact. Assets can be buildings, uniformed staff, vehicles, websites, marketing, advertising, content and search engine optimization. It can also include where the branding is visible and evident. Where possible, provide an opportunity to see the response in action to reinforce the understanding of the work that is under way to manage what has happened. The CEO has a key role as the most obvious visual representation of the business. What they say and do will be watched closely and they need to be aware of that when they speak publicly, meet employees and are responding to a challenging situation. They need to act with purpose and integrity to support the business' reputation.

TOP TIP

Remain alert to the societal views and issues that may impact on how assets and the visual representation of the business may be considered. Changes may need to happen, and possibly at speed, to ensure that the reputation is not damaged by appearing to be out of step with wider society.

Effective communication when addressing a reputational crisis

The development of effective communication is rooted in creating influence and not in imposing control over the situation. It therefore requires careful messaging that is aware of the wider circumstances, people's perceptions, and the views key stakeholders have of the situation and the reputation of the business. Underpinning the communication should be five key elements. The five Cs of effective messaging are confidence, clarity, commitment, compassion and competence. When communicating at a time of pressure on the business and its reputation these five points should be demonstrated:

1 **Confidence**
   Building confidence in the business and its response to any situation that has emerged is essential. This needs to be done using positive language that demonstrates how the business is aware of the issue, is listening to feedback about how it is viewed and is building an effective response. Wherever possible avoid words such as 'cannot' and 'is not', which will create a negative impression of the situation, the business and the response.

2 Clarity

Language that is used should be as clear as possible about the situation and the action that is being taken. Avoid using technical words or jargon that is not widely understood by those outside of the business. Messages should be simplified, explained and examples and illustrations used so that people can make sense of the situation and what is being done in relation to it. Be clear what people need from the communication around the issue and ensure it is reflected in the messaging.

3 Commitment

Demonstrate how the business is going to ensure the situation is brought to a satisfactory conclusion. Share details of what response is being put in place and how the business is responding. This needs to be in place whether it is a real issue or a perception that has developed. Be clear that the business is going to see things through while listening to feedback and any concerns.

4 Compassion

At the heart of all effective communication at a time of pressure is empathy and compassion. When a business' reputation is under pressure it is essential that there is a concern expressed and a level of understanding. Whether it is a tangible incident or perceptions, it is important to be listening in an open and receptive way. Failing to listen or demonstrate empathy can damage the response and the attempts to communicate about the situation, and at its worst can lead to moral outrage or accusations of gaslighting or other behaviour. This will be discussed in Chapter 8.

5 Competence

A key part of the reputation of the business is its legitimacy to operate. This is also important to the communication that is developed. It should demonstrate a competence to respond to the situation, listen to feedback and views, and make any necessary changes. Whatever the issue that has emerged or has been highlighted, the business needs to show they are aware of it and have the necessary skills and experience to respond to it.

Effective communication needs to be crafted so that it takes account of the five Cs and does more than just provide information. The communication provides an opportunity to show the action that is being taken, and to reinforce the values of the business. Remember, this is not just about the written words but should underpin the visual images used in relation to the situation. Understanding what communication to carry out and when should be part of the escalation plans that have been developed as part of the reputation management work. Ensure the business can speak first and speak frequently.

Readiness for a crisis affecting reputation

A significant part of an effective response to a reputational crisis comes from the business' readiness to be able to step in quickly and address what has emerged. It may be a sudden crisis that has hit or a long-running problem that has deteriorated. Every situation benefits from early identification and stepping in to act swiftly. This requires steps to have been taken that will put the business in the best place possible to be able to react at speed. Most businesses have major incident plans or business continuity plans that are developed to respond to operational and physical threats. Such plans need to include communication as a strategy part of the response, and they should also be ready to address significant reputational challenges and crises. The damage from a reputational crisis can be as substantial as any operational problem.

Ensuring there is an ongoing monitoring and consideration of risks and threats to the business' reputation is the first part of readiness. This is part of the reputation management framework that exists within the business. It should sit alongside the operational risk management, but communication and PR teams must have systems in place that can continually monitor the potential reputational challenges.

Having plans is important but they should be tested to ensure they would be effective at a time of crisis. There are a range of ways this can be undertaken, from a tabletop exercise through to a full simulation that uses software to replicate the social media and other elements. Artificial intelligence systems are increasingly able to assist businesses in developing crisis exercises. They can develop scenarios, provide inputs and assess the response. However, be aware of the potential security risks if using publicly available systems. All exercises should focus on the decision-making and actions that are taken by participants. It should test the response by the people who would take key roles and assess if the plans provide the necessary framework for support.

Crisis simulations are a way of recreating real-life situations with the viewpoints of all key groups represented. Software systems can replicate the customer complaints, media coverage, social media pressure, stakeholder requests and the internal demands. They can be developed to stress test any parts of the plan where there is concern about possible effectiveness. It provides pressure to the decision-making process and requires action to be taken. The performance of individuals and the systems and plans that are used can be assessed and improvements made. Where possible it is beneficial to bring in the external voices of those who are important to the business as part of the testing and exercising regime. Simulations and exercises should involve staff, customers, other community representatives, the board, trustees, investors or other key groups. This will ensure they can assess the approach, provide suggested improvements and assess the impact of the communication.

Exercising for reputational crises should be a part of every business risk, crisis and incident response preparation. Such situations require the same intensity of response, and this should be what is tested across the business. A crisis can appear at any point so the programme of testing should be in place throughout the year.

Six steps to an effective response to the reputational threat

An organization or business can be caught off guard when a reputational threat develops, and it may be a crisis before it is recognized. If the risk and crisis management framework is in place this can assist in early identification and response. For anyone needing to respond to a reputational threat or crisis there are six steps to take:

1 **Acknowledge the situation**
   Recognize that the reputation is under threat and that there is either a physical situation or perception that has emerged. Avoid attempts to ignore, downplay or gaslight people in relation to the situation. This will be discussed in detail in Chapter 8.

2 **Have a structure in place**
   Detail who is responsible for the response to the situation. Who is leading aspects of the response? What is the meeting structure that is in place? Be clear about the people involved, the expectations of them, and the governance structure to assist the response.

3 Gather the data and insights

Monitoring is the starting point of understanding the impact of the situation. Put monitoring in place and review it regularly as the response is put in place and communication is undertaken. Listen to feedback and views and understand what is being said, and what the perceptions are among key audiences.

4 Create a plan

If there is an outlined crisis plan within the major incident plans, then review it and consider whether it is suitable to be used for the issue that has emerged. It needs to consider the whole approach to the issue and not just the communication that may be required. Detail the proactive and reactive actions that need to be taken. The plan should also be in place for the long term to deal with the problems as they develop and the future.

5 Understand key relationships

Put stakeholder mapping in place at an early stage. This means understanding the most important and influential relationships, both internally and externally. Use the mapping to create a plan of who will be contacted, when, by whom and what information they will provide. Focus the attention on those affected and the most critical audiences identified in the reputation management processes.

6 Be human and show empathy

Ensure that the response is focused on addressing any human impact from the incident or what has happened. It is the human impact that will be the focus of media and social media coverage about the situation. Those who are disadvantaged or damaged will be put in the spotlight. Any approach that is taken must ensure there is support in place for those most seriously affected and that it is reflected in the communication.

CASE STUDY

Facebook and Cambridge Analytica

Background

In March 2018, Facebook became embroiled in a scandal related to the harnessing of information to use in political profiling. The information came to light through media exposures that alleged people's Facebook details were being accessed by Cambridge Analytica for use in its modelling. Around 87 million Facebook users were said to have been affected.[7] There were further covert tapes where senior executives at Cambridge Analytica were making claims of being able to influence elections.[8] Facebook quickly suspended the company's access to the data and within days had put more protections in place around the use of data. CEO Mark Zuckerberg talked to the media about building trust back into the company.[9] He also appeared before US congressional hearings where he apologized for taking the word of Cambridge Analytica when they said the data had been deleted.[10]

The issue was quickly of interest to governments around the world including the US, UK, EU and Canada. It led to changes in legislation including the EU Digital Services Act and Digital Markets Act.[11] The UK Information Commissioner fined Facebook £500,000 for breaches of data protection legislation related to the scandal.[12] Other social media platforms, including Twitter and Google, made changes to reduce the targeting of users, and alongside Facebook introduced transparency tools.[13] Meta, Facebook's parent company, has made payments linked to a class action in relation to allegations of privacy breaches.[14]

Reputation lessons

The situation may have been viewed as a system issue, but it was the impact on 87 million people, and what it may have meant to them and what they did, which became the focus. Facebook recognized that swift action needed to be taken to how they operated and what access third parties had to the data they held. CEO Mark Zuckerberg stepped in to be the visual representation of the business including making an apology and restating the position they wanted to demonstrate around care and ownership of people's data.

Other social media providers were quick to step in and demonstrate how they were responding to the issue of transparency and management of data. For Facebook, the operation of third parties had firmly put them at the centre of a scandal.

The reputational damage to Facebook had little long-term impact on the operation and the usage of the systems it provides. They are a key part of everyday activity, and the loss of data was not easy to quantify and understand on an individual basis, so most people continued unaffected. However, the issue of the way social media channels operate has remained a key issue for society and governments.

- Be prepared to manage reputational issues that can be linked to the operation of a third party such as suppliers.
- Understand what people are concerned about and how they view the impact on the business so that appropriate action can be taken.

- Ensure there are operational changes and actions linked to any reputational crisis.

- The CEO is an important figurehead that will be the visual representation of the business and its response when they speak. They need to be prepared and ready to reinforce the values and position being taken.

- Issues can lead to societal changes and government intervention which the business should not ignore and will have to take a position on.

Conclusion

An effective response to a reputational threat can both protect and enhance the way a business is viewed. It needs to be considered in both the short and long term, as reputational damage can take many months or even years to address. It is important to understand the details of the incident or issue, who it impacts upon and how it is being viewed by those audiences critical to the business' reputation. This will allow a whole business approach to be considered and action taken to address what has happened as well as communicate about it. Trying to communicate a way out of a reputational threat may bring only short-term relief.

A truly effective response needs to be underpinned by a robust framework or system of both risk and crisis management. The early identification will allow the plans to be implemented quickly. The framework needs to include major incident or crisis plans being prepared, policies to support the response being in place, and a system of meetings and decision-making spaces that are outlined. This approach must be ready to use to respond to both operational and reputational crises. Being crisis and issue ready allows a business to consider whether to take a proactive or reactive approach to the communication. But it also needs to be tested on a regular basis and key staff require ongoing training to ensure they know what to do and when.

The communication must be focused on the five Cs of effective messaging, where competence, compassion and commitment are demonstrated with clarity to build confidence. This is not just for messaging, and is essential for the visuals and images that are in place. Images of the business need to be assessed to ensure they are in line with the values and also the approach to managing the incident that is in place. Any business that is put under pressure should remember the six steps to an effective response and put them in place as quickly as possible. The approach must be ethical, honest and demonstrate integrity. Approaches where this is not evident or lead to public questioning of the business can have a further negative impact on reputation, as will be discussed in Chapter 8.

References

1 E Helmore. Activists sour on Oatly vegan milk after stake sold to Trump-linked Blackstone, *The Guardian*, 2 September 2020, www.theguardian.com/food/2020/sep/01/oatly-vegan-milk-sale-blackstone (archived at https://perma.cc/Q5GC-4PVF)

2 College of Policing. Independent external review of Lancashire Constabulary's operational response to reported missing person Nicola Bulley, November 2023, www.college.police.uk/article/review-nicola-bulley-investigation-published (archived at https://perma.cc/A5M8-KCGR)

3 L Dore. Alton Towers crash: Theme park owners will pay compensation and accept 'full responsibility', *The Independent*, 9 June 2015, www.independent.co.uk/news/uk/home-news/alton-towers-crash-owners-will-pay-compensation-and-accept-full-responsibility-10306635.html (archived at https://perma.cc/G57S-7LVB)

4 M Judkis, J Kingsbury, H Scribner and K Adam. How a doctored photo of the Princess of Wales triggered a media crisis, *Washington Post*, 11 March 2024, www.washingtonpost.com/style/2024/03/11/kate-middleton-photo-standards/ (archived at https://perma.cc/4XNG-RGNM)

5 R Neate. British Airways plans to make up to 12,000 staff redundant, *The Guardian*, 28 April 2020, www.theguardian.com/business/2020/apr/28/british-airways-plans-to-make-up-to-12000-staff-redundant (archived at https://perma.cc/UB98-MX8V)

6 S Goyal. Role and impact of visual imagery during crisis, in A Singh (ed.) *International Handbook of Disaster Research*, Springer, Singapore, https://doi.org/10.1007/978-981-19-8388-7_98 (archived at https://perma.cc/U7VK-W69H)

7 PBS Newshour. Zuckerberg: 'It was clearly a mistake to believe' Cambridge Analytica, YouTube, 2018, www.youtube.com/watch?v=mGpPHZB_fvI (archived at https://perma.cc/KW9S-LWP9)

8 S Meredith. Here's everything you need to know about the Cambridge Analytica scandal, *CNBC*, 23 March 2018, www.cnbc.com/2018/03/21/facebook-cambridge-analytica-scandal-everything-you-need-to-know.html (archived at https://perma.cc/KT9Q-7CWD)

9 NBC News. Mark Zuckerberg admits his data harvested by Cambridge Analytica, YouTube, 2018, www.youtube.com/watch?v=E-sMKNVAjcI (archived at https://perma.cc/2ANS-VUCK)

10 PBS Newshour. Zuckerberg: 'It was clearly a mistake to believe' Cambridge Analytica, YouTube, 2018, www.youtube.com/watch?v=mGpPHZB_fvI (archived at https://perma.cc/KW9S-LWP9)

11 K Harbath. History of the Cambridge Analytica controversy, Bipartisan Policy Center, 16 March 2023, https://bipartisanpolicy.org/blog/cambridge-analytica-controversy/ (archived at https://perma.cc/APN5-5SAP)

12 P Zialcita. Facebook pays $643,000 fine for role in Cambridge Analytica scandal, *NPR*, 30 October 2019, www.npr.org/2019/10/30/774749376/facebook-pays-643-000-fine-for-role-in-cambridge-analytica-scandal (archived at https://perma.cc/FL5L-PFGA)

13 Digiday. Goodbye, dark posts: how Facebook's and Twitter's ad-transparency tools work, 29 June 2018, https://digiday.com/marketing/goodbye-dark-posts-facebooks-twitters-ad-transparency-tools-work/ (archived at https://perma.cc/S5JK-9SPE)

14 A Hern. Facebook owner to settle class-action suit over Cambridge Analytica scandal, *The Guardian*, 23 December 2022, www.theguardian.com/business/2022/dec/23/facebook-owner-to-settle-class-action-suit-over-cambridge-analytica-scandal (archived at https://perma.cc/D57J-5N59)

8

A matter of ethics

Introduction

One of the most critical elements of reputation management is that it is underpinned by a strong ethical framework. Honesty and integrity are a significant factor in how organizations and businesses are viewed by others. They are also a key factor in how trust and confidence is built in the business. People will be heavily critical of a business that lies, manipulates and which acts in a way that is contradicted by the communication. Trust can also be damaged by a business that acts in a way that challenges its stated purpose and values. Ensuring there is an ethical approach is not just in relation to the communication but the whole approach by the business. From the CEO downwards there should be a focus on ethical decision-making that is based in principles of honesty, accountability and empathy.

Ethics is often referred to as doing the right thing, but this is a challenging concept to effectively define. It needs to be right in respect of the values of the business. It should be right in relation to societal norms and expectations. It must be right legally and in relation to any regulatory frameworks. It needs to be right from a moral perspective. This makes the phrase 'doing the right thing' meaningless when attempting to define and consider ethical perspectives on reputation management. Instead, businesses need to look to their agreed purpose and values that should encompass how they operate with respect and in consideration of what matters to others.

The issue of ethics is critical in a world that is affected by fake news and the developments in artificial intelligence. It is also affected by the post-pandemic trust deficit that is evident in many countries around the world.[1] People have an increased lack of trust in governments and institutions, which makes them question information that is provided.[2] Social media can also play a part in amplifying conspiracy theories that further threaten businesses.[3] The trust deficit puts additional pressure on businesses and communication to have a strong ethical framework that they work within. For communicators this means being able to identify and avoid propaganda, greenwashing, cover-ups, false information and dishonesty. Professional bodies supporting PR and communication put ethics at the centre of how they define the industry, and within training and continuous professional development.[4]

Ethical challenges to reputation management

The issue is where influence is and what becomes manipulation. This is a particularly challenging situation where behavioural communication and the development of fake news have become linked to communication. Much of the challenge is rooted in what is the truth and there is rarely a single agreed version of the truth of any situation. This means responding when there is a developing reputational crisis must be underpinned by ethical practices. There are a number of potential problems that can occur when developing reputation management:

- **Propaganda**
  This is a systematic dissemination of information, including rumour and lies, to influence public opinion and behaviours.[5] It is often shared using mass media channels and is often a state-sponsored manipulation of information. There is a co-ordination and deliberate approach to promote a particular position through the omission of key information or by lying. Examples of propaganda are often seen at times of war or conflict.

- **Manipulation**
  Manipulation through communication that aims to shape people's opinions, attitudes and beliefs without the person's consent and knowledge. It is used to impact on people's behaviour and views.[6] It involves deception and coercion with a view to benefiting the party delivering the information. Examples of manipulation can be seen in political and business environments.

- **Dishonesty**
  Providing deliberately inaccurate and misleading information happens in three ways deliberately, premeditatedly and innocuously. The communication

includes lies and deception. It often happens when businesses or organizations come under pressure because of something they have done.

- **Cover-up**
  Communication and activity may be put in place that attempts to hide wrongdoing, criminality or inappropriate behaviour. The business will potentially be dishonest or will manipulate the information to avoid the problem being exposed and identified by others. A recent example of an alleged cover-up is the UK Post Office scandal where subpostmasters were wrongly accused and convicted of criminality.[7]

- **False representation**
  When information is provided that gives an untrue or incorrect representation of the facts of a situation, it can be false representation. It is made with the understanding that the information is inaccurate. This can be seen in fraudulent activity and criminal attempts to gain by the misrepresentation. The use of bots, influencers and fake reviews can also be linked to false representation.

- **Spin**
  This is a form of manipulation or even propaganda that is provided to show a biased interpretation of an event or situation to influence public opinion about the person or organization that is delivering the information. It became a term widely used in the 1970s and 1980s where it was used to describe political communication and PR teams.[8] PR and spin are often confused, and the term spin has been a challenge to the professional and ethical operation of PR.

- **Greenwashing and other forms of washing**
  The term greenwashing describes using PR, advertising and marketing activity deceptively to persuade people of the environmental policies and green credentials of a business. It was first used in 1986 by environmentalist Jay Westerveld in an essay about hotel industry practices.[9] Companies that greenwash will make inaccurate or misleading claims about their environmental activity and impact. The washing element can also be applied to many other claims that businesses make including their inclusive and LGBTQ+ credentials, where there can be claims of pinkwashing.[10]

- **Privacy and confidentiality**
  A significant challenge to the ethics of communication and the way a business operates is the management of information. Where privacy and confidentiality are ignored or breached it has a significant impact on the

reputation of the business accused of the failure. Data management and protecting confidentiality appropriately need to underpin the operation of businesses. However, the use of non-disclosure agreements, which are legal documents to protect confidentiality, inappropriately can impact on the reputation of the business using them.[11]

- **Conflicts of interest**
  A situation where an individual's ability to act or make a judgement could be impaired or influenced by their connection to someone or something, is a conflict of interest.[12] It can be a significant challenge for people acting as Board members or trustees to a business where their other connections may be seen as affecting their views. Businesses need to consider where conflicts may arise when developing communication designed to boost the business' reputation. An example is a social media influencer that is discussing the benefits of a product while also being paid by the company making the product.

- **Gaslighting**
  Gaslighting is a form of psychological manipulation that aims to create self-doubt within the recipient. It is a term derived from a play and film called *Gaslight* where the husband convinces his wife she is imagining things that are actually happening.[13] It can be used both wittingly and unwittingly by businesses in response to a challenge or emerging problem. Examples of gaslighting include criticizing someone's response as irrational or overreacting and accusing them of exaggerating.

All of the above challenges are linked to the way a business operates and the values that it has. The behaviours that are accepted within the business and the boundaries that are put in place can allow approaches including cover-ups, manipulation and gaslighting to be viewed as acceptable responses to a reputational challenge.

The role of ethics in reputation management

It is important to understand the difference between ethics, morals and values. Ethics are the way people behave and what they do based on their views, attitudes and standards. These may change over time when we consider societal norms. Morals are the system of beliefs of what is right and wrong and will be underpinning the ethical actions. Values are more personal beliefs about what is acceptable, and these can exist within businesses through the business values of how it should operate. In addition, it is important to be aware of legality within consideration of the ethical approaches. What is legal may not be acceptable within society and could be unethical. Legal frameworks attempt to construct rules by which societies operate and these do not always keep pace with changing societal attitudes. For example, the developments within social media and more recently artificial intelligence have been slow to be covered by legislation.

The forced removal of a passenger from a United Airlines flight in 2017, was an example of legal but morally unacceptable behaviour. The practice of removing passengers from overbooked flights was commonplace and legally acceptable; it was viewed negatively when the video of the passenger emerged.[14] The response to the reputational crisis was seen to support the staff involved and to lack remorse or regret. This led to a backlash from some customers who cancelled flights, and criticism of the way the business operated.[15] The airline needed to understand the public viewpoint and to recognize the shifting position which made the action inappropriate.

Ethics are not universal and do not remain fixed over time. This requires businesses and communicators to understand norms of behaviour and what is acceptable by society at that point in time. Behaviour that may have once been seen as moral and appropriate can be seen as unacceptable with changes. For example, at some points in the past the use of plastic was seen as acceptable by a business but now, while legal, it is seen as inappropriate due to views on climate change. Many industries aim to provide an ethical framework for operation and decision-making including health professionals and law enforcement. This provides some agreed standards across the whole of the profession. In addition, there are governing bodies within sectors that aim to provide guidance on those standards. Within PR and communication each of the professional bodies have codes of ethics that detail what is acceptable from the membership. The Chartered Institute of Public Relations (CIPR), Public Relations and Communication Association (PRCA), Public Relations Society of America (PRSA), the International Public Relations Association (IPRA), International Association of Business Communicators (IABC) and the World Communication Forum Association (WCFA) all have either a code of ethics or conduct that detail what behaviour is acceptable.

Even with these codes there are moments when members breach the professional codes of behaviour. This creates a reputational crisis for the PR team or individuals that are involved in what is designated as unacceptable operation. In 2017, Bell Pottinger was expelled from the PRCA after an investigation found it had attempted to stir up racial hatred in South Africa.[16] Ensuring ethical operation within the PR and communication industry requires consequences to be in place for those who breach the codes of ethics and conduct. Bell Pottinger ultimately went into administration later that year. When the reputation of the PR operation is challenged it has a detrimental impact on the business as a whole.

Behaviour change and the ethical challenges

Behaviour change in communication is now identified as important to a lot of public sector and governmental communication and PR activity. It aims to influence the audience to act or behave in a particular way. It may be that the communication aims to encourage people to start a new behaviour, to stop a current harmful behaviour or to modify unacceptable behaviour. For example, behavioural change communication may work to prevent young people from starting smoking, find ways to encourage people to stop smoking, or identify how people could cut down smoking. The aim is to develop communication that addresses the capability, opportunity and motivation to make a change.[17] Using this approach brings ethical challenges from the influence that is placed and possible manipulation. It requires careful consideration and a justifiable position of why the change is required. Behavioural change communication can support risk communication by helping people to understand risks and how they can take steps to reduce them.

Attempting to use behavioural change communication when addressing a reputational challenge would be inappropriate. It would appear to diminish or even gaslight those concerned about the issue affecting the business. The influence could be misconstrued as an attempt to silence those with genuine issues to raise. Businesses may need to make changes to the way they operate rather than working to change the way their customers or service users act and behave. When responding to a reputational challenge or when attempting to improve the reputation of a business, operating honestly and ethically is essential.

The role of organizational ethics

Beyond the personal ethics and values that individuals have, there are organizational ethics. These are ways of working that define how the business operates and what is expected from the employees. Organizational ethics need to be understood in relation to the reputation of the business and its purpose and values. Organizational ethics need to be clearly laid out and understood as part of the expectations placed on staff. It must also ensure issues such as confidentiality, integrity, conflicts of interest and respect are defined for employees. Staff need to have the ethical framework explained and may require training to ensure they are able to implement what is required. Personal ethics can sometimes contradict or be put under pressure by organizational ethics. In such situations the business should be open to listening and understanding how employees may feel compromised so they can change, as necessary.

Where organizations fail to listen to the concerns and issues raised by employees, they may find whistleblowers emerge. Whistleblowers highlight wrongdoing and unacceptable behaviour by organizations and businesses. In the UK there is legislation in place that protects whistleblowers in a number of areas of work.[18] The information released needs to be for the good of others to be covered by the legal protections. Similar legislation is in place in the US where employees make protected disclosures.[19] Whistleblowers can seriously damage the reputation of the business as they bring unacceptable actions, operations and behaviour to public attention. It also demonstrates that the business is not listening to concerns and may not have the required organizational ethical framework in place. Addressing this is challenging and the most damaging approach is to try to silence whistle-blowers or to refuse to listen to the issues that are being raised. Instead be prepared to listen, to investigate and to act, as necessary.

Leadership and ethical business

CEOs and business leaders have a critical role to play in ensuring that business operate ethically and have a strong framework in place. They ultimately set the standards by which the business operates and designate what is acceptable behaviour. Boundaries are put in place with visible signs of behaviour that is rewarded or challenged. It is these values, expectations and boundaries that are part of what creates the organizational culture. The leadership of any business has to take the responsibility for establishing the values and ensuring they are fulfilled. Leaders also have a key role to play in linking the ethical approach to how reputation is defined and managed. They need to build reputation into the way the business is measured and how developments are implemented.

Leaders must also establish a strong risk management framework and ensure that the business is crisis ready. CEOs have a central role in both risk and crisis management. They must ensure the business develops and responds effectively to the current and future risks. When a crisis does occur, they have to take the ultimate decision-making position while listening to advisers. On a personal level they need to be open to different views and perspectives and be ready to listen and make changes, as necessary. When the business is under pressure and put in the spotlight, the CEO needs to be visible both publicly and to the workforce.

Embedding ethical behaviour within a business also needs training to be provided. This can be training on ethical decision-making or how to enforce the boundaries of behaviour. Encouraging staff to make decisions in a safe session or exercise can test the understanding of values and how to implement them. Training can also be included within ongoing training activities to reinforce the expectations at every opportunity.

TOP TIP

There is a growing move to expand the duty of candour that exists in health services into other institutions. The duty of candour requires organizations to be open and to tell the truth about situations and events. In the UK this is being considered for other public bodies but in December 2023, the UK Government rejected making it law and preferred to establish a charter.[20] Progressive organizations and businesses should consider the elements of openness, transparency and honesty in the charter as good practice to implement.

What to do when principles are challenged

Businesses need to have defined their purpose, values and the ethical framework that they work within. It is a key element to understanding their reputation and a part of how they view themselves and therefore want other people to view them. This will provide clarity about what matters as part of corporate identity. Corporate identity is about more than branding. The branding is just the manifestation and embodiment of the purpose that underpins the business. The principles can be challenged either from within or from outside of the business. As mentioned, staff can put pressure on a business when their values are not aligned to the corporate values. They can also challenge those running the business when they have concerns that are not listened to and may raise the issues publicly. This can also lead to the emergence of whistleblowers.

External challenges can come from perceptions and the emergence of fake news. Where people have developed inaccurate or erroneous views of the business it will take some time before they can be turned around and changed. It requires continued action over time to demonstrate how the views are inaccurate and do not represent the business or the way it operates. Fake news provides additional challenges for every business and organization. The emergence of clickbait and the use of artificial intelligence bots has the potential to damage a business' reputation. Clickbait is content developed just to attract attention and encourage the user to click a link. The AI chatbots are designed to engage as humans and can be operated to manipulate, persuade or share propaganda. PR and communication must ensure they are not using these techniques to manipulate, as they can be reputationally damaging to a business. When misinformation is caused by inaccurate information this can be corrected and the message amplified. But when it is disinformation that is intentionally being shared to damage the business, it needs a carefully considered plan of action. This should support the reputation management activity and the approaches identified in Chapter 7 to address problems.

Additional challenges can come from the connections and relationships that a business has with stakeholders. Unethical or problematic actions or behaviour from a third party can have a reflected impact on the reputation of those connected to them. Due diligence and attention should be taken when developing connections to any third-party group, organization or individual. For example, the actions of social media influencers that are working with businesses have become a risk that needs to be considered.

PR or communication officers can come under pressure to act outside of their ethical framework. This requires them to be clear with the business about the boundaries they work within. Where decisions are required that have ethical challenges attached, carefully working through the situation will assist in reaching a conclusion. The Chartered Institute of Public Relations developed an ethical decision-making tree in an attempt to support members who face challenges to their operating principles.[21] The tree looks at the legal implications, the impact on the CIPR's code of conduct and the

FIGURE 8.1   CIPR Code of Conduct Decision Tree (version 1)

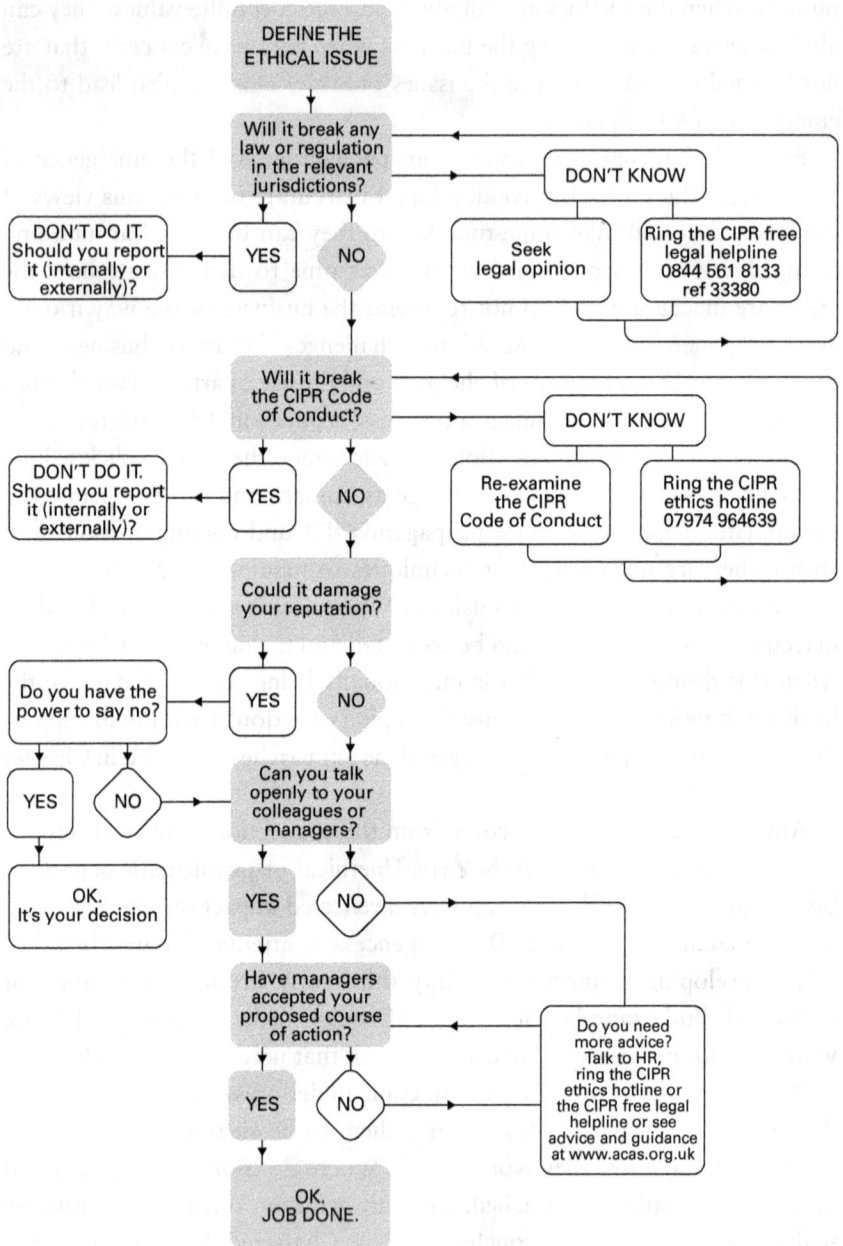

DEFINE THE
ETHICAL ISSUE

Will it break any
law or regulation
in the relevant
jurisdictions?

DON'T KNOW

DON'T DO IT.
Should you report
it (internally or
externally)?

YES   NO

Seek
legal opinion

Ring the CIPR free
legal helpline
0844 561 8133
ref 33380

Will it break
the CIPR Code
of Conduct?

DON'T KNOW

DON'T DO IT.
Should you report
it (internally or
externally)?

YES   NO

Re-examine
the CIPR
Code of Conduct

Ring the CIPR
ethics hotline
07974 964639

Could it damage
your reputation?

Do you have the
power to say no?

YES   NO

YES   NO

OK.
It's your decision

Can you talk
openly to your
colleagues or
managers?

YES   NO

Have managers
accepted your
proposed course
of action?

Do you need
more advice?
Talk to HR,
ring the CIPR
ethics hotline or
the CIPR free legal
helpline or see
advice and guidance
at www.acas.org.uk

YES   NO

OK,
JOB DONE.

SOURCE Reproduced courtesy of the CIPR https://cipr.co.uk/CIPR/CIPR/Our_work/Policy/Ethics.aspx
(archived at https://perma.cc/5TV9-79JJ)

potential for reputational damage to assist in the decision-making process. Anyone working in PR and communication will need to be able to provide other courses of action that are within the ethical framework when they are presented with challenging situations. They will also need to influence those making inappropriate requests by demonstrating the potential reputational damage of the action being requested, before presenting an alternative approach. Ultimately, when a business continues to suggest inappropriate approaches and whose values conflict with the communicator, it may require a move to alternative employment.

How situations can be made worse

Businesses can make challenging situations worse by taking action that increases the reputational damage. The approaches can be ethically questionable when considering the details of the situation and the impact it has had on the reputation. Reputational crises put the business in the spotlight and the response should focus on honesty and transparency. The following are commonly used approaches that can make situations worse either in the short or long term:

- *No comment* – a business may provide no information and refuse to discuss the problem that has arisen. This lack of information allows rumour, speculation and misinformation to circulate unchecked, which can further damage the business' reputation.

- *Ignoring the situation* – trying to detract from the problem by minimizing it and encouraging people to overlook what has happened. This can frustrate those affected leading them to speak out and for the situation to worsen.

- *Gaslighting* – as mentioned earlier in the chapter, it is a form of psychological manipulation to create self-doubt in the person raising the issue. This can be evidenced by the business taking a 'you don't understand the situation' approach to the situation that has emerged.

- *Minimizing the situation* – a business that refuses to acknowledge the complaint or people's concerns and be further criticized. It can demonstrate that the business is out of touch with its customers.

- *Sharing inaccurate information* – providing information dishonestly or as a smokescreen to the situation that has emerged can further damage the business' reputation. When a company or its PR and communication team become the instigators of misinformation it will be heavily criticized and will damage trust.

- *Dismissal of views* – as with gaslighting, when people have their views and perceptions ignored or dismissed by a business it fails to address the underlying situation. The problem may continue or will re-emerge at some point in the future.

- *Inciting conflict* – in an attempt to address a reputational challenge the business may spark a disagreement to deflect from the situation. This seeks to minimize the attention placed on the area of concern by putting the attention onto others.

- *Lack of authenticity* – when a business takes action that fails to align to the communication that is in place it can be criticized for lacking authenticity. This undermines the position of being honest about the situation and the response and can damage trust.

- *Creating confusion* – to limit the impact of a situation a business may try to make the issue so complex that people struggle to make sense of what has occurred and become disinterested. This can also be used as part of the communication response. The messaging is made overcomplicated in an attempt to encourage people to move on from what has happened.

- *Using PR stunts* – this links to the lack of authenticity as PR stunts are designed to attract attention using shock, awe or surprise. This can in itself become a reputational crisis if it is viewed as offensive, inappropriate or culturally unacceptable. The use of PR stunts to respond to a reputational crisis should be avoided.

- *Finances first* – where a business is managing a challenge and puts the focus on money at the expense of the people who are impacted by what has happened it will be criticized as insensitive and out of touch.

- *Misunderstanding the issue* – if the business fails to understand the details of the issue or situation that has emerged then its response will potentially fail. It will not address the concern about what has happened and the damage to the reputation if it is not clearly understood.

- *Lacking empathy* – failing to understand the emotion in the situation and how it has affected people will lead to accusations of insensitivity, callousness and inappropriate responses.

- *Non-disclosure agreements* – attempting to silence critics or staff who have identified inappropriate actions or behaviour within the business will be viewed negatively. Using non-disclosure agreements to prevent problems from emerging can lead to a bigger crisis.

All these approaches can be used individually or in a combined way. The damage from them can be significant as the problem is exacerbated. It puts further pressure on the business' reputation and can damage trust. It is important to use ethical decision-making when developing the response and to identify inappropriate responses before they are used.

Ethical training

The whole business needs to understand the ethical boundaries and framework. This requires effective communication of the approach, which is supported by training. The communication needs to be clear about the purpose and values as well as the ethical behaviour required from all employees. It needs to use external challenges and views that can provide a greater understanding of the implications of the actions and decisions. The communication and subsequent training can also support the development of cultural intelligence.

The training can involve any regulatory bodies that the business has to ensure employees understand how they are being supervised. This can help to reinforce the approaches that are required on a daily basis as well as when a problem has occurred. Training needs to test the approaches and decision-making in challenging areas where a number of actions could be implemented. This can be done through focused exercises that present a reputational challenge and require participants to respond and create a plan to address what has happened. Sessions can be developed solely to consider the ethical operation of the business, or it can be added into existing training sessions that take place. There are significant benefits to build it into all aspects of training and staff development that takes place as it can help to embed the behaviours that are required.

A key part of any ethical training in responses and decision-making is to ensure that it is regularly updated. Societal changes and the impact of emerging situations and technologies require employees to be aware of requirements and any changes. Such training should also be part of any induction or onboarding process that is in place so that every new employee in the business is aware of what is expected and the behaviour that is required.

Approaches for ethical decision-making

Underpinning the ethical approach is effective decision-making that takes account of the principles of operation. As well as understanding the legal and regulatory boundaries that the business works within, it requires acknowledgement of the societal morals. This can change over time so the approaches must continue to be challenged, refined and updated. There are five key elements for ethical decision-making: independence, beneficence, nonmaleficence, justice and fidelity:

1 *Independence* – people need to be allowed to make their own decisions and should be provided with the best possible information. This means having data and research that can assist in decision-making. For the communicator, it requires having access to insights into the reputation of the business and what it is among key audiences.

2 *Beneficence* – people should be focused on doing good and getting the best possible outcome for those involved. Actions that have the biggest positive impact and potential benefits should be prioritized.

3 *Nonmaleficence* – decisions should be focused on doing no harm to others both in a direct and indirect way. This needs to reflect the norms, behaviours and expectation of the society.

4 *Justice* – the decisions should be made to ensure that people are treated equally or in accordance with their requirements. If there is to be any deviation from this the business must be clear why it is necessary.

5 *Fidelity* – the decision should be made and then honoured. There has to be integrity within the approach that is taken. When actions are identified they need to be carried out or the business must be clear why they have not happened.

Before considering the five points it is important to be aware of the outcome that is required in relation to the decision being taken. This includes identifying who needs to be involved and can help the approach and outcome. Gathering the data required is the first step but it also requires horizon scanning and an understanding of different perspectives on the situation.

There are eight steps required for effective decision-making and ethics that should be in place throughout.[22] First, it is important to see the need to decide on an approach to take in relation to the situation that is being faced. Second, consider the circumstances surrounding the situation both internally within the business and externally. This includes horizon scanning and conducting scenario planning. With rapid changes in the world, media and the way issues are viewed, this is a critical step to effective decision-making.

Third, research the information and ensure the relevant data and insight is available to support the decision-making process. Fourth, look at the options that are available as a possible solution to the situation. Using the information a range of options will be identified. Fifth, evaluate the options that have been identified and consider the positive and negative aspects of each. Sixth, decide on the next steps and the action that will be taken. Seventh, put the decision on the required action into practice and be clear if additional support is required to effectively implement the action. Finally, step eight is to review the situation and consider whether it has brought the required outcome. If it has not, then additional decisions may be required and if it has, it should still be monitored for any changes or further developments.

CASE STUDY
Ohio train derailment

Background

On 3 February 2023, a train carrying toxic chemicals derailed near the town of East Palestine, Ohio, USA.[23] The small town had around 4,700 residents and shortly after the derailment between 1,500 and 2,000 residents were told to evacuate. The train operated by Norfolk Southern was carrying toxic chemicals including vinyl chloride. Three days after the incident the evacuation zone was extended and some of the toxic materials were released and burned off. On 8 February, residents were told they could return after air samples were below levels of concern. At the same time, the Ohio Department of Natural Resources said the spill affected seven-and-a-half miles of stream leading to thousands of fish being killed.

The Environmental Protection Agency (EPA) said there were no concerns, but at a residents meeting on 15 February, people talked of a lack of trust in officials and in the train operator Norfolk Southern who did not attend. Three days later, Norfolk Southern Chief Executive Alan H Shaw said the hazardous materials were being cleared up. But EPA made additional demands on the company saying they had to identify contaminated soil and water and arrange the clean-up.

On 23 February, the National Transportation Safety Board[24] produced a report and told a press conference that the incident had been preventable. The following month saw legislation being considered that would tighten the security around freight on the railways. Some residents were still living in temporary accommodation and there were reports of health problems. More tests were to be carried out. And the NTSB launched a special investigation after five accidents had occurred involving Norfolk Southern between December 2021 and February 2023. The Ohio attorney started a federal lawsuit and the Justice Department acting for the EPA claimed the company had prioritized profits over safety.

Twelve months on from the accident and residents were still discussing concerns about an odd odour when they first returned. There were claims that confusing messaging from EPA had added to concerns, division and distrust.[25] Some residents were still raising concerns about health issues,[26] but there were other groups in the community that wanted to move on and the situation created friction within the community.[27] The clean-up cost more than $800 million and the site was still under reconstruction 12 months on from the derailment.

Reputational lessons

The derailment was a major emergency that directly affected a community, forcing people to leave their homes and closing a business nearby. It was a complex situation that was difficult to explain but required simplification so that residents could both understand what had happened and feel reassured about the testing that was being undertaken. In addition, the operation of the business in the years preceding the incident would be scrutinized to assess the decision-making and what had been prioritized. The Norfolk Southern vision and values[28] state that 'everything starts with safety' and among the values is 'do what's right'. This is the standard by which the approach taken will be judged.

The reputation of both Norfolk Southern and the EPA was damaged by the response to the emergency that unfolded. This led to the decision-making being questioned and concern about the wider operation of the train company. There was also a lack of trust in the authorities and whether they could be trusted to provide accurate information.

- The impact of an emergency can be extensive and involve multiple agencies and organizations. Within this is the possibility that the damage to the reputation of one agency may be reflected onto others involved in the situation.

- The response to situations needs to be in place for the future and as long as the problem persists.

- Ethical decision-making needs to ensure that people are put before money and financial gain, particularly when dealing with situations that have negatively impacted on others. People and empathy remain the most important aspects of the response and in establishing a positive reputation when under pressure.

- The implications of situations need to be carefully considered and understood. Insight and feedback would have highlighted the requirements from the residents of East Palestine and could have helped to build trust by adjusting the response accordingly.

- Confusing and complex messages create distrust and allow rumour and speculation to spread. Providing clear and accessible information is vital.

- Businesses should operate in accordance with their purpose and values, and this includes in the decisions that are made. This should also be evident in the response that is put in place to manage a crisis. In the case of Norfolk Southern, doing what is right should have included comprehensive support to the affected residents.

Conclusion

Ethical operation and decision-making are a vital part of reputation management and addressing threats, risks and crises. In a complex and changing world it is important to have a structure, framework and process that can support staff at all levels. Operating ethically and within the boundaries and expectations that the business has laid down matters to all employees, from the CEO to the frontline staff. Leaders have a fundamental role to play in establishing the frameworks for operation and reinforcing them through reward and recognition and ensuring there are consequences for those who do not meet the requirements. They must also support the development and implementation of the business purpose and values, as well as the risk and crisis approach.

People working in PR and communication face additional ethical challenges as they have to navigate what is propaganda and manipulation and what is influencing and providing information. There is support available from professional bodies for PR and communication officers. Training and professional development should maintain an understanding of ethical challenges and how to approach the response. Failing to take account of the ethics of situations and the responses can leave communicators in a position where the action makes the problem worse. In the most serious cases it can further damage the reputation of the business. Reputations can be damaged where the business is viewed to have operated illegally, immorally or unethically. Ethical standards and what is acceptable can change over time and will be different within different societies. Understanding the societal norms is essential, particularly when working globally and in different contexts.

All businesses and organizations need to have a clear purpose as well as values and organizational ethics that underpin what they do and how they operate. This is particularly significant for communicators and PR officers who need to navigate the difficult ethical waters. They may be put under pressure to operate in ways that compromise their ethics, which requires clarity about acceptable communication operation and the ability to influence leaders to effect an alternative approach. Effective decision-making requires an understanding of what actions could further damage the business' reputation. The 14 approaches can be used without considering the impact that it could have on the way the business and the situation is perceived. The five elements of ethical decision-making can help in ensuring that inappropriate approaches are avoided. Ultimately, the communicator should have a decision-making process which can be used every day, but will be particularly beneficial when there is a crisis, and they are under pressure. Taking care about the decisions that are made and the approaches to take should continue throughout the crisis or time of pressure, through to the recovery phase for the business. The recovery phase of a reputational challenge will be considered in Chapter 9.

References

1 Ipsos. Veracity Index: Trust in politicians reaches its lowest score in 40 years, 14 December 2023, www.ipsos.com/en-uk/ipsos-trust-in-professions-veracity-index-2023 (archived at https://perma.cc/EE64-PA2H)

2 E Ortiz-Ospina, M Roser, and P Arriagada. Our world in data: Trust, *Our World in Data*, April 2024, https://ourworldindata.org/trust (archived at https://perma.cc/64L2-XR4E)

3 Conspiracy theories and social media platforms, Science Direct, https://www.sciencedirect.com/science/article/abs/pii/S2352250X22001282 (archived at https://perma.cc/HL6V-FJNY)

4 CIPR Code of Conduct https://cipr.co.uk/CIPR/CIPR/About_Us/Governance_/CIPR_Code_of_Conduct.aspx (archived at https://perma.cc/R7G3-KKK3) and PRCA Professional Charter and Codes of Conduct www.prca.org.uk/about-us/pr-standards/professional-charter-and-codes-conduct (archived at https://perma.cc/3AFL-4NXM)

5 Britannica. Propaganda, www.britannica.com/topic/propaganda (archived at https://perma.cc/R59Q-2A6K)

6 M Wyrostkiewicz. Manipulation and communication: manipulation as an anti-communicative act, *Biuletyn Edukacji Medialnej*, 2014, 12, 21–32,

www.researchgate.net/publication/271840013_Manipulation_and_
Communication_-_Manipulation_as_an_Anti-Communicative_Act
(archived at https://perma.cc/3M4C-T9QR)

7 H Price and T Beal. Secret papers reveal Post Office knew its court defence was
false, *BBC News*, 28 March 2024, www.bbc.co.uk/news/uk-68663750
(archived at https://perma.cc/TWJ3-NV4Y)

8 Iresearch.net. Spin doctor, https://communication.iresearchnet.com/political-
communication/spin-doctor/ (archived at https://perma.cc/ZK55-P9UZ)

9 B Watson. The troubling evolution of corporate greenwashing, *The Guardian*,
20 August 2016, www.theguardian.com/sustainable-business/2016/aug/20/
greenwashing-environmentalism-lies-companies (archived at https://perma.cc/
XQ2N-BTEJ)

10 I Garnelo-Gomez. Green to pink to blue: companies' dirty washing, *Henley
Business School*, 18 March 2022, www.henley.ac.uk/news/2022/green-to-pink-
to-blue-companies-dirty-washing (archived at https://perma.cc/3GP9-E563)

11 Intellectual Property Office. Non-disclosure agreements, Gov.uk, 12 March
2015, www.gov.uk/government/publications/non-disclosure-agreements/
non-disclosure-agreements (archived at https://perma.cc/CAH6-4G2R)

12 UK Research and Innovation. Conflicts of interests, 11 September 2023,
www.ukri.org/who-we-are/how-we-are-governed/conflicts-of-interests/
(archived at https://perma.cc/HBC4-3TTX)

13 M Conrad. What is gaslighting? Examples and how to deal with it, *Forbes*,
20 February 2024, www.forbes.com/health/mind/what-is-gaslighting/ (archived
at https://perma.cc/U9P9-Z5KF)

14 J Lartey. United Airlines passenger violently dragged from seat on overbooked
flight, *The Guardian*, 11 April 2017, www.theguardian.com/us-news/2017/
apr/10/united-airlines-video-passenger-removed-overbooked-flight (archived at
https://perma.cc/5LRS-6X79)

15 WGU. Ethical dilemmas: How scandals damage companies, 2 March 2021,
www.wgu.edu/blog/ethical-dilemmas-how-scandals-damage-companies1909.
html (archived at https://perma.cc/HU7T-GCKT)

16 M Sweney (2017) Bell Pottinger expelled from PR trade body after South
Africa racism row, *The Guardian*, 4 September 2017, www.theguardian.com/
business/2017/sep/04/bell-pottinger-expelled-from-pr-trade-body-after-south-
africa-racism-row (archived at https://perma.cc/Z6MP-K85Y)

17 Government Communication Service. Strategic communications: A behavioural approach, nd, https://gcs.civilservice.gov.uk/wp-content/
uploads/2020/03/Strategic-Communications-a-behavioural-approach.pdf
(archived at https://perma.cc/5455-NDGR)

18 Gov.uk. Whistleblowing for employees, nd, www.gov.uk/whistleblowing
(archived at https://perma.cc/2M8Q-YCNT)

19 US Department of Justice Office of the Inspector General. Whistleblower rights and protections, nd, https://oig.justice.gov/hotline/whistleblower-protection (archived at https://perma.cc/L7UV-5X6B)

20 J Bryson and A Lindsay. Hillsborough Law decision an insult, says victim's sister, *BBC News*, 6 December 2023, www.bbc.co.uk/news/uk-england-mersey-side-67634856 (archived at https://perma.cc/PMV2-CM9L)

21 CIPR Ethical Decision Tree, nd, https://cipr.co.uk/CIPR/CIPR/Our_work/Policy/Ethics.aspx (archived at https://perma.cc/5TV9-79JJ)

22 A Coleman (2022) *Everyday Communication Strategies: Manage common issues to prevent a crisis and protect your brand*, Kogan Page, London

23 C Hauser. How the Ohio train derailment and its aftermath unfolded, *New York Times*, 23 June 2023, www.nytimes.com/article/ohio-train-derailment-timeline.html (archived at https://perma.cc/2FG6-MCKF)

24 National Transportation Safety Board (2023) Norfolk Southern railway train derailment with subsequent hazardous material release and fires preliminary report, 3 February 2023, www.ntsb.gov/investigations/Documents/RRD23MR005%20East%20Palestine%20OH%20Prelim.pdf (archived at https://perma.cc/JX27-RFMJ)

25 B Goodman. People in East Palestine were told their homes were clear of toxins last year. That might not have been the case, *CNN*, 9 March 2024, https://edition.cnn.com/2024/03/09/health/east-palestine-derailment-home-screening/index.html (archived at https://perma.cc/5GPE-676W)

26 J Funk and P Orsagos. A year on, a small Ohio town is recovering from a fiery train derailment but health fears persist, *AP News*, 2 February 2024, https://apnews.com/article/norfolk-southern-train-derailment-east-palestine-ohio-eab23ed0fd6577a5cf96e8fd301da681 (archived at https://perma.cc/YQ66-ZL9L)

27 S Detrow, E Ryan and T Ermyas. 'People do avoid me': How a toxic train derailment split a village in two. *NPR*, 5 February 2024, www.npr.org/2024/02/05/1228772709/east-palestine-train-derailment-norfolk-southern-lawsuit-epa (archived at https://perma.cc/PW99-S8EC)

28 Norfolk Southern website. Vision and values, nd, www.norfolksouthern.com/en/commitments/who-we-are/vision-values (archived at https://perma.cc/2NA7-57YT)

9

Post-crisis reputation recovery

Introduction

When a business has been faced with a challenge to its reputation or has suffered some reputational damage it needs to be concerned and proactive. Developing long-term plans to repair and improve the reputation, to understand what happened and to make any organizational changes is essential. There are occasions where the problem can persist over an extended period of time, as has been seen with the Post Office in the UK where a situation 20 years ago is still affecting their reputation.[1] In addition, there may be occasions where there are legacy issues that remain after the crisis has concluded. Businesses may be keen to return to normal, but in doing so fail to recognize the problems that may be lurking in the background linked to their experience.

Reputational damage can continue for a long time after the situation itself has concluded. Issues remain indefinitely on social media channels and in search engines. Perceptions of the business may have changed and rebuilding trust in both people's hearts and minds will take some time. Every crisis, damage or threat to the business provides an opportunity to learn and change. The business must address what went wrong in people's views and what the reputational monitoring and evaluation shows in relation to changing perceptions.

Further work, to move from crisis into recovery and then on into business development and any change activity, is necessary. At a basic level it is about considering the long-term impacts and any action that may be required. But for serious issues with a significant impact there needs to be proactive management, the development of a recovery communication strategy and further work on the reputation management plans and framework. The timescales for the move to recovery and beyond will need to consider the level of impact, extent of the damage, and potential for outrage or breaching societal norms. Reputation management is a key part of the drive to move the business forward, particularly after a crisis or incident.

Why recovery matters

The recovery phase is often neglected but is the moment to take stock of the situation and what has happened. Recovery is the final phase of the crisis management process that starts with preparation. Time needs to be taken to really understand what is at the heart of the issue and the areas that are affected or involved. It is also a chance to look at what changes may be required in relation to the business and how it operates to prevent a reoccurrence. After every situation there is a requirement to make some changes and identifying what these are should be the role for a recovery team. They can assess the circumstances that led to the crisis emerging and the issues that the response raised. It is important to involve external views and perspectives at this stage if they have not been part of the crisis response. How are people viewing the business and its response? Do they see it as having brought a satisfactory conclusion? Are people angry or frustrated at what happened or how it was addressed?

Communication is part of this but, as outlined in Chapter 1, rebuilding a reputation is about more than PR activity. PR and communication activity will be necessary going forward and this may benefit from being outlined in a specific recovery communication strategy. It is about more than throwing PR and good stories at the situation, as this will fail to address what has been at the heart of the issue and the response. Using reputation monitoring is an important part of assessing the impact and the changes to the way the business is perceived. There may also be aggravating factors and connected issues that the crisis and its response have raised.

A firm foundation for the future can be developed through the careful consideration of the incident and its effects. This phase is a further opportunity to build back trust in the business. It can help people to move forward with confidence in the business and the way it operates and to re-establish the purpose and values that are at the heart of the company.

The four Rs of recovery

The impact of a reputational crisis can last for an extended period of time and may be forever linked to the business through search engines and social media channels. This requires a considered approach to the recovery phase focusing on the four Rs – review, rebuild, resources and re-establish:[2]

- **Review**

  Understand the issues that were raised during the crisis or risk, and the level of severity linked to the situation. Be clear how many people were affected and how badly it affected them. Assess the success of the response and the approach that was taken. Any information from debriefs will also be beneficial in capturing the learning from the experience. Gather feedback from all key groups including customers, employees, stakeholders, board and trustees. Consider the key audiences identified in consideration of the key groups to the business and its reputation. Be aware of any backlash from the problem or the response that was taken. Communicators can play a key role in uncovering the relevant data and insights related to views and perceptions. But there is also other data that would assist, including business information, the level of complaints, and employee feedback and statistics. Consideration should also be given to understanding the external factors that may have had an impact on the situation, response or people's views.

- **Rebuild**

  Incidents and reputational crises do not happen in isolation. They mark a moment in time for the business, which requires an examination of what was in place or happening before the problem occurred. If the business was experiencing financial challenges, had internal staffing concerns, or needed to make changes to products and services, all these things will still exist once the crisis has concluded. They will need to be reconsidered in light of what the review of the situation has identified. In this phase it also requires a consideration of the history of the business and any previous crises or reputational problems that have happened. This information will be critical when establishing the way forward and creating a recovery plan and associated communication.

- **Resources**

  The time and effort put into the recovery phase of the crisis response will need to be quantified. Businesses need to put staff and in some cases funds in place to support the changes and activity that may be necessary. From a communication perspective it requires staff to be put in place to support the activity as well as to revise approaches to PR, marketing, advertising and other aspects of the business' promotion. If the business does not have reputation tracking in place, then funds may need to be put into being able to monitor the impact and any changes related to the activity and actions.

- **Re-establish**
  The end phase is to re-establish the business' reputation through setting appropriate plans and actions. The plan will consider the short- and longer-term areas to develop and improve. The re-establish phase is when the recovery plan should be developed taking account of the findings of the review and rebuild phases, and using the resources identified to support the plan. The recovery plan needs to have a communication plan in place covering all aspects of the promotional activity. It can support the reputation management strategy to ensure the business can move forward effectively.

How long will recovery take?

The time that it takes for the damage to be undone or the recovery to be completed will depend on a number of variables. But it is important to understand the impact the situation has had and not to rush forward in an attempt to move on from the problem. Moving too quickly will be seen as a cynical attempt to dismiss the situation and its impact. It is vital the business accepts the perceptions that have been created and left by the events that happened. This can then underpin a strong recovery addressing the problem and taking account of the changes in the views of the business.

The variables that will decide on the length of the recovery are impact, people affected, views of staff and stakeholders, level of culpability, visual legacy and the contamination within the business:

- *Impact* – identify whether the situation has had a broad impact or is contained within a certain group or area. This includes understanding the amount of interest in the situation and whether the spotlight is still placed on the business. The bigger the impact and interest, the more challenging it will be to move forward quickly.

- *People affected* – understand how many people are affected by the situation and which groups are connected to what has happened. The perceptions of groups and individuals who are important to the reputation of the business will be critical. If the numbers and groups affected has been limited the move forward will be easier.

- *Views of staff and stakeholders* – if the views of key groups are negative or they feel the business has not responded appropriately, recovery may take an extended period of time. Employees and key groups must be ready to accept the business is changing and moving forward.

- *Level of culpability* – where the business has had to accept responsibility for what has happened, the move through recovery can take longer. Until the business acknowledges its part in the situation that has occurred, it will challenge them. The reputational damage can continue, which delays the ability to move forward.

- *Visual legacy* – if the issue or problem has left a very visible representation that can be viewed by people it will take longer to recover. The images will continue to place the focus on the problem. For example, if you have damage to a building or location, or a failed advertising campaign it will keep putting the spotlight back on the crisis.

- *Contamination within the business* – if the situation affects the whole business, then the impact is broader, and the recovery time will potentially be longer. If it only affects a division or department, then unless it is a fundamental element of the purpose of the business, the steps to recovery may be quicker.

All these factors will dictate the pace of the recovery and the amount of change that may be required following the crisis. Some situations are so serious and have such a significant impact that the recovery from them for a brand can take decades or even require generational change. In those situations it is important to have an embedded long-term recovery plan that considers organizational change and reputation management. It will be crucial to ensure that new staff joining the business are clear about what happened, the impact and the ongoing plans for recovery. This will support the future developments within the business and ensure the knowledge and experience is not lost when staff leave. Long-term crises and recovery that takes time can attract media attention or even documentaries to consider the situation and its impact over time. Communicators and senior leaders need to be prepared for the continued interest in the business and the issue and should ensure it features in the recovery plans.

Crises, issues and critical situations do not neatly happen one at a time, and it is very possible that the business could face a further problem while already managing a reputational challenge. It is important to remain vigilant to any further problem, even while dealing with a critical issue. If the second problem is serious it may require a joint and revised response and communication plan. When there is additional pressure on a business' reputation it should not be dealt with in isolation as both issues will have the potential to impact on people's perceptions.

Recovery short-term actions

Where the reputational damage and crisis are short lived or a single issue it may be easy to contain it and prevent further spread. There will still need to be some short-term actions taken to ensure that the business can move forward and rebuild its reputation:

1 **Consider immediate threats and risks**
   After a problem has emerged and been addressed, there are still issues that may remain as a further threat to the reputation. These should be added to the risk management processes to ensure that they can be spotted at an early stage. In many situations where problems have occurred, the public, media and stakeholders will be keeping a close eye on whether they re-emerge in the future.

2 **Take some positive action**
   After every crisis and reputational challenge there will be aspects of the business and communication approach that need to change. This should be seen as a positive opportunity to boost the business and to transform where it is needed to increase resilience for the future.

3 **Review against the four As of issues management**
   The four As of issues management are: assess, analyse, articulate and act. When a problem has concluded, and the business is moving to recovery, take a moment to reflect on what happened and the actions that were taken against the four elements. Use it to consider what further activity may be required both operationally and in the communication from the business.

4 Offer support to staff

Incidents do not need to be life threatening for them to have a significant impact on the employees who have to respond to them. Staff can be exhausted by what has happened and when the business is being heavily criticized on social media and in the media, it can affect them. The CEO is key to supporting staff by being visible and ensuring they feel valued.

5 Alert stakeholders to the next steps

In an effective response to a reputational challenge stakeholders will have received information quickly, and frequently. They remain a critical audience to keep connected to into recovery and beyond. Ensure that plans are in place and that they feature in any recovery communication plan. Stakeholders need to understand and be supportive of the next steps that will be taken.

6 Keep the situation under review

Monitoring and reputation tracking should be in place all the time. But when a problem has occurred and been managed it is vital to keep a close watch on people's views and perceptions of the business. If there is starting to be chatter on social media about the business and its operation this should trigger the escalation plan and a consideration of taking some form of action. The same is the case if there is a noticeable reduction in the reputation of the business.

7 Establish a recovery plan and escalation plan for any recurrence

Co-ordinating and managing the recovery phase after a reputational crisis is critical. This requires a recovery plan to be in place together with an escalation plan that details further actions that may need to be taken, as outlined at point six. This work can drive any change that is required, and this includes to revise and update communication, advertising and marketing.

The key in the short term after a reputational crisis is to be ready to respond and move back into response mode, as necessary. Monitoring, evaluation, acting and pulling this together into a plan for the whole business is the key to moving forward.

Recovery long-term actions

The impact of a reputational crisis can take a long time to recover from and this means considering the long-term actions that are needed as well as short-term monitoring for any reappearance, as has been outlined. A crisis will have learning attached to it, which is why media statements often talk about learning the lessons. The phrase has come to have little meaning and is often viewed very cynically by the public who question whether anything is changing. This makes showing change the priority in the long-term recovery phase. Showing how the business is changing and developing. Showing how structures, products and services have been analysed and amended. Showing that the business has listened to what has happened, and people's views. To maintain or rebuild trust and confidence, the business needs to make changes and talk about them so people can see what is happening. Moving forward and trying to avoid referencing the situation that occurred will add to the damage and can block the ability to move forward. There are substantial long-term actions that should be considered:

1 **Recognize the need to make changes**
   The CEO and C-suite have to recognize the need to take long-term action to be able to rebuild the reputation and move forward. Without this activity it will be left to chance whether the problem re-emerges, or the reputation is rebuilt. In the same way, a crisis must be identified before it can be adequately addressed so must the need to change in the aftermath for effective recovery.

2 **Review the structure, governance systems, policies and processes – possibly even the purpose and values**
   The fact the problem occurred or that people had a negative perception of the business shows that something went wrong. If the business is going to move forward and build a strong recovery, then it needs to be clear what works and what needs to be changed. This starts with considering the structure and how the business works across all departments and teams. It must then consider the governance that is in place on a day-to-day basis and if that is effective. Policies and processes connected to the part of the business that has been at the centre of the crisis must also be reviewed. In the worst cases where the reputation has been severely impacted, the business may have to go back to look at its purpose and values. If those are damaging to the reputation or have been viewed as a problem, either by the public or by staff, they may need to be revised and updated.

3 **Develop a comprehensive recovery plan involving organizational change**
   Once the short-term issues have been considered and reviewed there

is a need to develop a longer-term recovery plan that grasps the organizational change that may be needed. If there has been a failure in the governance, then it requires a review to replace and update the governance system. If there has been criticism of the business' culture and the behaviour of staff, it needs a plan to address the issues and ensure there are clear expectations that people are adhering to.

4 Consider if the right people are involved in the recovery

The employees that are involved in the crisis response may not be the right people to be part of the recovery process. They may lack the skills and experiences necessary to move the business forward through the change process. They may also have been severely impacted by their time as part of the response and need to be given time to recover. Staff can also get so invested in the situation that they struggle to be able to make objective decisions. Have the right skills and experiences that come together to lead the recovery and change work.

5 Review the branding, marketing and communication assets

Once the purpose and values have been reconsidered then the branding needs to be reviewed taking account of any changes. Does the brand reflect those values and are there any elements of it that feel out of touch given the situation that occurred? The same review needs to take place of marketing and communication assets to be clear that they are supporting the revised business. If this does not change to reflect what is happening within the business, it can have a further detrimental impact on reputation. People will see a mismatch between what the business is doing and what it is saying, and this must be avoided.

6 Keep the situation under long-term monitoring for legacy issues

Short-term monitoring is important to consider whether there is any immediate recurrence of the problem. But the same monitoring has to be in place to ensure that the legacy issues can be identified quickly if they appear. The legacy can be those impressions or perceptions that have become entrenched due to the circumstances of what has happened. The perceptions can be of the business, its operation, the staff or how it manages challenging situations.

7 Refocus and develop the reputation management plan and risks and issues management

Part of the long-term recovery is about bolstering the approach to risks and issues management. Developing systems and processes that have been redesigned based on the experiences will build future resilience. The recovery communication will be replaced at some point with the reputation management plan and process including communication. It will involve the whole business, as outlined in Chapter 2.

8 Develop training and support to staff
Consider what has happened and the details of why it occurred. It may become obvious that staff training is needed. There may have been a requirement to improve the customer service experience, or to change the product development processes, and all these need to be supported with adequate training. Even if formal training is not needed there may be a requirement for updated guidance or other systems to support staff.

9 Redefine the relationships with stakeholders, boards and trustees
The board and trustees connected to a business may have specific requirements and actions that they want to see from the management of the business. Often these may relate to the governance and other systems and processes that may need to be revised and improved. Where there has been a loss of trust from boards and trustees the relationship may need to be redefined. The same may be required for other stakeholder relationships that have been impacted by the situation and the aftermath.

10 Put well-being support in place to support change and any staffing impact from issues
Employees need to be supported through any business changes that are being planned. People can fear change and may also be affected by any potential criticism felt in relation to the plans for the future. Taking care and being sensitive to the views of staff is important and where possible they should be involved in implementing the changes.

Any significant reputational crisis needs to be grasped with changes and future developments emerging from the learning and feedback. The business and senior leaders must avoid the attempt to move on too quickly or to try to airbrush the events out of the history of the business. Use the events to rebuild, redesign and repair the business for the long-term future. Throwing positive communication out without carefully considering the legacy issues and perceptions that have developed can be dangerous. It may create a backlash or further damage the reputation of the business. Take a moment to stop, reflect and shape the future.

Reputational crises and the importance of change

Every crisis should be followed by some form of change. It may be a change to the business operation, to the communication approach, to the way issues and incidents are managed. This is where a business can avoid a return to the situation or additional problems in the future. Using debriefing of staff will help to identify what changes need to be made. Debriefing should be based around what worked, what did not work and what would be done differently. This should involve all the teams involved in the response who should provide input from their perspective. The crisis and issues management process should have a structured debrief process included as part of the move to recovery and beyond.

The structure of the recovery and change activity needs to ensure that the strategy for the future has been set with supporting meetings taking place. Those involved should be held to account for whether they have implemented the required changes. A recovery communication group and meeting will help to ensure the actions align to the business development and also listen to the voices of staff. Ultimately the strategy, meetings and actions will allow the CEO, board and trustees to be confident that the situation is being taken seriously and addressed for the future.

There are five principles of change management that must be considered:

1 It needs to be focused on organizational, team and individual levels. The change needs to be clear at each stage.

2 It needs to connect the purpose to the organizational results. People need to see the part they play and how it fits within the purpose of the business.

3 It needs a planned and managed approach to the change process.

4 Leaders need to be equipped to support the change process.

5 Ongoing communication, connection and consultation are vital for effective change management.[3]

Recovery communication strategy and roadmap

After using the four Rs of recovery that were outlined earlier in this chapter, what comes next? From a communication perspective having a clear recovery communication strategy and roadmap is essential. It should be developed by carefully considering all the information that is available, but it should include as a starting point: the purpose of the plan, organization and communication objectives, details of the priorities, key audiences, narrative, stakeholder engagement, employee actions, communication actions, timescales linked to an organizational roadmap, critical success factors, budget and evaluation.

The recovery communication strategy is a positive step that allows the business to be clear about the activity that is being planned. It can avoid conflict with those developing the recovery activity and ensure that misinformation and disinformation can be addressed. For those reading it there will be clear continuity from the crisis communication strategy and plans:

- **Purpose and approach**
  Consider what the plan is trying to achieve, and how it links to the current, and possibly reviewed, purpose and values of the business. Be clear how the communication will support the purpose and embed the changes that may have been made. Refer to the definition of what is important to the reputation of the business to help in defining the purpose. In this section, detail the principles of the recovery communication and the approach that the business is going to take. This may be to prioritize direct communication to customers or to ensure honesty and transparency in the future communication.

- **Organization and communication objectives**
  Detail the organizational objectives and any revisions that make it clear what the goals are for the business. Alongside this identify the recovery communication objectives and show how they are directly supporting the business objectives.

- **Priorities**
  Use the information from the review and any additional research to detail the priority actions. It may be customer service, staffing, or product development, but whatever the most important activities to be undertaken are, outline them. This may benefit from a phased approach with phase one as critical. The focus must always be on supporting those who may still be affected by what has happened as well as rebuilding and supporting the positive reputation of the business.

- **Audiences**
  Outline the audiences that will be the focus of the activity and group them into those directly affected and others. Use any mapping that has been

carried out during the crisis to support the development of the recovery communication activity. But be aware that there may have been changes to those impacted during the crisis so ensure the mapping is updated.

- **Narrative**

  Have a section detailing the clear narrative about what the business wants from the future and how it wants to be viewed. This should be developed from the issues that have emerged during the crisis. Perceptions that developed or the misinformation and disinformation that caused concerns can be addressed through this section. The narrative should be three to four paragraphs that explain where the business is and where it wants to be.

- **Stakeholder engagement**

  Detail who the key stakeholders are for the recovery communication and have an engagement plan that considers who will be contacting them and how frequently. This builds from the activity undertaken during the crisis but can address any concerns or issues that emerged during the response.

- **Employee engagement**

  In the recovery communication strategy this should be focused on helping employees move forward and understand what the business is doing as part of the recovery. It can start to explain the change management processes and other steps that may be put in place to address the situation. It should also outline how staff will continue to be made aware of well-being and welfare support that they may need going forward.

- **Communication actions**

  In this section provide details of the actions that will be taken to communicate about the business. What channels are going to be critical moving forward? How will media relationships be managed? Will social media be a part of the recovery and which platforms are a priority? Does the SEO need to be amended and how will advertising and marketing be undertaken? This can consider who will lead on what actions and particularly where it may be the responsibility of another department or team.

- **Timescales**

  The recovery will need to be developed over an appropriate period of time which can be dictated by the impact the crisis has had or on the time taken to make some of the business changes. The change process should have a clear organizational or business roadmap that has the actions and when it will be introduced. This helps to link and develop the change in phases, so it is easier for people to understand. The communication strategy needs to use this roadmap to develop a communication roadmap that supports the introduction of any changes.

- **Critical success factors**

    Be clear in this section what problems may derail or create a setback to the communication strategy. It could be a re-emergence of the crisis or a new problem emerging that can limit the steps that can be taken to rebuild the business. This section needs to assess the risks and issues that could relate to the recovery communication.

- **Budget**

    Effective recovery communication will need resources to support activities and to allocate staff to the work. This needs to be clearly identified so those involved in other aspects of the recovery do not assume that it can be managed within the existing communication budget or resources. If additional staff are needed make it clear within this section, as well as if money needs to be spent on consultation, focus groups or reputation tracking software.

- **Evaluation**

    Using the AMEC integrated evaluation framework[4] ensures the communication activity is evaluated to understand what works and where changes may need to be made. The recovery communication strategy may have to cover a 6-to-12-month period, so it is important that changes are made if the evaluation shows that the business' reputation is not improving. The actions taken may need to be updated. The outcomes and organizational impact are critical to rebuilding the reputation.

A recovery communication strategy can help the business understand what is happening and what is being done. It is also important where there are regulators or others who will be scrutinizing the business' response to the situation that has emerged and holding them to account for changes that need to be made. The recovery communication strategy is not just for any PR and communication team, it has to be a key part of the business' approach to recovery.

Structures for the future

Moving forward after recovery there needs to be a review of the approach to the business' reputation management. If it was not adequately addressed before the crisis, it needs to be put in place for the future. The following areas need to be revised or be put in place:

1 *Reputation monitoring* – ensure systems and structures are in place to track the business' reputation and provide an early warning to any further problems or recurrence of previous issues. Consider where the business wants to be against any competitors for both business development and reputation.

2 *Reputational risk management* – put reputational problems into the risk management process. This means the PR and communication team involvement in identification and highlighting potential problems and threats before anything happens.

3 *Staff training on vision and reputation* – staff need to understand the importance of living and demonstrating the values of the business. This may require additional training on key areas to ensure the business has the culture that supports where it wants to be. It should consider behaviours as well as expectations.

4 *Reputation crisis management and planning* – crisis planning, and approaches should include reputational crises. Plans should be universal and ready to be used for operational and reputational crises. Exercises and crisis simulations should include reputational elements or be solely focused on a reputational problem.

5 *Leadership training on reputation* – senior leaders need to understand what is required of them in supporting the development of a positive reputation for the business. This is both on a personal and professional level. As the boundaries have become blurred with remote working post-Covid, what people do outside of work can be a reputational threat to the business. A CEO that is found to have behaved inappropriately or has spoken negatively in some way outside of work can still have an impact on how both they and the business they lead is viewed. This should be considered in training and any communication.

6 *External consultation* – being able to access the views of customers and others outside the business will help to provide details of views and perceptions. It can help the business to make changes at an earlier stage and prevent an issue developing into a crisis.

Recovery checklists

Staff, including communication staff, may be exhausted by managing the crisis so checklists can assist in ensuring that key aspects of the recovery are not overlooked. There is a checklist provided for both the communication approach and the wider business approach to recovering from a reputational crisis.

Communication/PR checklist

- Review and evaluate the crisis communication activity and identify feedback, risks and areas of concern.
- Put reputation monitoring in place or ensure close assessment of the media and social media activity.
- Conduct a severity assessment to assess where the biggest impact is and on which audiences or stakeholders.
- Be clear on the objectives and how they will be evaluated.
- Create a structure for the recovery communication response which sits within the wider business response structure.
- Put an escalation plan in place that details when additional communication and PR actions may be required.
- Put stakeholder mapping in place and have a stakeholder management plan.
- Consider consultation with key groups to assess the impact and inform the future plans. This should include building staff engagement and involvement.
- Ensure adequate staffing is put in place and bring in additional specialist support, as necessary.
- Share the plan with the recovery team and C-suite to ensure they are aware of their requirements and the actions that are being taken.

Business recovery checklist

- Review the business values and purpose and ensure they are appropriate.
- Develop a recovery strategy that details the actions required and who will be responsible for them.

- Create a response structure that will bring key departments and teams together in a co-ordinated way. This may use the Gold, Silver and Bronze approach.

- Ensure leaders have been visible to the workforce, both those that have been involved in the response and those keeping the business functioning.

- Discuss approach and planning with regulators, board and trustees.

- Assess what policies and procedures may need to be amended in light of the impact.

- Conduct a business severity assessment to understand the nature of the impact and how serious it is. This should involve reputation management and tracking data.

- Define the change process and what actions are needed in the long term.

- Ensure well-being support is still in place for anyone affected.

TOP TIPS FOR TRACKING REPUTATION IN THE FUTURE

Every business will potentially face reputational threats at some point during its operation. The scale of these may vary and steps can be taken to identify problems at an early stage to act and avoid deterioration. Below are some tips for tracking and managing the reputation in the future:

- Understand what matters to the business' reputation. The purpose of the business and what it wants to achieve needs clarity. This can then underpin the reputation management framework and approach.

- Recognize the triggers that can prompt outrage or negative feedback. Where situations have emerged in the past, be clear what led to the problem developing. The business' operation may have sensitive areas or activities that are more likely to be seen as controversial.

- Continue to monitor views and perceptions. This should be undertaken on a regular basis to help the understanding of how people feel towards the business and to drive the communication and business development activity.

- Act early to step in and prevent issues becoming crises. Ensure that communication is ready to respond to deal with problems swiftly and that the business can step in and support. Use an escalation plan to recognize when action needs to be taken and when communication needs to be in place.

- Use focus groups internally and externally to review plans before implementation. As part of efforts to prevent problems emerging, ensure staff can raise concerns about issues and developments before they are implemented. Similarly, use external focus groups to assess views of the business, marketing and advertising, and other key areas of the operation.

- Continue to review and evaluate the communication approach and activity. The PR and communication activity should be continually evaluated to know what is and is not working. This can support the reputation management approach.

- Develop the use of artificial intelligence to support the tracking processes. The developments in artificial intelligence should be monitored to identify ways of evaluating the data and insight.

- Monitor recruitment and staff retention information. The reputation of the business may be under threat if recruiting new employees becomes challenging or if staff are not remaining within the business. Use this data to support the development of the reputation management strategy.

- Assess the market share and profitability of the business. The financial details about the business and its operation are crucial to being able to assess any emerging reputational challenge. Know the market, the market share and the profitability of the business so any threats are identified early.

- Understand the sector issues and potential changes in the future. Horizon scanning is an important part of the reputation management process. Being aware of reputational crises involving competitors can be an early warning to a wider industry issue. And monitor for new regulation or sector changes that may need to be proactively managed.

- Be aware of the longevity of crises and issues that have affected the business. As has been seen with Covid-19 and its legacy, and the Post Office Horizon IT scandal, reputational challenges can remain for a long time. Build response and recovery plans that will support the business for the full length of the crisis.

- Ensure the details of ongoing issues are understood if they are long running. Keep educating staff about issues and the responses that are required. If they have not been involved or are new, they may not understand the complexities and details of what has happened and how the response has been developed.

- Build resilience through education and training. Reputation management can feel like an alien concept for some within the business. Make it easy to understand and relevant to staff so that they can maintain a positive reputation and be ready to respond when a problem emerges.

CASE STUDY
Capita cyberattack

Background

On 31 March 2023, Capita plc highlighted a cyber incident that was part of a ransomware attack affecting software and which led to the personal data of staff working for the company and many of its clients being hacked. The clients involved included local authorities, the military and the NHS. Capita is one of the UK's largest pension scheme administrators, which put the personal data of a large number of people in the schemes at risk.

The business explained that specialist advisers and forensic experts were used to investigate what had happened. In the communication it talked about Capita itself interrupting the attack and therefore limiting the damage caused.[5] It highlighted that data had been taken from less than 0.1 per cent of the server estate.[6] Capita explained it had been working to recover the data and through regulatory authorities, notify affected people. The cost to the business was anticipated as being between £15 million and £20 million but was then increased to as much as £25 million.[7] Despite the business highlighting that trading performance remained as expected, it was reported to have a pre-tax loss of £68 million for the first half of the year.[8]

In a report almost a year later the Pensions Regulator said the case demonstrated the importance of preventative measures being in place and having robust cybersecurity plans.[9] There was a requirement on that framework to include roles, responsibilities, processes, systems and to have exercises that have tested the plans. It also included recognizing the risks involved.[10]

Reputation lessons

There was a recognized complexity about the information and the situation which created difficulties in the explanation and also the delivery of communication. Clients and pension trustees had the responsibility of communicating to those affected. This was in addition to information that Capita published. The Pension Regulator identified that although messaging was agreed with Capita and shared, some trustees developed their own communication, which created delays.[11]

A significant challenge for Capita was the concern about the operation that had been in place before the cyberattack and what protections there were. Many people received letters to warn them that their data may have been compromised through letters circulated by trustees. There was a contact number circulated for people who had issues to raise but this was problematic to access. Those affected were encouraged to be aware of potentially fraudulent activity and to remain alert. This put the responsibility onto those affected.

- Understand the structures and situations that are in place and may impact on the response to a crisis.
- Providing details of the 0.1 per cent affected could be perceived as an attempt to minimize the impact of the cyberattack and downplay the severity.
- Develop communication that is clear and can make a complex situation simple to grasp. This is particularly important when those affected may need to act or protect themselves.
- Explain what has changed and how things would be improved in the future. This would include a response from Capita to the Pensions Regulator report.
- Other pensions operators and those holding data on behalf of others needed to provide reassurance about how prepared they are for a cyberattack and the protections in place to manage personal data.
- Any further cyber incident or data breach involving Capita would spark further and possibly intensified criticism of the business operation. Changes and long-term developments were necessary in light of the significant impact the situation had.

Conclusion

Recovery after a reputational crisis is a critical piece in the jigsaw. It can address any outstanding areas of concern and build resilience for the future. But it requires a business to recognize it is a key phase of the crisis response and management. It also needs senior leaders to be ready to review and develop the way the business operates, taking on board the feedback and learning from the situation that has been faced. Recovery is a whole business approach and requires the same structures and strategies to be in place that are used during the crisis itself.

Communication is an important part of the recovery phase but must be in support of business changes and developments. In that situation a recovery communication strategy and roadmap can be a key part of the move to rebuild the reputation. This strategy has to be documented and clearly explained to the business so that resources and support are available to make it happen. This is an opportunity to address concerns and make changes that will improve the business and how it is perceived.

Ultimately, the recovery phase of any crisis should become a change management process. It becomes part of business development and operational improvements. This also needs support from communication to reconnect people to the purpose and vision or connect them to a new purpose and vision. Even when a business has been reputationally damaged during a crisis there remains an opportunity to rebuild and re-establish through the recovery and, then, change phase.

References

1 Post Office Horizon IT Inquiry, nd, www.postofficehorizoninquiry.org.uk/ (archived at https://perma.cc/K6F7-L67J)

2 A Coleman (2023) *Crisis Communication Strategies: Prepare, respond and recover effectively in unpredictable and urgent situations*, 2nd edition, Kogan Page, London

3 W Heckleman. Five critical principles to guide organisational change, *OD Practitioner*, 2017, 49, (4), https://wlhconsulting.com/wp-content/ uploads/2018/11/ODP-Five-Critical-Principles-to-Guide-Organizational-Change.pdf (archived at https://perma.cc/VT29-AHED)

4 AMEC. AMEC Integrated Evaluation Framework, https://amecorg.com/ amecframework/ (archived at https://perma.cc/B3V6-FXS6)

5 Capita. Update on actions taken to resolve the cyber incident, 10 May 2023, www.capita.com/news/update-actions-taken-resolve-cyber-incident (archived at https://perma.cc/2U4B-66RS)

6 Capita. Update on actions taken to resolve the cyber incident, 10 May 2023, www.capita.com/news/update-actions-taken-resolve-cyber-incident (archived at https://perma.cc/2U4B-66RS)

7 J Partridge. Cyber-attack to cost outsourcing firm Capita up to £25m, *The Guardian*, 4 August 2023, www.theguardian.com/business/2023/aug/04/

cyber-attack-to-cost-outsourcing-firm-capita-up-to-25m (archived at
https://perma.cc/PW7P-9HEF)

8 J Partridge. Cyber-attack to cost outsourcing firm Capita up to £25m,
   The Guardian, 4 August 2023, www.theguardian.com/business/2023/aug/04/
   cyber-attack-to-cost-outsourcing-firm-capita-up-to-25m (archived at
   https://perma.cc/PW7P-9HEF)

9 The Pensions Regulator. Capita cyber security incident – Regulatory intervention report, 2 February 2024, www.thepensionsregulator.gov.uk/en/
   document-library/enforcement-activity/regulatory-intervention-reports/
   capita-cyber-security-incident-regulatory-intervention-report (archived at
   https://perma.cc/38GZ-PLY8)

10 The Pensions Regulator. Capita cyber security incident – Regulatory intervention report, 2 February 2024, www.thepensionsregulator.gov.uk/en/
   document-library/enforcement-activity/regulatory-intervention-reports/
   capita-cyber-security-incident-regulatory-intervention-report (archived at
   https://perma.cc/38GZ-PLY8)

11 The Pensions Regulator. Capita cyber security incident – Regulatory intervention report, 2 February 2024, www.thepensionsregulator.gov.uk/en/
   document-library/enforcement-activity/regulatory-intervention-reports/
   capita-cyber-security-incident-regulatory-intervention-report (archived at
   https://perma.cc/38GZ-PLY8)

10

The future of
reputation management

Introduction

In a world of social media, fake news, instant updates and 24-hour news, reputation management remains an essential element of running any business. It is about really understanding the impact that the business has on people through how it operates, what it produces and how it communicates. Communication and PR is important, but it is only part of what matters to reputation management. It is about what the business does as well as what it says about itself. Ultimately, reputation is a strategic business issue that needs to be discussed, developed and managed across all parts of the business. Managing reputation is better described, as James E Grunig does in Chapter 1, as influencing reputation.

Every business needs to have a reputation management or influencing process in place and a plan for how it will be addressed. In a world where perceptions are people's reality and there is a challenge to engage and build trust, being prepared to build and maintain a reputation is a strand of business activity. Underpinning this work is a reputation plan that can outline the framework for the approach, the principles involved and the actions to put in place. This can be done with the support of a reputation management toolkit that will be outlined later in this chapter.

The development of reputation as a part of the business and one that matters to everyone needs to be shared with everyone. Awareness and an understanding of the issue and how they can make a difference in relation to it must be put in place with employees. Staff may need to be educated about why it matters and the impact a positive reputation can have on the development and security of the business. Reputation needs to be included in all training sessions so that employees can see how it relates to what they do. Whether they are a product developer, are involved in making or packing products, or are part of customer services, what they do can have a positive or negative impact on reputation. As well as recognizing this they need to understand what is in it for them if the business develops and maintains a positive reputation. This could be reward, recognition or simply having more job security. Explaining the situation with tangible and relatable examples and information will help to connect the whole workforce to reputation management.

Communication and PR has a key role to play in the management of a business' reputation. They can help to amplify the positive messages and actions and can minimize the damage from negative events and actions. But they should not be the driving force. Instead, they are the influencers within the business helping to connect everyone with building positive views of the business. The management team and the CEO need to be steering the business in the way it approaches reputation management. Operational competence is not enough in a world of image management, perceptions, reviews, influencers and media scrutiny.

The approach to reputation management and the structures relating to it need to be in place prior to any risks, threats or issues being identified. This will put the business in a strong position to recognize problems early and take steps to address them before they can develop into full-blown reputational crises. Putting the framework in place will also allow a business to respond quickly when a crisis has happened, working to limit the impact and spread of the problem. But it needs a different approach and view of business competence and management to be in place. It is not just about having a great product or service, nor is it about being profitable. It is recognizing that the way people view and consider the business is as important as sales figures, investment and profitability.

Reputation as a part of business resilience

Building a positive reputation is part of creating a resilient business that will be in a strong position to withstand the issues, threats and crises that may occur. This elevates reputation management or influence from the realms of PR and communication and places it as a strategic business function. Having a framework for the management of reputation across the business is a critical development. Communication and PR needs to be invested to be able to support the activity and take the opportunities that exist to build and maintain the public face of the business. The resilience comes in creating a culture and approach that accepts and works to understand and manage risk rather than avoid it completely. The brave business that takes action to develop alongside building a strong reputation will be in a strong position to face the inevitable challenges that will arrive. Businesses that try to remain under the radar and that take a risk-averse response to issues and threats can face more severe damage as they struggle to develop a convincing approach.

A business that is able to develop with systems, processes and policies that consider reputation will be in a robust position. When there is work to create positive perceptions of the business it can help create goodwill that supports the management and then recovery from crises. The bounce back from whatever has happened or from negative views of the business will be potentially swifter and stronger when there is a background of support. It may be viewed as a short-term blip which goes against the broadly positive narrative and activity around the business. Where there is a resilient business, it also supports the creation of team and individual staff resilience. They can see the robust position and have more confidence in the response and the strategic direction of the business. For example, the earlier case study that considered policing in the UK (Chapter 1) has seen a deteriorating reputation and reduction in public trust according to IPSOS MORI's Trust Veracity Index 2023. This has a further impact on the morale of officers, which has led to a survey finding 91 per cent of officers that replied felt morale within the police was low or very low.[1] The lack of reputation management and a consistent approach has left little resilience for the police forces, and this has impacted on officers.

The resilience needs to be built with an ethical approach to reputation as outlined in Chapter 8. It is vital that there is an honesty and integrity to the actions that are developed and implemented. A reputation that is built using unethical approaches of manipulation, greenwashing or other washing or propaganda will be on shaky foundations. All the activity has to be rooted in an ethical operation of both the business and the communication. It supports the resilience of the activity. Resilience comes from a positive reputation that will buy the business some time to allow a full and comprehensive response to manage the issues, threat or crisis.

Principles for trust

There are 10 principles that help to build trust and in turn to support the development of a positive reputation. Remember that these principles are important elements to underpin the operation of the business on a day-to-day basis. They are not to be put in place purely to manage a problem or risk. The principles will link to the business' values and how it defines its purpose. There are strong connections between the 10 principles for building trust and the principles that underpin the management of a crisis.[2] It is when a crisis happens that the reputation of the business is at the most risk and put under the most significant pressure. This is the time when trust and confidence in the response and the management of the issue is essential. The 10 principles for trust are:

1 **Honesty**
   Trust can only flourish where there is an acceptance of what is said and done by the business. People must be comfortable that they are being told the truth and that the business has an integrity in their operation.

2 **Openness**
   Being proactive with the activity and communication so that people are able to connect with the business is vital. People need to feel they have access to the business and to those leading the business. This can be through opening up communication channels and ensuring there is visibility of the business.

3 **Transparency**
   Withholding information without a clear and understandable reason will damage trust in the business. People need to have access to information that they trust, and this can only be achieved if a business works to be transparent about how it operates, what it does and how it responds to problems.

4 **Responsibility**
   A business needs to demonstrate how seriously it takes the operational activity, the way it develops, the support to employees and how it acts with a focus on the best possible outcome. In the post-Covid world it requires a focus on being a responsible employer, a responsible and ethical business and sustainability. Such elements are the societal focus and may change or develop in the future.

5 Accountability

When the business has done something wrong, or a process or situation has failed, or there is a negative development, it has to accept where it is culpable. This means it may need to apologize, to provide recompense, to repair damage that it has caused. Failing to do this will lead to considerable damage to trust and ultimately will damage the reputation of the business.

6 Proactivity

The development of trust between an individual and a business requires a level of proactivity in both the actions and the communication. A business that is reactive in its communication will struggle to build trust as it is blown from crisis to crisis and problem to problem. It is important to put energy and effort into creating a reputation management framework that allows for proactivity on a daily basis.

7 Empathy

A business that fails to take account of people's concerns and challenges and that does not respond with humanity will struggle to connect effectively with people. Where there is a trust deficit, as exists in 2024, businesses need to demonstrate they understand and are listening to people's issues, comments and concerns.

8 Responsiveness

Trust requires a business to be able to act quickly to remedy any problem and take action to minimize any concerns. A business needs to be able to change in response to what customers and employees are saying, and in relation to external developments that impact on the business and its sector.

9 Humility

A business can only develop when it and those in senior positions are humble enough to accept that they do not have all the answers. They need to take the views of others and use them to build a strong and resilient business. Trust can be created where a business does not act with superiority.

10 Authenticity

All the actions, comments and the behaviour of the business need to be undertaken with a genuine approach. It needs to operate authentically and where it is in line with its purpose and values. Where the business attempts to create a fake persona purely in order to build customers or establish a position, it will be uncovered at some point and will damage its reputation. It can even become a reputational crisis in itself. Effective trust can only be built where there is a genuine relationship.

Building strength to withstand damage

There are some businesses and brands that are able to withstand the pressure that comes from incidents, events and even negative perceptions. As mentioned in Chapter 3, Amazon, Apple and Meta, parent company of Facebook, are all able to continue with negligible impact from threats and crises that may affect them. Amazon offers a simple system that is easy to use and gives customers the instant response that they desire. They are able to meet demands for purchased products to arrive within a day or two. It is easy for people to use, and their expectations are met in the majority of cases. In the case of Amazon founder Jeff Bezos, even when there was criticism of him spending substantial amounts of money to send a rocket into space while there were concerns about the working conditions of his employees, it failed to dent the operation of the business.[3] People may have been critical and highlighted the juxtaposition of the situation but there will still be significant numbers logging in to purchase products using the platform.

Apple has been one of the most recognizable brands creating the iPhone and continuing to develop products that people rush to purchase. The iPhone 15 launched in September 2023 in 40 countries around the world. It still managed to attract queues of people waiting outside stores to be among the first to buy one.[4] Fortune put Apple at the top of corporate reputation with a $2.8 trillion market share.[5] For many years it has been seen as being at the cutting edge of technological innovation and developments. This is pushing the business into a challenging situation with US authorities as they launched a landmark lawsuit against Apple claiming it has been creating a monopoly.[6] But Apple has been able to create a loyal following that continue to see the business as being at the forefront of technology making products that are able to satisfy people's expectations.

So, what can other businesses learn from these giants and are there any actions that can be taken to build protection from reputational damage? Put simply yes, there are aspects of how Amazon, Apple and others have developed that can be principles others can learn. But it is important to remember what the business is about and where the purpose lies. For Amazon, Apple, LEGO and others they are in the area of enjoyment and fun, which gives them a higher starting point on the ladder towards a positive reputation. If the business is responsible for some dry, practical aspect of life it starts from a lower position. For example, a business in drainage can build a positive reputation but has a challenging starting position.

The big robust brands have created a strong brand and a useable product that is responsive to customers' feedback and continues to innovate. This means other businesses can focus on products and services that people want and need, and then continue to invest in developing them. The aim is to be one step ahead of the market, of trends and changes in societal attitudes. This needs to be supported by internal systems and processes that capture trends and attitudes towards the product as well as responding positively and effectively to any concerns or criticism. Customer service responses and the individual experiences people have when there is a problem with the product or service has to be good. A poor response will leave a negative impression that it is more likely people will share, and now they can share it far and wide using social platforms providing reviews and leaving feedback that can remain forever.

Big brands will invest in managing the reputation through the business structure and framework but will also ensure adequately funded communication, PR and marketing functions. They recognize the importance of managing risk and responding quickly when something happens. They put effective PR as a strategic function that continues to keep them in the forefront of people's minds and relevant to modern life. Being heard and standing out against the opposition is an important part of building a robust business. Managing relationships beyond the customer but with stakeholders, shareholders, investors and others is important to avoiding conflict or concerns being raised. Stakeholder engagement needs to be in place to support the business' development.

Managing risks is a critical part of creating a strong business. This means understanding what they are and actively managing them. It can also require a risk acceptance position where risks and issues are addressed. For example, the issue of LEGO and the sustainability challenge outlined in Chapter 2. If the situation had been ignored it threatened to chip away at the reputation over time and to put the business out of sync with the societal position. Risk management has to be part of the business framework with everyone recognizing their role and responsibility to identify and highlight emerging areas of concern. This is also the case for communicators who need to be able to spot reputational risks early so the business can address them. Crisis management and response as well as business continuity are an important part of the business' systems.

A business also needs to have a clear purpose that is understood by all and that is reinforced by creating the right culture. This means having systems and processes that are aligned to the purpose as well as investing in employees. It is about more than effective internal communication and is about the right employee experience to drive engagement with the development of the product or service. Reward and recognition alongside addressing problems early can support the organizational culture. Alongside this having a strong and effective governance process which can allow the business to move quickly to respond to requirements, feedback and changes and deal robustly with organizational challenges.

The key points to being robust like the big brands are:

1 Attempt to become a valued product and service, and if possible, liked.

2 Stand above the competitors in a positive way.

3 Invest in product innovation and development to be one step ahead of others.

4 Ensure a reliable product or service coupled with excellent customer service.

5 Deal with problems early through effective issues management as well as a crisis management system ready to use when needed.

6 Address the risks, issues and concerns about the business and product or service.

7 Create the right culture with effective governance and reward and recognition to support the development.

8 Invest in reputation management across the business through training and revising policies and procedures.

9 Put effective PR, communication and marketing in place that supports the business' approach, purpose and values.

10 Bring outside voices into the business and ensure proactive listening to inform growth or maintain stability.

Toolkit for effective reputation management

The toolkit is outlined in three sections: organizational/business, staff and employees, and communication and PR. The toolkit provides details of systems and processes that can support the development of a positive reputation and the actions that may be required. Using the toolkit cannot always guarantee success but it will help to put a business on the road to developing and maintaining a more positive reputation. It may also assist in avoiding or addressing problems that emerge. Before using the toolkit, it is important to have undertaken a review to consider what currently exists and is in place. What assets does the business have? What documentation and structures exist? What is the presence both online and offline? This will assist in identifying the elements of the toolkit that may need to be implemented.

Section A – Organizational/business

1 Purpose, vision and values

The business needs to have a clear purpose that it is focused on achieving. This needs to be supported by a vision and values of both what will be done and how it will be done. It needs to drive the business plans, approach and activities. It is not enough to have a few words that are shared with staff and placed on a wall; the whole approach to the operation needs to be rooted in the purpose, vision and values. This will ensure an authenticity in what the business does. In addition, staff need to understand the purpose, vision and values and, importantly, what it means for them. Individual goals and objectives need to be connected to the broader strategy that has been developed for the business.

a Develop a purpose, vision and values in consultation with employees.

b Ensure everyone understands it and what it means for day-to-day activity.

c Root all the business developments and framework in the delivery of the purpose.

d When a challenge occurs review whether the purpose, vision and values are still relevant or if there was a problem in them and how they are used and integrated.

e Create a reputation management plan that supports the purpose and activities of the business. (See also in Section C.)

2 Risk management

A successful business needs to be alert to risks and threats so it can avoid them and put mitigation in place. Being able to identify problems quickly is critical in a world of instant news that goes global within minutes. All parts of the business need to understand the risk management framework and their responsibilities in relation to it. It also needs to be supported by a strong crisis and major incident response plan. The risks that are considered need to include the reputational threats that can be highlighted by any part of the business. The communication and PR team need to be involved in risk management so it can inform their activity.

a   Create a risk management system that includes a risk register with a plan and meeting structure.

b   Ensure that everyone is involved in risk management and knows what to do when issues are identified.

c   Develop a communication and PR potential critical incidents list that can be considered within the risk meetings.

d   Keep the risk management updated so that new and emerging threats both from within the business and outside are identified with mitigation or management put in place.

3 Training plan

Effective reputation management needs to be supported by appropriate training for staff at all levels within the business. This means from the CEO and C-suite right through to frontline staff. Training on reputation can be included in other courses and sessions so that it becomes a recognizable thread through the business. But employees do need to have training in risk management and responding to crises that may occur. Training is not just about telling people what they need to do but why they need to do it to secure the future of the business or brand.

a   Review existing training and identify opportunities for reputation management to be included.

b   Ensure training reflects the purpose, vision and values of the business.

c   Provide training on risk identification and management, and crisis response. This should include exercises that test the plans and approach both in relation to an operational problem and reputational issues.

4 Consultation and feedback

Establishing feedback loops both within the business and with customers and stakeholders outside is critical. This helps to understand where problems may be emerging, and changes may be necessary. It also prevents complaints developing unchecked. This can be achieved by developing a customer feedback panel or staff network that is used on a regular basis. These established groups can also help when a crisis occurs by providing immediate feedback on the impact of what has happened on the business' reputation. If a business loses the connection to its customers/service users or staff, it may be ignoring vital information to keep it at the forefront of its sector.

a Establish a staff engagement panel where employees can give feedback on developments, approaches and actions.

b Create an external customer panel to provide insight into the views of those using the product or service.

c Gather data on customer service, complaint levels and the issues that are being raised.

d Use the data and insight to support the business' development both in operational activity and the PR and communication approach.

5 Cultural intelligence

Creating the right culture within the business is a crucial factor in building a positive reputation. This needs to recognize the requirements of the workforce and to build cultural intelligence throughout the business. Cultural mistakes can create a reputational crisis as well as impacting on recruitment and retention of staff. Managers need to have cultural awareness and intelligence. This creates the right culture for the business and avoiding insensitivity.

a Raise awareness among employees of diverse cultures, customers, beliefs and approaches.

b Create an open and welcoming environment that allows people to feel connected to the business.

c Build culture intelligence into the consultation and feedback loop.

d Be open and willing to learn when problems occur and use the information to further develop the business' approach.

6 Innovation and development

Being on top of changes and developments can help build a resilient business. It helps to keep it ahead of competitors and able to identify new opportunities. A business that is adaptable and can flex the strategy and approach to take account of what is happening in the wider world will be able to respond swiftly to challenges. When the Covid-19 pandemic hit, businesses that could change and develop quickly to comply with the new restrictions were able to weather the impact better.

a Ensure business development exists and is horizon scanning for changes in the world, sector and among customers.

b Create lean systems that are able to flex and adapt to the changing environment.

c Review approaches to corporate social responsibility and the environmental, social and governance framework to ensure they are appropriate for that point in time.

7 Change management

Introducing changes within the business needs to have a structure and framework that will manage the impact and bring the required outcome. Communication is a key part of this work and requires careful consideration. It requires engagement and an explanation of why the change is needed, not just sharing the information. Ensure there is a process for change management that identifies the required approach and embeds it within the business.

a Understand how change is introduced within the business and consider if a clearer structure is needed.

b Train communicators in change management and the principles of behavioural change to improve the internal communication of changes.

c Involve the workforce in identifying changes and being part of the approach to keep the business as a leader in its field.

8 Measurement

There needs to be a suite of measurements in place that assess the operation of the business. It will include if the business is profitable and what the bottom line looks like but should also assess the reputation of the business. Communication and PR needs to evaluate effectively and put in place reputation trackers that can act as an early alert of potential issues. The measures must also help to drive the business development, change and risk management.

a Create a measurement dashboard that covers all the key aspects of the business and particularly those that are important to the reputation.

b Communication and PR needs to develop an evaluation framework that can help develop an evidence-based approach to the work.

c Put reputation tracking software or systems in place that can assist in identifying changes and issues so action can be taken.

Section B – Employees/staff

1 Expectations of staff

Employees need to understand what is required from them and why it is needed. This includes recognizing the ethical considerations, regulatory issues and societal norms that may affect the work. Setting boundaries and outlining expectations will assist in connecting the staff to the purpose and vision of the business. It is more than having a job description or a contract of employment. Those documents provide tactical and practically necessary information but do not assist the development of the culture and the vision.

a Review the onboarding process for new staff to ensure the expectations are clear and understandable.

b Build reputation management into the job descriptions and requirements from employees.

c Establish clear boundaries that set the ethical, regulatory and other considerations for staff.

2 Role of managers

Managers play a key role in driving the business and also the culture of the business. They need to both understand the expectations of them and how they are managing staff. Managers also are important to sharing the information about the way the business is developing and why. Having a cascade briefing system assists the two-way flow of information. Ensure new managers are given support, training and mentoring to ensure they are driving the business the right way.

a   Establish a training and support programme for new and existing managers.

b   Create a checklist of what is required from managers and particularly in relation to reputation management.

c   Implement a cascade briefing system that will support the two-way flow of communication and information.

3 Well-being offer

Employees need to have support to ensure any issues can be raised and addressed. Assisting employees when they have challenges or when they have been called to respond to critical issues affecting the business is essential to its reputation. Bad reports on systems such as Glassdoor and Google reviews can affect the ability to recruit and retain staff. In the post-Covid world employees will leave if they feel neglected by the business.

a   Ensure there is support available for employees who may be under pressure.

b   Monitor the exit interviews and information about how employees feel and the morale levels.

c   Put well-being into HR and change processes to manage the impact and offer assistance.

d   Prioritize staff and gathering the views of employees so they can be understood, problems can be addressed, and the business can remain resilient.

4 Training and development

As mentioned in Section A, a training and development plan is needed to support employees in their work and in managing the business' reputation. Ethical operation should be part of this training along with cultural awareness and intelligence. Further specialized training on managing problems and working with customers to secure an early resolution is required.

a   Consider organizational touchpoints with customers and key areas of the business and ensure they have the necessary training.

b   Review training to ensure that it is supporting the business' purpose and vision and addresses the approach to reputation management.

c   Implement new training quickly when situations emerge that require changes to the operation of the business.

5 Position of CEO and C-suite

The CEO and C-suite have a vital role to play in establishing the frameworks and the culture that supports effective reputation management. They have to embody the values of the business and assist in creating positive perceptions of the business both when they are at work and outside of work. For example, Richard Branson is seen as the embodiment of Virgin as a business, and this is related to everything that he does. Training and support from communicators can assist the senior leadership in establishing themselves.

a Put training in place to support senior leaders so they understand both reputation and communication and what is required from them.

b Establish a communication plan to assist the C-suite listening to the workforce and being visible to employees.

c Create a culture of feedback and challenge so that senior leaders are aware of views and perceptions of them and how they operate.

6 Role of board and trustees

In the management of a business' reputation there is a clear role for boards and trustees. They hold the business to account and will be overseeing how it operates and the work that is undertaken. This gives them a key role in understanding the approach to reputation management and ensuring that it is ethical and has integrity. Boards and trustees also have a key role to play when there is a crisis or reputational problem.

a Develop a training and information sharing process that helps boards and trustees understand the reputation management approach taken by the business.

b Establish a clear role for the board and trustees in managing incidents and issues.

c Anyone operating as a board member or trustee needs to be comfortable in challenging the business for how it is influencing and developing its reputation.

Section C – PR and communication

1 Reputation audit

There needs to be an understanding of the communication, PR and marketing assets that may impact on, or affect, the business' reputation. This also needs to be supported by an understanding of what the reputation is and what is affecting it. An audit of the reputation management process can support the drive to improve it. This needs to have a strategic and tactical approach.

a Audit the communication, PR and marketing approach and the assets that impact on reputation.

b Understand what is having an impact, what is working, and areas of work that have little impact.

c Assess how reputation is tracked and what evaluation is carried out.

2 Reputation management plan

Develop a reputation management plan which should exist for the whole business but will have a key connection to the business' communication strategy. The plan should focus on what is important and where the business can have an impact on views and perceptions. A plan can approach the timescales and milestones for actions that will be taken. It can also detail the roles and responsibilities that are required from all parts of the business.

a Create a reputation management plan for the business looking at where it is and where it wants to be.

b Detail the timescales to implement actions and to make any required changes.

c Ensure the plan has roles and responsibilities that exist across the whole of the business.

3 Measurement and evaluation

PR and communication measurement is an essential part of reputation management. Building evidence-based communication is vital to really understand different views and perceptions of the business. Time and resources should be invested in ensuring that the communication activity is making a difference to the views of the business and is also assisting in managing any reputational challenges.

a Create a suite of measurements that can be used to evaluate the impact of the PR and communication activity.

b Build the measurements into the reputation management framework and ensure they are helping the activity to be strategically focused.

c Ensure measures cover across the external and internal communication and are used to refine and develop the actions.

4 Stakeholder engagement

Build stakeholder engagement into the management of reputation and the development of communication plans and activity. Effective relationships can provide information that assists the business to develop and is vital when managing any challenges or potential issues. This is not just the responsibility of the communication and PR team and requires support from across the business.

a Conduct stakeholder mapping to ensure the key relationships are identified and the information can inform reputation and communication work.

b Have a stakeholder management framework that can be used to promote the business but also support the work to address any reputational challenges that emerge.

c Prioritize engagement with other key organizations and businesses when threats or issues emerge.

5 Crisis and risk management

Communication is a critical and strategic part of risk and crisis management. It needs to understand the business and the potential impact of the issue or problem that has emerged. The crisis communication plans need to be more than posting out information and have to consider the reputational impact, and how to respond to it. The risk framework needs to identify reputational risks and build them into the wider operational threats. Planning for crises, testing and exercising the plans are essential to move quickly to manage problems.

a Create a risk management framework that focuses on the reputational risks.

b Ensure a crisis communication plan is in place, that staff know what it says, and that it is tested on a regular basis.

c Build the PR and communication approach to risk and crisis into the business framework and activities.

6 Recovery communication

The crisis management needs to ensure that recovery communication is in place to be ready to rebuild the reputation once a problem has developed and been managed. It needs to focus on how to repair any damage, implement changes and then demonstrate how the business has improved and developed in the aftermath of the situation. Recovery and change will be required across the business and the communication needs to work with the operational activity.

a   Ensure crisis communication plans include recovery communication with details of what it will do and how it will operate.

b   Develop a recovery communication plan when dealing with the aftermath of a problem.

c   Have a process that moves from crisis to recovery and then into change communication that may be required.

7   SEO, branding and content marketing

The position of the business and how it is seen and heard by others is a critical part of the perceptions that people develop. Search engine optimization, branding and content marketing all need to reflect the purpose and values of the business that have been laid out (see Section A). They also need to be refreshed when any changes are made and to be revised in the aftermath of a crisis or issue.

a   Ensure SEO, branding and content marketing are all reflecting the business as it is and wants to be. Audit the activity and approach.

b   Build SEO and content marketing into the crisis communication response and the recovery communication activity.

c   Use feedback and consultation both internally and externally to revise and develop the approach.

8   Innovation and development

Communication and PR is continuing to develop and change over time. The impact of artificial intelligence presents both challenges and opportunities to communication. Deepfakes, misinformation and disinformation threaten to impact on the perceptions people have of any business. Being ready and able to respond to them requires communicators to understand them and how to address them.

a   Build innovation and modern technologies into the approach to PR and communication.

b   Ensure teams are trained and ready to be able to maximize the opportunities and understand the risks from developments.

Implementation and use of the toolkit

The toolkit should be used to consider the approach the business already has in place and identify any gaps that may exist. It can also be used when a problem or reputational threat has emerged to ensure that there is a robust response in place that can help to limit the impact of the situation. It should not be used as a tick-box exercise and a business needs to authentically engage with the actions that may be required from assessing against the toolkit. There has to be a willingness to change the approach and make necessary improvements.

Effective relationships need to be in place across the business and with other groups and individuals. Reputation needs to be considered from the position of key stakeholders so any issues can be understood. Gather data and insight that will assist in understanding how people view the business, its activity and how it is developing. The challenge of data and insight into the reputation of the business and how it is viewed may be assisted by maximizing developments in artificial intelligence. Algorithms and AI can help in understanding customer satisfaction data, areas of concern, cultural challenges and in highlighting risks and threats.

Using the toolkit can support the implementation of a reputation management framework that will be underpinned by operational competence. It is necessary to ensure the business has a legitimacy to operate and can build the resilience seen by global brands such as Amazon and Apple. Perceptions are important to the way a business operates and need to be addressed, whether they are linked to actual events or have developed from views. Reputation is impacted by both equally and with the modern technology and societal norms views are shared as fact instantly. The use of the toolkit can support the creation of the whole business reputation management system.

Conclusion and building for the future

Reputation is increasingly problematic to manage and influence. There are many fragmented groups and communities who may or may not be important to the business. But the way they view and then share those thoughts with others can damage the reputation. In the worst cases this can lead to operational damage such as a lack of investment, problems with recruitment and a lack of innovation. Building a business that sees reputation management as important as the profitability and financial viability, is required for the resilience to survive the challenges of the modern world. It starts with understanding the current position and what the reputation of the business is within the identified groups.

Do not assume that there is one reputation measure for the business. There are different groups with a different weighting of importance and the reputation should be assessed from the perspective of those groups. Monitoring the reputation needs to be a broader activity and can be approached in a number of ways. Customers, investors, regulators, employees and others will have an expectation of the business and what it should be doing. Understand the key groups and then measure the way they view the business. Do this when there are no significant problems or challenges so that when the worst happens the impact of it can be assessed.

This is a changeable world with considerable challenges that can emerge swiftly and have a devastating impact on a business. Being ready to address the problems and learn from them is essential for a business to survive, grow and thrive. Responding quickly to problems and then making changes that are needed are critical. No business can be successful if it continues to operate in a bubble and does not take account of the way the world is developing. Reputation is not just a problem for the PR and communication team. Effective reputation management needs the whole business to be involved and to take the steps that have been outlined throughout the book. Strategic reputation management starts at the top of the business but filters throughout it at all levels. Reputation is a complex issue but with some thought, determination and a willingness to change and develop any business can take steps that will identify problems, manage performance and strengthen the brand for the future.

References

1 Police Federation. Poor pay and treatment pushing officers towards resignation, 20 March 2024, www.polfed.org/news/latest-news/2024/poor-pay-and-treatment-pushing-officers-towards-resignation/ (archived at https://perma.cc/6985-RSKZ)

2 A Coleman (2023) *Crisis Communication Strategies: Prepare, respond and recover effectively in unpredictable and urgent situations*, 2nd edition, Kogan Page, London

3 A Gabbatt. Bezos blasted for traveling to space while Amazon workers toil on planet Earth, *The Guardian*, 20 July 2021, www.theguardian.com/science/2021/jul/20/bezos-space-travel-blue-origin-amazon-criticism (archived at https://perma.cc/VBF6-7C4V)

4 *Times of India*. The great iPhone rush: Apple brings the buzz back with iPhone 14 series, 22 September 2023, https://timesofindia.indiatimes.com/gadgets-news/the-great-iphone-rush-apple-brings-the-buzz-back-with-iphone-15-series/articleshow/103867372.cms (archived at https://perma.cc/UBL3-MTTR)

5 D Chang. Apple is named the world's most admired company in the world by Fortune continuing its 17-year run in the top spot, *Mail Online*, 31 January 2024, www.dailymail.co.uk/news/article-13028801/apple-named-admired-company-fortune.html (archived at https://perma.cc/L78W-JSA7)

6 D Chang. Apple is named the world's most admired company in the world by Fortune continuing its 17-year run in the top spot, *Mail Online*, 31 January 2024, www.dailymail.co.uk/news/article-13028801/apple-named-admired-company-fortune.html (archived at https://perma.cc/L78W-JSA7)

INDEX

NB: page numbers in *italic* indicate figures or tables

Looking for another book?

Explore our award-winning
books from global business
experts in Marketing and Sales

Scan the code to browse

www.koganpage.com/marketing

More from Kogan Page

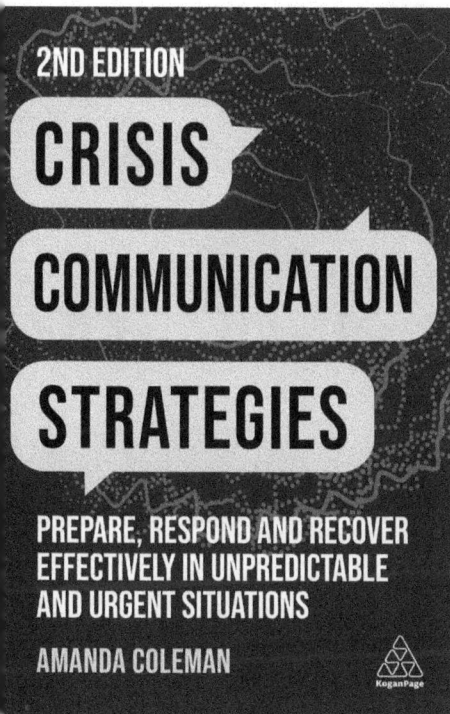

2ND EDITION

CRISIS

COMMUNICATION

STRATEGIES

PREPARE, RESPOND AND RECOVER EFFECTIVELY IN UNPREDICTABLE AND URGENT SITUATIONS

AMANDA COLEMAN

KoganPage

ISBN: 9781398609419

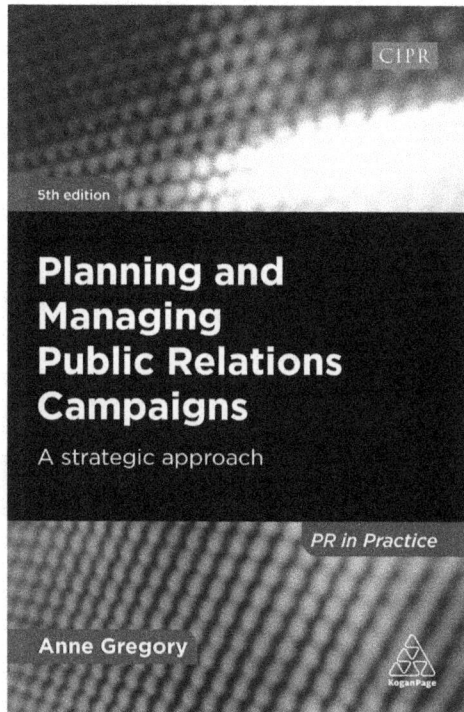

CIPR

5th edition

Planning and Managing Public Relations Campaigns

A strategic approach

PR in Practice

Anne Gregory

KoganPage

ISBN: 9781789663204

www.koganpage.com

KoganPage

From 4 December 2025 the EU Responsible Person (GPSR) is:
eucomply oÜ, Pärnu mnt. 139b – 14, 11317 Tallinn, Estonia
www.eucompliancepartner.com

www.ingramcontent.com/pod-product-compliance
Lightning Source LLC
Chambersburg PA
CBHW071556210326
41597CB00019B/3267

9 781398 617308